SAMBA IN THE SMETHWICK END

REGIS, CUNNINGHAM, BATSON AND THE
FOOTBALL REVOLUTION

SAMBA IN THE SMETHWICK END

DAVE BOWLER
AND JAS BAINS

MAINSTREAM
PUBLISHING

EDINBURGH AND LONDON

First published in Great Britain in 2000 by

MAINSTREAM PUBLISHING COMPANY (EDINBURGH) LTD

7 Albany Street

Edinburgh EH1 3UG

This edition 2001

ISBN 1 84018 188 5

A catalogue record for this book is available from the British Library

Typeset in Janson Text

Printed and bound in Great Britain by Creative Print and Design Wales

To my family
Jas

To Mom and Dad. Thanks for passing the Albion down through the family. It's been very character-building
David

ACKNOWLEDGEMENTS

Many people have helped in the compilation of the book and we are grateful to them all. Our greatest thanks go to Cyrille Regis and Brendon Batson who were extremely supportive of the project and gave unstintingly of their time. A number of others endured our interviews, offered help or suggestions, so we would like to thank Gordon Taylor, Neil Kaufman, Frank Woolf, Bobby Fisher, Tom Collins, Bob Badhams, Carl Taylor, Geoff Taylor, Charles Ross, John Richards, John Trewick, John Wile, Bryn Jones, Larry Canning, Tim Beech, Simon Wright and Bobby Gould.

Everyone at Mainstream has been very enthusiastic about the project, so thanks to all in Edinburgh, particularly Bill Campbell and Judy Diamond. The BOING newsgroup was helpful with support, suggestions and answers to numerous questions, so our thanks go to all the members.

Further information is available at www.baggies.com. Those wanting to buy copies of the photos can fax Laurie on 01375 413123, or e-mail Dave at kcd53@dial.pipex.com.

Thanks too to our families who have put up with us while we've been putting this together.

This book is based on an original lunch with Ian Preece. Thanks Ian.

PREFACE

Over recent seasons the rivalry between West Bromwich Albion and Wolverhampton Wanderers has intensified to unprecedented levels, bringing with it an unsavoury aspect, the more extreme factions associated with both clubs orchestrating their own pathetic boy soldiers games, where the victims, caught in the crossfire, have largely been the innocent. Nor has this increasing bitterness among these century-old rivals, both founder members of the Football League, been wholly confined to the lunatic elements. The weekly radio phone-ins, now an ingrained part of the modern football culture, have provided a platform for the supposedly more responsible fans to reveal growing hostilities. The stakes have become so high in this increasingly pressurised results-orientated football environment that we have all seemingly entered the asylum. So when my co-author, Dave Bowler (a lifelong Baggie) approached me (a lifelong Wolves fan) to work with him on this book idea my first reaction was to (politely) tell him where to go.

But then, and this may sound like heresy and treachery all rolled into one to fellow Wolves fans, I have long held a soft spot for our nearest rivals. Like many other football neutrals in the late 1970s I became enchanted and intrigued by these three black players who came to symbolise a game that I, as a non-white, could more comfortably relate to. The fact that they played for the Baggies became irrelevant. The vitriolic outpourings of the ignoramuses towards these players largely escaped me until they lined up against the Wolves. One such occasion will remain imprinted in my mind, forever.

Standing at the back of the old Smethwick End terrace, with its corrugated steel sheets ready to provide a metallic accompaniment, I looked on with utter bewilderment and humiliation as a mass of white fingers came over shoulders, pointing at Batson, Cunningham and Regis and chanting, 'Pull that trigger, shoot that nigger'. As a 15-year-old this was something I had never seen before in 'my country'. This was a throwback to what had gone on in the southern states of America. But England? Surely this could not be happening here. If this was my country then clearly I, and many others, did not belong. Ever since that day, I have retained an affection for the Baggies.

Which is one of the reasons why I felt Jas had to be involved. Apart from having an address book of Biblical proportions, he's been on the sharp end of the racism that this book is, in part, about. I can do the worthy, white liberal, hand-wringing, bleeding heart bit, but it's like being in a car crash – until you've actually experienced the ugliness of it, you don't really know what it's like.

I hope I'm right in saying that racism has never been an issue for me. White or black makes no difference. Gold and black, on the other hand, is a completely different matter. The Albion is a hereditary disease in our family, a century of it. When I told my dad I was doing this book with a Wolves supporter, I'm sure it crossed his mind to drop dead just so that he could have the satisfaction of turning in his grave. And much as I tried to show Jas the error of his ways, he has remained true to his erroneous calling and is still a Wolves fan. Still, nobody's perfect.

But he's right. What was once a joking rivalry, even if it had it's darker undercurrents, has become openly hostile in recent years as both clubs have suffered. With neither side threatening the Premiership, the derby game has become too important, the be-all and end-all of the season. But if rival fans can co-operate on a book like this, maybe there's hope for us yet?

INTRODUCTION

In the dim and distant past we used to be an industrial nation, producers and purveyors of goods of quality and distinction. One lengthy, too lengthy, Conservative administration later and that has all but disappeared. Manufacturing has been supplanted by giant shopping malls, service companies, intangible productions. Among these, nostalgia is one of the great boom industries. Perhaps it's inevitable that, in a world that changes as rapidly as this, people will want to hold on to a time when things seemed more permanent, secure, solid, when life seemed simpler, even though it probably wasn't. Maybe we were doing the very same things at the time, in what we now regard as the good old days, romanticising times 20 years or more further back into the past. Sometimes, by clinging so fervently to the past, we miss the glories of today. But sometimes, the past is all we've got. And if you happen to be a supporter of the 'big four' in West Midlands football, then let's face it, 20 years ago we *were* enjoying a golden age, because there's been precious little to be thrilled about ever since. In the halcyon days of 1979, few could have predicted that the Divisional gang of four would now include the previously ignored Walsall as substitutes for the region's most successful side and only Premiership representatives, Aston Villa. And to add insult to injury, 'little' Walsall would be regularly turning over their more illustrious neighbours.

At Villa Park, Aston Villa were reaching the end of their long march under Chairman Doug and his Little Claret Book from the depths of the Third Division to the heights of the League Championship and then the European Cup. Massive crowds continued to support the club even in the darkest days and the money they generated helped Villa rebuild. In Wolverhampton, the best team assembled at Molineux since the halcyon days of Wright, Mullen and Hancocks reached a UEFA Cup final and won the, then mercifully unsponsored and still meaningful, Football League Cup on two occasions. Fair enough, Birmingham City didn't actually win anything nor ever look like doing so, but then that's their lot in life, isn't it? As Jasper Carrot – who was to the Blues in the late '70s what Frank Skinner now is to the Albion – pointed out, 'The only way Birmingham City will get into Europe is if there's a war.' But for all their regular flirtations with relegation and promotion, Birmingham spent most of their time in the top flight, played some nice football, enjoyed a Cup run or two, and had teams filled with good players and great characters such as Trevor Francis, Bob Latchford, Frank Worthington, Alberto Tarantini, Kenny Burns and Bob Hatton.

Then there was West Bromwich Albion. Like Birmingham, they came out of those days with nothing concrete to show for their efforts, no trophies. And yet Albion were perhaps the most significant of these big four West Midlands sides, proof if it were ever needed that in sport not everything can be measured by medals won. Whisper it now for fear of triggering a wave of cardiac arrests among the banking fraternity in these money-obsessed Premiership days, but if you want to find the soul of football, if you want to uncover why it really counts, you don't look at league tables. You look into people's hearts.

What made that Albion side so special? It would be wrong to suggest that they brought a new dimension to the English game in terms of tactics or performances because they plainly did not. What they did do was reapply principles that had lain dormant through much of the English game in the 1970s, a dour, defensive decade where having a slickly run off-side trap was deemed to be far more important than playing with panache, scoring goals, entertaining supporters. Albion themselves had flirted with that idea, under the stewardship of Don Howe, the high priest of defensive organisation who had masterminded Arsenal's dismal double in 1970–71. Finding Albion in transition, Howe had three fruitless seasons in the Black Country, taking the club to relegation and then nowhere near promotion, before the board decided against renewing his contract. Instead, they appointed Johnny Giles, midfield lynchpin of the great Leeds United side and before that a graduate of the Busby school at Old Trafford.

Giles was the master of possession football and schooled his players accordingly, assembling a side that played in his image. By the time Giles had had enough of management after two years, he had won promotion and crafted a thoroughly capable First Division outfit. With the confidence of a year in the top flight behind them, Albion simply soared, briefly under Ronnie Allen, then memorably under Ron Atkinson. They played with an unadulterated joy last glimpsed a decade earlier when Manchester United and their Holy Trinity of Best, Charlton and Law ran amok. Fittingly, perhaps, that Albion side reached its zenith at Old Trafford, Christmas 1978, when they simply dismantled United 5–3, thankfully a game caught by TV cameras and still given regular outings, even on MUTV.

If United had a Holy Trinity, then the Albion had the Three Degrees, perhaps the most radical feature of the side. Laurie Cunningham, Cyrille Regis and Brendon Batson were the standard bearers for the wave of black footballers that now accounts for around 20 per cent of all professionals in England. There were other black players plying their trade – Viv Anderson at Nottingham Forest, Bob Hazell at Wolves, a number in the lower divisions. But Albion were the team of the time, much as Newcastle were recently under Kevin Keegan, briefly top of the First Division and playing some enthralling football. And in Regis and Cunningham in particular, Albion had two players who were undeniably glamorous, exciting, and as good to watch as anyone in the country.

Regis was a powerhouse in those early seasons, an elemental force who you simply put on the field and let rip. Cyrille was built like a heavyweight boxer and you could guarantee that during any given game he would get the ball on the halfway line, turn and tear off towards goal, ending the run with a thunderous shot.

Cunningham had more subtlety in his skills. He was more the magician, with a beautiful touch and absolute mastery of the ball. Bobby Gould, later his manager at Wimbledon when Laurie collected his FA Cup winners' medal, points out, 'If you identify great players, Ronaldo, Pelé, Cruyff, Best, they have rhythm and balance and Laurie had that. And forwards were tackled when he played, but he knew how to ride them, his body bent with it. He had a pin-toed run, there was only one lad who ran like that, he was beautiful to watch. He took ballet classes and that was instrumental in his understanding of body movement.'

With all due respect to Brendon Batson, himself an accomplished and polished attacking full-back who often linked intelligently with Cunningham down the right, it was Regis and Cunningham who truly captured the public's imagination. Isn't it always the forwards that do that? From a black perspective, it needed a charismatic goalscorer to burst on the scene to put the issue in the public mind. Albion provided two of them, the addition of Batson merely underlining that there were no barriers to where a black man could play. Nor should there be, but the level of prejudice was so great, that only practical demonstrations against that stupidity could hope to change attitudes. Regis and Cunningham were fortunate to have each other and Batson as a support network in the glare of the fiercest publicity, just as the black community were fortunate that they were just so good, so exciting. Had they proved to be a flash in the pan, famous for Warhol's 15 minutes but with nothing else to offer beyond that, the progress of black footballers would have been put back several years, reinforcing thoughtless stereotypes and ingrained bigotry. But the three were footballers of real quality, of First Division quality at the very least and, to most observers, worthy of higher rewards. Furthermore, the subsequent success of Batson and Regis in other footballing spheres continues to dismantle prejudices. Twenty years ago, their pictures graced bedroom walls not just in West Bromwich, but up and down the country, striking both overt and subliminal messages against racism as every drawing pin went into white bedroom walls. And so, by the simple virtue of being superb footballers, the Three Degrees had perhaps the greatest sociological impact on English football in the years that separated the abolition of the maximum wage and the Hillsborough tragedy.

For a brief few months, maybe a little longer, the West Midlands was the hub of English football, the place to be. Liverpool still continued to dominate with their forensic pass and move game. Forest, all economy, all efficiency, harried the Reds to the glittering prizes, usurping them as European Champions for two seasons with Brian Clough's trademark blend of the physical and the intellectual. But West Bromwich Albion grabbed the headlines and shone a spotlight on the whole region. For a few moments, the region was alive. It was sexy in a way it never had been and never has been since. It was even possible to believe that a Midlands footballer might actually get picked for England on a regular basis, though that was quickly shown to be heresy.

As quickly as it had risen, so the Midlands fell back into virtual obscurity. Albion faltered at the last when, following the terrible winter weather of 1978–79, a fixture backlog denied them a genuine chance of the Championship – now that's a *real* winter of discontent. That summer, Laurie Cunningham left the club and the Two Degrees didn't have quite the same ring to it. And though the local clubs still spent big, breaking the national transfer records on a number of occasions, and enjoyed several more years in the top flight, they never had the same glamour, the same appeal. That golden atmosphere had evaporated. The Midlands was once again that characterless lump that separated London and the North once again. As the region moved into its first lengthy economic recession since the war, so its football clubs fell into disrepair. After the golden age came the wilderness years, years that still linger on, years that have seen Wolves, Birmingham and Albion all flirt with bankruptcy to a greater or lesser extent, years that have seen them cast out from the Promised Land of the Premiership and years where Aston Villa failed to build on their European Cup success and underachieved on a consistent basis. The very writing of this book underlines the problems the region faces – you'd have been able to buy it six months earlier if it hadn't been for the fact that every time we thought we'd finished the last chapter, the Albion managed to turn another drama into a crisis, do something ridiculous, and we were left to revise it for the umpteenth time. The people of the West Midlands, as fanatical about their football as any Geordie, Scouser or Mancunian, have been ill-served by their football clubs in recent times and have only been able to find comfort in the comic misadventures of their local adversaries, pretty cold comfort at that.

From a samba to a lament, these are the sounds of our times.

ONE

'If you want a nigger for your neighbour, vote Labour.' Recognise the tone? Is it the National Front? The British National Party, perhaps? No, it's the voice of sweet reason that has for so long characterised the Conservative and Unionist Party.

That was an 'unofficial' slogan that the Tory candidate for the Smethwick constituency used in the October 1964 General Election, a campaign organised by the controlling Tory council administration from Marshall Street, now a crumbling site of soon-to-be-demolished Victorian-built terraced houses. At an election where there was a significant national swing to the Labour Party, enough to enable them to end 13 years of Conservative rule and form a government, that odious line was enough to win the Conservative candidate Peter Griffiths a formerly safe Labour seat, unseating Patrick Gordon Walker, the Foreign Secretary designate. Overturning a Labour majority of 3,544, Griffiths won the seat by 1,774 votes to become Smethwick's first post-war Tory MP. Gordon Walker's defeat was wholly, and rightly, attributed to the anti-immigration campaign waged in the constituency by the Tories. It was felt Gordon Walker had been made to pay for his supportive stance on immigration, a position he had made clear during a major speech in 1961. This had earned him the label 'Nigger lover' and following his electoral defeat he was asked 'Where are your niggers now?' While Gordon Walker was making pro-immigration speeches, Griffiths, then leader of Smethwick's Tory councillors, was advocating that any immigrant who had been unemployed for more than six months should be deported. Something had to give way. Sadly for Gordon Walker he had shown himself to have badly misjudged the situation. Smethwick, for its part, was to become a barometer for the Tory national election campaign.

It's one of the few times that Smethwick has made national news. Like everything else in the Black Country, even the origin of the name is open to dispute. Depending on your preference, it means either a smith's dwelling or a village on the plains. What is beyond dispute is that the town was built on industrial foundations, so successfully that 120 years before the immigration of the 1950s, Smethwick was host to migrant workers from France and Belgium who had come to work at the Spon Lane gas works. Pretty much from the dawn of the industrial age, Smethwick had been a success, and by the outbreak of World War II it was a manufacturing town that made a virtue of variety, dealing in highly skilled engineering processes. What came out of Smethwick? From table glassware to lighthouse lenses, metal window frames to railway rolling stock for the London Underground, any and every component the automobile industry required and engineering supplies for the aircraft industry. You wanted it? You could get it in Smethwick. A skilled, motivated workforce could meet all the challenges you could throw at it until the fight became unequal and Thatcherite economics strangled the area and extortionate interest rates prevented investment in the new skills, technologies and materials that would have helped Smethwick continue to compete on the global stage. As the British motor industry was raped, Smethwick bore the collateral damage. But then this was the dull, thick Midlands, not the racy cosmopolitan south. Who cared?

In 1964, this parliamentary constituency battle was probably the most important event in British politics for black and Asian people. Griffiths told the Midlands correspondent of *The Times*: 'I would not condemn anyone who said that [referring to the rhyme]. I regard it as a manifestation of popular feeling.' Although the new Prime Minister, Harold Wilson, took a less sympathetic line on immigration than his predecessor Hugh Gaitskell, he still urged that Griffiths be treated as a 'parliamentary leper', a tag that stuck until he was ousted by Labour's Andrew Faulds at the 1966 General

Election. Years before Wolverhampton MP Enoch Powell delivered his infamous 'rivers of blood' speech in nearby Birmingham in April 1968, the Black Country was already disfigured by racial mistrust and prejudice.

Thirteen years later, 31 August 1977. A sparsely populated Smethwick End at The Hawthorns, home of West Bromwich Albion, the bulk of fans standing on the Birmingham Road End terraces. A routine Football League Cup fixture, First Division Albion against Third Division Rotherham United. Albion 2–0 ahead, a penalty awarded. All round the ground, the call goes up, 'Cyrille, Cyrille'. It's directed at a young man making his debut, a lad straight out of non-league football. Cyrille Regis is given the ball, smashes home the penalty, then scores another goal to finish a 4–0 victory, and, within 90 minutes, he's made himself the new hero of The Hawthorns, supplanting Jeff Astle as 'The King'. And the new King was a black man. More than that, Cyrille Regis was the living embodiment of that vicious, pathetic cartoon that Powell and those of his ilk tried to draw of the black population: physical supermen waiting to beat up old ladies at the ends of darkened alleys. Strong, powerful, it always seemed as though it was impossible to create a shirt that could contain Regis's muscular presence. He looked like he'd changed in a phone box and came out on the pitch, muscles rippling, ready to save the world or at least, and more importantly, the Albion. More prosaic, perhaps, his Albion colleague Brendon Batson reckons, 'He used to wear his shirt two sizes too small to emphasise his physique.' It had the desired effect. The white masses should have been terrified of him. Instead, Cyrille Regis was, still is, adored by the Albion faithful, many of whom came from that same Smethwick constituency that had voted so shamefully just 15 years before. Smethwick had, apparently, come a long way.

A couple of weeks later, the same Smethwick End, packed to capacity. This time, it's full of Wolves supporters for the local derby. At the back of the terraces are corrugated iron sheets. Throughout the game, the Wolves supporters drum on these in a jungle rhythm, and thousands of voices chant 'Nigger, nigger, lick my boots' or 'Pull that trigger, shoot that nigger', abuse aimed at Regis and Albion's other black genius – and the word is used advisedly and deservedly – Laurie Cunningham, who wasn't even on the field that day. So maybe the Black Country hadn't come such a long way after all, particularly when you recall that Albion's travelling supporters made reciprocal, if slightly less heated, attacks on Bob Hazell and George Berry at Molineux.

Nigger. If you're white and can read that word without flinching, you really haven't been paying attention these last thirty years, have you? Lenny Bruce might have simultaneously tried to desensitise the word and re-emphasise its bleak meaning with the machine gun savagery of his comic delivery. John Lennon might have tried to use it as a term relating to slavery in general rather than one of racial abuse. But it's still there, one of the great taboo words, one of the most vicious, insidious, nasty words in our vocabulary. For the moronic white supremacist, it's that word more than any other that supposedly signifies the superiority of the white race over the base black man, although any people that can only define themselves and proclaim their perfection by abusing others has far more problems that it can ever deal with. For many a white liberal, it's the term that strikes fear into the bleeding heart, in case it should suddenly leap into the brain, unwanted, unbidden, but there, there, there, making us wonder if deep down we don't all have a germ of prejudice in us. For the black community, it's yet another word from the great litany of possible abuse. Sometimes vitriolic, sometimes casual, always offensive. The smart communicators, most notably musicians such as NWA and Public Enemy have attempted to seize the word, take it back, use it on their terms in their own way, with some success. But it remains a hateful, shameful word.

One word. In 1964, it won a parliamentary constituency. In 1977 it was central to the transformation of football. Much of that transformation was wrought in the Black Country.

No one club can claim the credit for the introduction of black footballers. There had been a smattering of them in the Football League since the war, such as Middlesbrough's Lindy Delaphena from Jamaica, South African Albert Johanneson at Leeds, Charlie Williams, later to find fame as a comedian, at Doncaster and Bermudan Clyde Best at West Ham. But these were isolated individuals. Indeed, those who had come to Britain in the first real wave of immigration just after the war had yet to put their head above the parapet and make any impression on public life in this country. Most had come to this country simply to take up those jobs that remained unfilled in a country basking in full employment, a concept almost incomprehensible today. At the risk of descending into stereotype, the huge majority were engaged in low-skilled, low-paid jobs that the white population did not want, nor need to do. Through the 1950s and 1960s how many black people achieved fame in this country?

Such black icons as there were tended to be American. Aside from civil rights leaders like Martin Luther King or Malcolm X, those with a global impact were generally entertainers of one sort or another, who acted as inspirational figures for black youngsters in the UK. Musically there was a rich post-war heritage – Miles and Coltrane, Little Richard and Chuck Berry, Stax and Motown, ska and reggae, Hendrix. Sidney Poitier was causing a stir in Hollywood, even as the 1960s closed, with his powerful performance opposite Spencer Tracey and Katherine Hepburn in *Guess Who's Coming To Dinner?*. These were all people capturing the imagination of the wider British public, black and white alike, surely laying the foundations for a wider acceptance of ethnic diversity.

Perhaps the most obvious examples of black success came in the sporting field. Boxing on the world, i.e. American, stage had long been a black preserve, as commentators cast around desperately for a 'great white hope'. But boxers had never been intellectually threatening. Until the arrival of Cassius Clay, later to become Muhammad Ali. Not only was Ali the supreme athlete of the twentieth century, not only was he 'The Greatest', he was a social phenomenon too. David Remnick's study of Ali, *King of the World*, makes it obvious that he was the figurehead of a changing attitude by black Americans and towards black Americans: 'In the early '60s

Floyd Patterson cast himself as the Good Negro, an approachable and strangely fearful man, a deferential champion of civil rights, integration and Christian decency . . . Ali would declare himself independent of the stereotype Patterson was beholden to. "I had to prove you could be a new kind of black man . . . I had to show that to the world."'

But these heroes were from across the Atlantic, inevitably so, for the black community was neither so large, nor so rooted in Britain as in America. Black Americans were there largely because their ancestors had been stolen from Africa, hauled across the world to work as slaves. The black community in Britain was mostly there from choice, even if it had been the Hobson's choice of moving to the UK or staying at home and surviving in harsh economic conditions. In that sense, black Britons are not dissimilar from 'European' Americans, for example. Broadly speaking, the story of those migrants is of families moving to America in the hope of a better life and initially settling into fairly menial employment in the hope that their children would have greater opportunities in the future.

It is a generational issue. Few of those mass migrants had the skills to immediately break into the higher earning bracket. And with the other attendant difficulties of settling in a new country, dreams often had to be shelved as day to day problems were faced. But look at how many successful Americans now have European parents or grandparents. There is a very powerful argument that suggests that migrants are, almost by definition, a more driven group than an indigenous population. As 'outsiders' there is a desire to fit in, to become a vital part of the new society. And as people from the outside looking in, there is fresh perspective, a greater awareness of new opportunities, opportunities that those who have lived in a country for generations take for granted and often fail to see. Equally, as people who have usually left behind very hard lives, there is often a greater appreciation of what is often, economically at least, a far better situation than they might have ever dreamt possible.

These are sweeping generalisations of course. Nobody could

suggest that life for the migrant is all milk, honey and happy chocolate. And that's particularly true of black migrants coming into a predominantly white society. If a South African, an Australian or a New Zealander moves to the UK, their accent aside, there is nothing to distinguish them from the rest of the population and so assimilation is much easier. People of colour, by definition, stand out as 'different' and in a society which, despite protestations to the contrary, does not celebrate 'difference', that automatically makes life a tougher prospect. Of course things have improved over the fifty years since immigration first became a real issue. Race relations have improved beyond recognition though many, many problems still exist. Few would deny that that improvement has been greatly accelerated by the rise to prominence of black Britons in a host of fields, notably football.

It was not until the early 1970s that the sons of the early wave of Caribbean immigrants began to make a concerted impression on the English game, passing through the time-honoured system of school, town, district, county teams, invitations to train with professional clubs, the chance to sign on schoolboy forms, then apprenticeships for the lucky few. London clubs had the greatest pool of black talent on which to draw simply because of the concentration of immigrant families in the capital city. Millwall and Orient were in the vanguard, as were Arsenal who recruited the young Brendon Batson among others.

Batson's early experiences are quite typical of many of his contemporaries. Born in Grenada on 6 February 1953, 'I left when I was six, then spent three years in Trinidad. My mum then sent my brother and me to stay with my uncle, my father's brother, in England. We come from a typical West Indian background where families are split up because parents are working away – my mother worked on a ship. She had seen the world and felt our future would be enhanced if we came to England, which we did in 1962.' Like many West Indians, Batson hadn't really been exposed to the joys of what in England is the beautiful winter game, playing the beautiful summer game instead. 'I consider myself fortunate to have found a career in professional football because in the West

Indies I had never played the game. I don't recall myself being active in any sports, but I do remember running along the beach and occasionally a game of cricket, but I showed no real aptitude towards sport.'

Any child moving to a new town and a new school with no friends is going to face a tough time. A black youngster moving to a new country is sure to have it even harder. Batson recalls, 'We were the only black family in Tilbury. My aunt was the local midwife and helped deliver most new babies in Tilbury so everyone knew of us. The lads I happened to fall in with were the sporty types and it was through them that I got involved in football. We used to play on a big open field near the house. The maths teacher – Mr Fitzgerald – used to be involved with the football team. One night I asked my friends what events were taking place on the field. They told me it was football practice – the only advice they gave me was to say I wasn't a goalkeeper. I had no boots, I used the plimsolls I had for athletics. My first trial turned into an absolute nightmare. Mr Fitzgerald saw me at the end of the session and asked me where I came from. I said Grenada at which point he said, "Maybe your game is cricket." He must have seen the look of disappointment on my face. Rather than tell me not to bother again, he felt sorry and told me I could come back next week. I went back, did reasonably well, and before long was in the school team, then got selected for district teams and got to win a runners-up trophy within a couple of years, my first ever trophy. My mother joined me after a couple of years and we moved up to Chadwell and then Walthamstow. By this time I was playing for a team in Barking.'

For a youngster who had never kicked a ball until he was nine years of age, Batson showed a great aptitude and appetite for the game and made rapid progress. Perhaps because he hadn't played as a young child he hadn't developed any bad footballing habits. Perhaps by coming to the game later, he didn't take it for granted as much as some of his contemporaries. Or perhaps he was simply a naturally gifted player. Batson recalls that by the time he was 13, he was 'playing for the district team and I got spotted by George

Male, one of the Arsenal greats of the 1930s, the Herbert Chapman era. I used to train out at Highbury twice a week. From there I progressed into the professional game. I was offered apprenticeship forms in 1968 when I was 15, but I chose to stay on at school for another year. On signing as an apprentice I was paid £16 a week and my mother was paid the same for digs money. I signed pro forms on my seventeenth birthday at £28 a week.'

His smooth progress from one level of the game to the next and then the next was not entirely typical of a professional footballer, black or white, but it was encouraging at a time when prejudice was rife. There is more than enough documentary and anecdotal evidence to show that during the 1960s, as Batson was beginning his rise through the ranks, black people were finding it very difficult to find work of any but the most menial kind. The days of full employment were beginning to ebb away and as work became more scarce many employers were only too happy to find an excuse not to employ black staff. The trade unions were rarely any more supportive and indeed were often the instigators of this shop-floor apartheid.

Sport, however, is one field where ability and achievement can overcome prejudice. To lapse into footballspeak for a moment, the game is all about opinions, but, at the end of the day, it's the 90 minutes that count and the team needs to get a result on Saturday afternoon Brian. In plain English, the be-all and end-all for a football club is its results on the field. Everything flows from that. Though 'outsiders' do face prejudices about their ability to cope with the English League – black footballers did, Europeans did, Asian footballers still do – if a player can demonstrate he has the ability that might just win your team an extra four or five points in the season, the points that might mean the difference between survival or relegation, that might win promotion, a place in Europe, or even a Championship, he's in. In that sense, football is incredibly democratic. Because a game that is focused so completely on winning can't afford not to be. To its credit, football showed a good deal of foresight in recruiting from the black population. In some quarters there continued to be the 'they don't like it up 'em, they've got no heart, they don't like it when it gets cold' stereotypical rubbish, but a large number of football's scouts, coaches and managers chose not to leave their brains in the gutter and judged players on the grounds of ability, attitude and application. Little wonder, since their jobs depended on their judgement.

One outstanding individual who made a great impression on the young Batson was Arsenal's manager, Bertie Mee. 'He was a fantastic man. He did wonders by instilling good qualities in all the young pros. He was a small man in size but a huge man in stature, his motto being "remember who you are, what you are and who you represent". I carry that philosophy with me today. I recall the season Arsenal won the Double, 1970–71, the youth team won the FA Youth Cup. Bertie Mee took us out that night to a really top restaurant. His philosophy was that as young men growing up we would need to get used to this sort of environment. He wanted us prepared for this type of situation. That's why we also played in international youth tournaments abroad. He wanted us accustomed to living like tourists, which involves a lot of hanging around. I saw him sack lads because they did not conform to the Arsenal "code of conduct".'

Mee was a disciplinarian of the old school, one who preached the gospel of high standards in everything, of achieving quality at every step. In some ways he was a man out of time, for the 1960s and 1970s were times of ever-increasing individualism. But Mee was not foolish enough simply to dismiss a player because he had his idiosyncrasies, his own way of doing things. Arsenal were an extremely organised unit, but Mee and his coach Don Howe knew that you needed to add flair to turn a team that was hard to beat into a side that won regularly. Providing a maverick was sufficiently willing to toe the line, to harness his abilities to the good of the side and to be enough of a team player not to cause disruption, Mee was happy. In Charlie George, he had such an individual, the star whose moment of brilliance clinched the FA Cup and, with it, the Double in 1971.

If a footballer would not meet those Arsenal standards, showed no sign of conforming, then Mee and his staff had no compunction in saying goodbye. That was the fate that met young Laurie Cunningham when he trained with the club as a schoolboy. George Petchey, later Laurie's boss at Orient, recalls, 'He was kicked out of Arsenal because he was unpunctual and an erratic sort of kid.' Unlike Batson, Cunningham was a London lad, born in Holloway on 8 March 1956, the son of a Jamaican racehorse jockey, which may go some way to explaining his grace and his ability to weave in and out of opponents. Also unlike Batson, Cunningham was a more introverted type of character. As Batson admits, 'I always had something to say for myself' but Cunningham kept himself to himself. Some saw that as a sign of arrogance, others as a lack of confidence, but it was neither. The truth was simply that Laurie Cunningham did things his own way, had his own ideas and neither needed nor sought a lot of advice. He lived life the way he saw it and that was it. According to John Wile, Cunningham's captain when he arrived at West Bromwich Albion, 'He was a bit of a loner, especially when you compare him with Cyrille and Brendon who were very approachable and happier with the attention they got. Laurie was more introverted, shy, and I think that sometimes all the press attention got to him a bit. He wasn't always comfortable with it.' According to former O's team-mate and close friend Bobby Fisher, this was not the man he knew during his time at Orient. 'When we were younger, Laurie was always laughing and joking.' Yet Wile's account of Cunningham is corroborated by Fisher, after he visited him in Madrid. 'In the time I was with him in Spain, I saw him laugh just once, which was incredible.' By then, whether pained by the failure to fulfil his early promise, by injury, by racism or by cultural alienation, this was no longer the confident young man destined for true footballing greatness.

Press attention must have seemed a million miles away when Cunningham was dumped by Arsenal. Joining him at the exit door was Glenn Roeder, himself a future England international. Within 18 months of walking away from the marbled halls of Highbury, both Cunningham and Roeder had made their first-team debuts, though Cunningham needed some persuading before he would go to Orient. Youth coach Bob Cottingham recalls, 'He was staggered when Arsenal turned him down. I had to drag him almost bodily to Leyton. He had such talent. Sometimes it seemed as if he was going through his opponents, not round them.' Bobby Fisher adds, 'I first saw him in the season of 1972 and I sensed there was something totally different about him. I knew he was going on to do something really big in the game. I just had this feeling that this skinny black kid, with no weight to him, had that something special.' Cunningham accepted that, in terms of physique, he was no Cyrille Regis, saying, 'I was a little titch when I joined Orient. In fact I used to like running the hurdles at school but it looked as though I would be better off going underneath them! I was that small.' But George Petchey knew enough about the game to see beyond that and recognise his supreme gift. 'I saw him play for his school and a local Sunday side, so did Arthur Rowe. It was obvious he had natural ability.' That Rowe should spot Cunningham and have a role in his eventual success as a professional post-Arsenal was a nice irony given that Rowe was the mastermind behind the great Spurs push-and-run side.

At the club, Cunningham teamed up with other promising apprentices and played in a talented youth squad alongside Roeder, Tony Grealish and Nigel Gray. Frank Woolf has been associated with the club for almost a lifetime, first as a fan, then as Commercial Manager before becoming Club Secretary. Woolf shows his encyclopaedic knowledge of post-war Leyton Orient as he walks round the tidy little Brisbane Road ground, pointing to the Laurie Cunningham bar in the main stand, reeling off statistic after statistic. From football's traditional wing, Frank Woolf is struggling to ingratiate himself with the modern game which he considers may eventually lead to the demise of clubs like his. He does however remember very clearly the excitement a new batch of youth team graduates caused in the mid-1970s. 'Normally, you get one or two youth players into the senior team. With that lot, it was five or six of them.' Cunningham was a member of the Orient team that finished runners-up in the South East Counties League, winning the London Youth Cup into the bargain in 1973–74. That same season he made his first impact in Europe when he was voted

Player of the Tournament in a youth competition in the Netherlands. The Orient boys, in many cases two years younger than their opponents, lost the final on penalties to a Borussia Moenchengladbach side who they had beaten in an earlier round.

Given the run-ins Cunningham had had with the Arsenal establishment, Petchey might have expected him to grasp this second opportunity with both hands, knuckle down and play by the rules. But that wasn't Cunningham's style, partly because he simply couldn't help being an individual. He began as he meant to go on. Bobby Fisher recalls his first day at the club, the all-important trial match. 'Everyone else was waiting, the first team players, manager, reserves, and suddenly Laurie just strolled over. The rest of the guys said he must be either very stupid or he must be one hell of a player. And it turned out to be the latter.' Timekeeping remained a particular weakness. During his time at Orient, he was known to pay off fines by going out to perform a dance demo at a local discotheque. Frustrating, exasperating and genial, all rolled into one. If a footballer is touched with genius on the field – and Cunningham was – if he can do the unexpected, the impossible, if he can show the imagination, the flair of the true artist, if he breaks all the rules on the field, can we then expect him to live by the rules in conventional society? Did we criticise Dali or Hendrix for not popping into the office and doing a bit of work from nine to five, Monday to Friday?

Dali had the great advantage of having nobody to answer to, nobody to rely on and nobody who relied on him. Laurie Cunningham was just one in a team, something which makes individualism a tricky path to follow at the best of times. Petchey admits, 'We had one or two problems with him in the early days. At times he didn't take too kindly to training. He had to struggle in life and was the sort of youngster who was used to living on his wits. He was suspicious of people outside his own circle. He took a long time to trust other people.' Part of Cunningham's difficulty was due to his being a non-conformist – how many other hopeful footballers were taking ballet classes? But equally, as a sensitive youngster, Cunningham had been scarred by the racism, casual or aggressive, that was endemic in England, in London, throughout his formative years. Any kid who has ever been bullied knows that it's not wise to stand out from the crowd. Most can shrink out of the way and not be seen. But if you're a black kid in a white country, how do you hide? And if being black wasn't enough for the simple racists, stir in the fact that the boy was the best footballer any of his contemporaries would ever play with, the kid who could destroy any opposition, and you've got somebody who is a real target.

He became a full professional on his eighteenth birthday and made his first team bow against West Ham in the Texaco Cup at the start of the 1974–75 season, creating quite an impression. 'Laurie Looks Great' said the *Sun* newspaper headline. The accompanying article written by Alex Montgomery went on to say, 'O's manager, George Petchey, is certain the debut winger is going to be a great player. And, on the evidence of what I saw at Upton Park, Petchey could be spot-on with his prediction. Petchey enthused, "It took him a little time to get adjusted to the pace of the game but I was delighted from the way he played from then on. He has a natural talent. He has the speed and ability to take on men. He never gives up. There's a big future ahead for him." Frank Woolf remembers his league debut a few weeks later. 'We were 2–1 down to Oldham when Laurie came on. He created havoc among their defenders and almost helped turn the game round for us.' During that first season, Cunningham went on to play 15 games, scoring a solitary but nonetheless spectacular goal. A few months on from making his debut, however, he was to be given a salutary reminder that the game was not all sweetness and light. Welcome to the real world son.

The opposition: Millwall. The venue: The Den, Cold Blow Lane. Even the name sends a chill down the spine to football followers of a certain vintage. It was a period when the association between Millwall, hooliganism and racism was at its height. Academic and fan Les Back talks about it as a period when 'Millwall reigned supreme'. Enough said.

Fisher recalls, still with some trepidation, an encounter with some of Millwall's notorious fans. The Orient team's arrival at the

Den witnessed National Front activists distributing racist propaganda. Inside the ground, they were met with a torrent of abuse and spitting. Then, all-square, one minute to go, up pops Laurie Cunningham to score the winner. It was the ultimate insult to the uncompromising white male culture of white working-class dockland. Objects rained onto the pitch, the most striking a six-inch carving knife. In these more enlightened days of the anti-racist campaigns, it's easy to forget the experiences to which the black players of that era were exposed. More often than not, they returned to unsympathetic dressing-rooms and club officials, unable to call upon the authorities to take their problems seriously. Both comfort and strength had to be drawn from within. Responses varied from the passive to the provocative. Bobby Fisher recalls, 'Me and Laurie did the black power salute a couple of times. To be honest, we didn't properly understand the significance. All we knew was that some black American athletes had done it at the Olympics, and that was good enough for us.' The reference was to Tommie Smith and John Carlos, winners of gold and silver for the 200 metres at the 1968 Mexico City games when Smith broke the world record into the bargain. Their athletic achievements were somewhat overshadowed when both Americans stood on the podium and raised their right fist in the air. Smith and Carlos said they were using this high profile opportunity to show solidarity with fellow black Americans who were in the midst of civil disobedience actions against state and national government. In fact, the coining of the phrase Black Power was a pragmatic rather than provocative act. Black American activist Stokeley Carmichael used it simply as an antithesis to the term 'white power structure' that was then current in the American civil rights vocabulary. In 1967, the definition was widened to say that black people should pursue their rightful, equal place in society 'by any means necessary'. It was the latter definition that riled many white Americans who found the term to be overly threatening. Smith made the point 'We are great American athletes for 19.8 seconds, then we are animals as far as this country is concerned.'

According to Fisher, the salute seemed an appropriate retort. 'It was at a time when we were getting a lot of stick, abuse, spitting, objects thrown at us. We wanted to do something to get people to sit up and take notice. With no support from anybody it was our only way to make our point.' They were black football's Tolpuddle Martyrs or suffragettes. That said, one could only speculate on the likely effect which many incidents of this type had on the psychological wellbeing of black players and in particular on a young player whose confidence had, seemingly, no bounds. Later on, in February 1979 when he'd become an England international and was winning rave reviews at West Bromwich Albion, Cunningham admitted that he had undergone something of a journey of discovery, about himself as much as anything. 'There have been times when I've been mixed up about the race thing. A couple of years ago I thought that to be black in England was to be a loser. You know, back of the queue for decent jobs. Suspicion on you before anyone knew what you were about. I did have a feeling for 'black power'. It seemed to meet the mood of frustration. It could give you some pride. Then I changed. It sort of struck me that the great majority of people, black and white, are in the same boat, fighting for a decent living. It also struck me that down at Orient I was getting a very good break. I got on well with George Petchey. It didn't matter to him whether I was black, white or Chinese just as long as I could play. And then along comes a guy like Johnny Giles, who knows so much about the game, and lays out all that money for me. I want to tell a lot of those black kids out there the same kind of thing can happen to them.'

Cunningham's arrival on the scene coincided with a major revival in the O's fortunes. According to Tom Collins, a supporter now working as an education officer with the Football Unites Racism Divides project, 'There was much anticipation that soon 'little Orient' would be getting ready to take on the mighty Spurs and Arsenal.' Sadly, financial difficulties resulted in a break-up of the team and the fans were left clinging to their dreams, but not before they had some fun and a collection of happy memories, many involving Cunningham. Collins is another who marvelled at his ability, and he offers a perspective from an unusual vantage point. 'I used to watch him from ground level in the enclosure. I was amazed at how this young man with sinewy legs managed to survive against those tree-trunk-legged defenders. Many a time he would ride over challenges from guys with hate tattooed on their foreheads, who'd then end up crashing into a heap on the walls of the enclosure.'

What made Cunningham all the more incredible was the poor quality of the Brisbane Road pitch. According to Frank Woolf, 'The state of our pitch was a long-standing joke in those days. At one point we were unable to play on it for three months. It had something to do with the failure of the river authorities to open the gates of the River Leigh, which runs beneath the ground. The only way we could stop it waterlogging was to throw tons of sand on it.' While Cunningham played as if he were a Brazilian ball-juggler at the Maracana, mere mortals struggled to perform the basics. If one ever needed proof that he was something special, then it was necessary to look no further than Brisbane Road. According to Collins, as well as talent, Cunningham had 'attitude'. It is something he associates with his racial identity. He feels that Cunningham's blackness was an important component of that 'attitude'. 'He was the one with attitude, ability, in a team full of triers and workhorses. It was almost as if he was imposing a reverse superiority, telling all around him that black people were superior to their white players.'

Ultimately, West Bromwich Albion and its use of the famed 'Three Degrees' made the most significant contribution towards ensuring the English game opened its eyes and eventually its heart to the previously suppressed black footballing community. In some ways, it's unfair and unjust to Leyton Orient. At a time when the Baggies were fêted for employing three black players, Remi Moses coming into the team soon after Cunningham's departure for Spain, Orient were regularly running out with five or six. Whilst many of the Brisbane Road faithful remained impassive or bemused by the situation, a small but vocal band of younger white followers rejoiced at the idea of their team reflecting the local multicultural community. In an era when much was said and written about the influences of far right-wing groups in football, here was an example of the opposite. Young white working-class men, influenced by the politics of the left, keen to celebrate the ethnic diversity of British society, were not prepared to concede ground to the racists. Collins says, 'Among my friends, there was this very proud thing about the likes of "Fish" and Laurie being at the Orient. We knew that we had something special and could never understand the hate and vilification towards black people. It was great growing up in this rich, vibrant and dynamic environment. I still have vivid memories of watching black women in their big smart hats going into those music-loving Pentecostal churches.'

Two decades on, it's inconceivable to think of circumstances in which followers of a team containing several black faces would actively celebrate that situation. Young children may wear the shirt of a black hero, terrace types may sing the praises of their star black player, but we remain a long way away from fans celebrating their team's ethnic diversity. What makes the chanting of a song sung by a small band of travelling Orient fans, to the tune of Boney M's 'Brown Girl in the Ring', all the more remarkable was that it happened all that time ago. According to Collins, 'We used to substitute the words with "there's a black team in the league". Us, this motley band of white fans. Opposition fans could never work out why we were singing the song.'

These days, it's not uncommon to see teams containing four or five black faces, the ranks of professional football being swollen by black players. It's a situation that has given way to passive acceptance of the permanent presence of black players in the game, but we remain a long way from the day when we hear fans 'sing a rainbow': 'black and yellow and white and brown, our team is a rainbow, a ****ing rainbow and we'll rain on you.' The taunting of Leicester City fans, a city with a large Asian community, by Leeds United followers, with the song 'A town full of Pakis' suggests we're a long way from a repetition of 'There's a black team in the league.'

Unfortunately for the O's, even having a team half filled with black players couldn't attract a significant new black following to

Brisbane Road, as they continued to feel unsafe in the football ground environment. 'A lot of my black mates changed their allegiance from Spurs and Arsenal to Orient and carried around pictures of Laurie, but didn't feel confident enough to come with us.' Collins is saddened by the fact that so few black people were able to share with him the 'privilege', as he calls it, of seeing the genius play. Arguably, had Leyton Orient been a more fashionable club in a higher division, then it might have been them rather than West Bromwich Albion around which this story unfolds. What is indisputable is that the club played a highly significant part in the development of black players in this country.

For Laurie, three seasons on from his debut, ninety-one starts, thirteen substitute appearances and eighteen, mostly spectacular, goals, it was time to move on. For almost two seasons scouts had been pouring into Brisbane Road to observe this outstanding young player. There was reported interest from several big clubs. It no longer remained a question of 'if'. It was 'when'. Ironically, the club's notorious quagmire pitch forced their hand. A succession of postponements resulted in major cash flow problems. Manager George Petchey said, 'I did not want to sell him, but we were over our limit at the bank and West Brom were ready with a cheque.' Other clubs were interested, notably SV Hamburg – who three months later were to buy Kevin Keegan from Liverpool – and St Etienne, who would express similar interest twelve months later in a young forward called Cyrille Regis. Neither of those major European clubs felt ready to take the plunge on Cunningham, still just a young player who had yet to succeed at the highest level. Cunningham was ambitious and admitted, 'I jumped at the chance of moving into the First Division with West Brom. It was progress as far as I was concerned and I was impressed with Johnny Giles's approach to the game.'

Cunningham moved to the Hawthorns in a deal valued at £110,000, which included a player swap element, Albion's Allan Glover and Joe Mayo moving south. He moved 'too cheaply' according to Frank Woolf. No one was more sad to see him go than the man Cunningham was to regard as the manager who best knew how to handle him, George Petchey. 'There was a time when Peter Angell [coach] and myself wondered if we could win Laurie over. He often turned up for training when he liked. The old eyes flashed when we fined him, but for all that, I loved the spark that made him.' Within 12 months, the inevitable break-up of the team had begun. Glenn Roeder soon followed and with that went the last hope for the O's to exchange fixtures with Millwall and Brentford for altogether more enticing games with Arsenal and Spurs.

He was a tube ride away from family, friends and familiar environments and at a club where not only did the fans adore him, but where he played for a manager he truly respected. It's not difficult to see why Cunningham seemed at his happiest here in this southern corner of London. Home.

TWO

That Laurie Cunningham should end up at West Bromwich Albion was somehow appropriate. Albion had long had a reputation for playing attractive football, particularly for their use of skilful ball players, intelligent wingers. Cunningham was merely the latest in a post-war line that included Billy Elliott, George Lee, Frank Griffin, Clive Clark, and the darling of the crowd, Willie Johnston. Johnston was a crowd-pleaser par excellence. Bought by Don Howe from Rangers for a club record £135,000, Johnston had played the pivotal role in the Glasgow side's European Cup-Winners' Cup win, and made an immediate impression on Albion fans. He was quick, skilful and had people on tiptoes or out of their seats whenever he got their ball, the sort of footballer people are happy to pay good money to watch. He was also a man of unreliable temperament who regularly found himself finishing the game earlier than the other 21 players, on one memorable occasion launching a kick at a referee as Albion slumped to a League Cup defeat at home to Brighton. How could you not love a footballer like that?

Cunningham was fortunate that he hadn't been bought to replace Willie, but to complement him on the other flank, though on occasion he played more centrally as an inside-forward. That Albion were willing to sign such a player and to embrace such an attacking formation was final proof that the brief traumas of the earlier 1970s were over, and that Albion were again a force to be reckoned with at the top level. Throughout the 1960s, Albion had had a superb Cup team. They won the Football League Cup 5–3 on aggregate over two legs in 1966, against a West Ham side that included Moore, Hurst and Peters, just a couple of months before those three earned immortality in the World Cup final. But Albion were always terribly fallible – current supporters will doubtless recognise an emerging theme here – and the following year, in the first League Cup final to be held at Wembley, Albion crashed to a 3–2 defeat against Queen's Park Rangers of the Third Division, having led 2–0. The FA Cup returned to the Hawthorns the following year, when Jeff Astle's thunderous shot beat Everton. That win means Albion were the last West Midlands side to win the Cup. Back at Wembley a couple of years later, again in the League Cup, an early goal from Astle wasn't enough to prevent Albion losing 2–1 to Manchester City.

That Wembley defeat signalled the end of an era, as the team began to age and break up. Manager Alan Ashman was sacked in 1971, despite his Cup successes, for failing to turn the team into championship challengers. Don Howe, a former Albion full-back, fêted for his role as coach to the Arsenal Double-winning side, returned to The Hawthorns as manager, but succeeded only in taking the side down in his first season, ending a 25-year run in the top flight. In fairness to both Ashman and Howe, Albion haemorrhaged an enormous amount of talent in a short space of time. Centre-halfs John Kaye and John Talbut and full-backs Dougie Fraser and Graham Williams all came to the end of their careers at around the same time, leaving successive managers to put an entirely new defence in place. Shortly thereafter, midfielder Bobby Hope was allowed to leave the club too soon to move to Birmingham and Asa Hartford eventually left for Manchester City after a move to Leeds broke down on medical grounds. Worst of all, the King, Jeff Astle, was beginning to struggle with regular injuries. Astle was an Albion talisman, natural successor to the likes of Ronnie Allen and Derek Kevan as the side's great goalscorer, always good for twenty-five or thirty goals a season. With him gone, the goals dried up and with a brand new back four letting in too many as they bedded in, relegation was inevitable.

Relegation from the First Division in the early 1970s, though desperately disappointing, was not the traumatic blow it is today. A number of clubs used a year in the Second Division as an opportunity to regroup, introduce new blood and then attack the First Division anew – Manchester United were a classic example of that. Losing Best, Law and Bobby Charlton in quick succession, they were relegated, but came straight back up with a clutch of promising new players who cut their teeth in the less pressurised environment of the Second Division. Most observers saw this as Albion's lot. The master tactician Don Howe would use the year to restructure the team, to change the style of play a little and to mould together a strong unit. He certainly had promising raw material – John Wile, Alistair Robertson, Len Cantello had come in to join Willie Johnston, Tony Brown, John Osborne. A team was forming.

Yet Howe was unable to get the best out of the players he had. Johnston complained later that 'the side became bogged down in a blackboard jungle' as Howe tried to introduce the Arsenal philosophy of football to the club, in itself an idea that did not go down well with supporters who demanded that the side attack rather than defend. As he has shown time and again, Howe is a very successful coach with very definite ideas on the game, most of which are based on using a watertight defence as a springboard. Howe's view was that that was all the more important in a team that was in transition. Unfortunately, the side lacked quality up front and with such a concentration on defending in numbers, the forwards rarely got much support. Albion legend Tony Brown continued to post his share of goals, but the likes of Joe Mayo and Ian Edwards were, if wholehearted, simply not good enough to replace the King. Albion spent a couple of seasons in the upper reaches of the Second Division without threatening promotion. The Albion board chose not to renew Don Howe's contract and the club were looking for a new boss to take them into the 1975–76 season.

John Wile, who, with Alistair Robertson, eventually created a central defensive pairing as utterly uncompromising as any in the land, argues, 'Don was unlucky because he didn't get any credit for what he'd done. He gave us a very good grounding, taught good habits, particularly defensively, which became the foundation for our success later in the 1970s. I think that in essence, Don's problem was that some people are very good coaches, some are very good managers. There is a difference between the two jobs and Don wasn't so good as a manager. He started to build a team but didn't get time to develop it. I think he wanted to bring John Giles in as a player, and that would have been an excellent move.'

In September 1974, Giles had been widely linked with a move to Tottenham, to form a new managerial partnership alongside Danny Blanchflower in succession to Bill Nicholson. That ultimately fell through, but it alerted the wider footballing world to the fact that Giles was ready to leave Leeds and move into football management. In suggesting that Giles might have a role to play at the Albion, Don Howe might well have committed professional suicide. Why bring him in as a player when you could dispense with Howe and have Giles doing two jobs for the price of one?

The player-manager was still a comparatively new idea at the time, certainly in the top two divisions. But it was critical that Giles continued to play. Giles was the fulcrum of the wonderful Leeds side under Don Revie, and remained a superb reader of the game, a player who could dictate the pace and control the direction of any game. As John Wile says, 'John Giles took up the good things that Don had done with the defence and built on it. A lot of the success we had that season in particular was to do with his presence as a player. That was John's most effective contribution, certainly initially. Because of his ability, and the way he brought players on, we developed into a very good side.' According to Willie Johnston, 'We worked with the ball nearly all the time . . . Johnny was an intelligent manager, a majestic and graceful player and a great guy.'

But life wasn't all plain sailing under Giles as John Trewick, then an up and coming youngster, remembers. 'We'd struggled early on but he was strong in his beliefs, just kept us passing the ball, and eventually we got the groove. We became known for it and it worked, even though people were impatient initially. It took time to get the fans on the wavelength.' Slowly but surely, the Giles philosophy began to pay dividends. With the manager pulling the strings in midfield, players like Len Cantello, Bryan Robson and Trewick himself began to get on top of First Division sides, feeding Johnston, creating for Tony Brown, while at the back Wile and Robertson were steadfast. Giles also bought wisely, both that season and the next, as Wile recalls. 'Paddy Mulligan, Ray Treacey, Mick Martin were all very good signings for us, didn't cost a lot but gave good experience to the squad, helped bring on the young lads. John was very quiet, we crept in to the last promotion spot, a hell of a run from Christmas, just kept going and then won that last game at Oldham to go up, caught everybody by surprise. John kept a lid on it, there were no expectations, we just got on with our work.' Albion clinched the third promotion slot on the last day of the season when Tony Brown launched one of his trademark volleys from the edge of the box at Boundary Park. Albion were back in the First Division.

The close season wasn't without its traumas. Giles decided he didn't enjoy the precarious nature of football management and handed in his notice. He was persuaded to change his mind, but that, along with the fact that Albion had only just scraped into the top flight, left most commentators predicting relegation. It was a reasonable assumption, but the step up into the top flight wasn't as daunting then as it is today, as Wile admits. 'The gulf between the First and Second Divisions wasn't as immense. In essence now, you get promoted to the Premiership and you're really going up two divisions. You've got the bulk of players who would have been playing in the old Second Division now in the Premiership as squad players, which makes for a big gulf. The players we bought in, as well as a lot of our own players who were already at the club, like Tony Brown or Willie Johnston, would now be in a Premiership squad somewhere, they wouldn't have been playing in the Second Division. So the good players were more evenly spread around the country.'

Albion got off to a good start, soon crushed Manchester United 4–0 and looked every inch a First Division side. John Trewick remembers, 'We surprised people, but we weren't frightened of anyone. Maybe it was reckless or stupid, but we just had that "roll up the sleeves, we'll beat anybody" attitude.' The way in which Albion played was as big a surprise to many as the results they got. They finished the season in seventh, just short of a UEFA Cup place, and dumped Liverpool out of the League Cup to boot. Albion were established and could move into the transfer market in a more expansive fashion. They bought David Cross for £100,000 from Coventry to provide the target man they'd lacked since the days of Jeff Astle, and then brought Laurie Cunningham to the club in a deal valued at £110,000.

The arrival of Cunningham was of immense significance. Although he was not yet a nationally known figure, within the game there was a general appreciation that here was a very special talent. Question marks remained about his temperament, but his ability was never in question. When Albion moved to sign him, it was a signal to the rest of English football that the club meant business.

Cunningham continued to have trouble fitting in, at least initially. Trewick remembers, 'The first impression was he was a bit arrogant. He came into a dressing-room where we'd known each other for years, and he was a bit aloof, but when you got to know him, he was one of the good guys, a lovely bloke. The biggest memory I have of Laurie was he was such a wonderful mover, like a ballet dancer. The stretch he had was phenomenal. He played with such grace. The first day of training, he stretched his leg up over his head to bring a ball down, controlled it. Pulled it down. He had such subtlety, lovely touch, very quick, great individuality but he knew team play too. A terrific player. We'd done well that year and adding quality with Laurie at the end of that season had to improve things. I was getting experienced, Derek Statham was coming in, Bryan Robson was getting experienced, we were looking a good side.'

Cunningham made his debut in a 2–0 win at Spurs, his home debut four days later against Ipswich. Bobby Robson's side finished third that season and had already thumped Albion 7–0 at Portman Road. Albion swept them aside 4–0 and Cunningham grabbed a goal and became an instant hero, even though Bryan Robson grabbed the headlines with a hat trick. With Cunningham, immediately nicknamed 'the black flash' by the local press, out on the right, Willie Johnston on the left, Albion were suddenly a potent attacking force, capable of creating chances out of nothing. Though Cunningham didn't unleash his full repertoire of tricks, mostly keeping it simple on his debut, his pace and his superb close control made it clear that Albion had bought themselves a real footballer who could make a real impression on the club. Wile recalls, 'We'd played against Laurie when Orient were in the Second Division, and he was one of a bunch of good young players they had. He was tricky, but there was no end product, lots of ability, but very young. When he came here, it was obvious that that ability was something very special. He'd do tricks in training that would take your breath away. People thought he was a smashing player anyway, but if he'd done some of those things in games, they'd have been astounded.'

If Cunningham's arrival heralded a new ambition on the playing field, it was equally significant on a social level. Laurie Cunningham will always be known as the first black player to play for West Bromwich Albion. The Hawthorns is situated slap-bang in the middle of an area with a substantial immigrant presence. Just to the south of Smethwick lies Handsworth, perhaps even more significant than Smethwick, for where Smethwick's immigrant population was substantially Asian, Handsworth had a greater number of Afro-Caribbeans. Neither community had made its presence felt on the terraces, understandable in a period where contemptible groups such as the National Front were infiltrating football crowds and at a time when general, indiscriminate football violence was at its worst. If that were not enough to put any sensible person off going to the game, the football arena was an intimidatingly white one. Crowds were solidly white working class, but so were the teams. Who could black supporters identify with? Where county cricket offered that opportunity with players like Kanhai and Kallicharran at Warwickshire, football did not. The arrival of Laurie Cunningham signalled a change in that imbalance.

For Cunningham, the switch to the Midlands meant a complete

change in his life. Living outside London for the first time, he was now with a club that claimed a large amount of coverage in the local media where Orient had barely merited a few lines in a city that included Arsenal, Spurs and Chelsea. Cunningham was now in a goldfish bowl, a situation exacerbated by his position as a role model for the black community, a position he neither sought nor particularly welcomed, but which he could not escape. Equally, from being the star man at Orient, he now found himself in the middle of a dressing room that had been together for some time, closely knit, full of hardened professionals and players of genuine stature who had proved themselves in the First Division. Though Cunningham was an obvious talent, probably the most naturally gifted player at the club even on arrival, he wasn't going to be allowed to get away with anything. John Wile remembers, 'Laurie was a one-off in lots of things – the way he played, his dress sense, he was into fashion, he was a bit outrageous in his clothes. He didn't find mixing with other people easy. And at times he didn't endear himself to the rest of the players because he did act as an individual when we were very much a group. But Laurie would be late for training, he stretched things a bit, which went against the grain because the essence of the club was the team ethic, that we were all together. We had strong characters, but basically good pros, that was it, that was how the Albion was even when I came, with men like Graham Williams, John Kaye, John Talbut, Dougie Fraser, John Osborne and that had carried on even as the players changed. The managers and coaches couldn't disrespect those players, they had to value their opinions, they had strong ideas about the game and about their colleagues. If someone stepped out of line, often as not the players would deal with it. Laurie had his own ideas and sometimes that didn't make him too popular. It never became a big problem, but he did upset people now and again.'

There was a genuine fear that Cunningham would not fit in, and that here might be another in the line of hugely talented players who failed to fulfil their potential because of temperamental weaknesses. Cunningham's waywardness was all the more frustrating because he was such a nice man, wasn't deliberately wilful, wasn't 'behaving badly' to get attention. He wasn't trying to prove any points, he was just one of those characters that simply march to the sound of a different drum, that are simply incapable of conforming and find it baffling when that irritates others. He expressed some surprise when Johnny Giles fined him for missing training towards the end of that 1976–77 season. He felt if he was doing his job – and six goals in thirteen games suggested he was – that was enough. But, as Tony Brown said at the time, 'Johnny Giles set the pattern. He told us what he wanted and insisted that as professional players we shouldn't need reminding.' In some ways, Cunningham was a man out of time, for there was still a very definite hierarchy operating within football clubs, and not just at the Albion, as John Trewick explains. 'I first came here at 12 or 13 as a schoolboy, joined the club full-time at 15. The club trained at Spring Road, opposite the ground. The first-team dressing-room was sacrosanct, out of bounds, and you had so much respect for first-team players, if they spoke to you, it was a big thing. You looked at them with stars in your eyes. Things have changed a bit now. The world changes so the game changes. Kids have a different handle on things, it's not a lack of respect so much, but they don't have that awe we had. It kept you in your place and if you progressed, you felt you'd earned it. You were with the kids, suddenly you'd be in the reserve team dressing-room stripping with them, and if you're there at 16, you know you're progressing, it was a measure. The big thing was getting the peg in the first-team dressing-room. At 17 or 18, that was wonderful. Those measures aren't in place any more, it's much more a group thing, we're all part of the club. A lot is right about it, but it's different, you cannot compare.' Perhaps Cunningham would have felt more at home in the less reverent atmosphere of today, but that said, the discipline exerted at the Albion was good for him, as he conceded. 'I've taken a lot of unfair criticism but I would be mad not to admit that I have things to learn. I've made mistakes which I won't ever make again. When you are 21 and in your first year of First Division football you have a lot of things to sort out. I'm sorting them out now. Don't worry, I'll make it.'

More problems were around the corner. Having played some

sublime football at the Albion, he was instantly elevated to the England Under-21 side and on 27 April 1977, he became the first black player to represent his country at that level, playing in a 1–0 win over Scotland. Two months on from being just another anonymous footballer at a struggling Second Division club, Laurie Cunningham was one of the most talked about players in the country. And he was a target for the racists, both here and abroad. There was trouble on the Under-21s' summer tour of Scandinavia. Cunningham was provoked in a nightclub which had a colour bar, and then he was taken to task for behaving disrespectfully during the Finnish national anthem prior to an international. Certainly he made mistakes and to behave in such a fashion towards a host nation's anthem was stupid in the extreme, but then Cunningham himself wasn't always shown the respect he deserved either, in the main because of the colour of his skin. How would you react to abuse on that level?

Cunningham was isolated and exposed because he was the trailblazer, the pioneer. Cunningham was the laboratory rat in the experiment with the black footballer. He was the only black player in the England team, one of few in the First Division and certainly the most visible, the most eye-catching. He came under tremendous scrutiny from players, coaches, fans and administrators alike. For every person who wanted him to succeed and thereby end the spurious debate about the role of black players, if indeed they had one, there was at least one more who would have loved to see him fall flat on his face and put a halt to the spread of 'his kind'. Opposing fans hurled abuse, opponents weren't above doing the same. Whenever Cunningham went down under a heavy tackle, there were many only too happy to point out that black players didn't have the heart for the English game. When he picked himself up, he was a cheating black bastard who hadn't really been injured after all. That these morons were questioning the courage of a man subjecting himself to this torrent of abuse while they hid behind the anonymity of packed terraces like the pathetic cowards they were never occurred to them. But then racists have never been noted for their intellectual rigour, have they?

Anyone with eyes to see and a brain with which to think – leaving out of most of his colour-blind, mentally challenged detractors – could see that Cunningham was a marvellous footballer whose presence we should cherish, a man with a gift so rare it had to be nurtured lest we all lose out through its destruction. Isolated as he was, it would have been easy for him to fall apart under the strain and disappear into obscurity. That he did not surely gives the lie to those tales of him as a fragile individual. Cunningham was hard enough to survive but it was a lonely business.

That was soon to change as black players began to make a mark in many teams up and down the country. On a personal level, perhaps the greatest stroke of good fortune that befell Cunningham was the arrival of another young black striker at The Hawthorns. Cyrille Regis was plucked from the non-league game and signed for the club in May 1977, though he didn't actually arrive for training until pre-season work began in July. The signing of Regis was one of the last acts of Johnny Giles's time as manager of the club. As in the previous summer, he decided he needed greater job security than that offered by conventional football management and this time he could not be dissuaded. That might have been a blow for Regis, had Giles not been replaced by Ronnie Allen who had been instrumental in signing him for the club. 'From what I'm told, Ronnie Allen heard about me, heard I was this big, raw black guy, and came to see me playing for Hayes. He tells the story that he saw me go up for a ball and put the ball in the net along with four defenders and decided "that'll do for me!" He had to persuade the board to buy me, eventually he said he'd buy me with his own money and that persuaded them. I had a one-year contract, the club paid Hayes £10,000 altogether after so many games, and that bought the lights at Hayes, and they're still there! Then Johnny Giles resigned and Ronnie Allen took over as manager, so that helped me.'

Regis had a lot in common with Cunningham, having spent much of his life in London. 'I arrived in England, in London, from French Guyana when I was five. When I went to school I preferred athletics and cricket to soccer and I didn't take it seriously until I went to senior school. I didn't even become interested in the game until I was 12 and I didn't get in the school team until I was 13. By the time I'd left I was determined to learn a trade and play football just for enjoyment. I just played for a club called Ryder Brent Valley. That was mostly the Borough of Brent side who played at my school and then played Sunday mornings. I was round about 17, we played in the Regent's Park League. It was just a load of kids getting changed in the back of a Ryder Van, because the manager worked for Ryder Truck Rentals and he used to get a van, so if he was late we had to get changed in the back as we were going along! It was there that John Sullivan, who was owner-paymaster of Molesley Football Club, saw us and he invited two or three of us to go along at the end of one season, then invited me back for the next, quite liked me and I stayed there a year. I did well while I was there, got 20-odd goals, could have gone to Boreham Wood but the manager said I was under a professional contract, "you can't move". At that time I was too young to be under contract, but I didn't know. After that season, the Hayes goalkeeper, Ian Bath, came to Molesley and recommended me to Hayes. I was naïve, I said, "I can't go, I'm under contract"! He had a mate in the FA who looked into it, discovered there was no contract, and I was disgusted really, so I just walked out. I went to Hayes which was great, another level up, closer to home, met some great London boys from Chingford, and I got 25 goals again for them. The year I'd been at Molesley, Trevor Lee and Phil Walker from Epsom went to Millwall from that league and made a bit of a name for themselves, two young black boys. Then the year after, Gordon Jago was after me for Millwall but the directors vetoed it because they thought I was too raw. But there was a bit of a buzz that I'd got to a big club, but I just loved playing football and if it happened it happened. I liked my job, I was an apprentice electrician working on a building sites all over London. It was hard work, getting across London to play, coming home late after a few beers after the game, getting up for work, the whole drill of non-league life, but I enjoyed it and I grew up in that time. And it helped that from 17 I was playing against big men, so when I got to the Albion and played against men, it wasn't intimidating. When you come through the ranks at a club, you're always playing in the same age group until you get to the first team. Then you're playing against men and there's that physical aggression, and that's a real barrier, so I didn't find it a problem, which it can be for a lot of players.'

When Regis arrived at the Albion, nobody expected him to play first-team football in the near future. Laurie Cunningham looked likely to be Albion's only black player for quite some time to come. Funny how life changes, isn't it?

THREE

A change of manager is as regular as a change in the weather at The Hawthorns these days, but to be changing after just a couple of very successful seasons under Johnny Giles wasn't something anyone wanted. Replacing Giles with Ronnie Allen was an excellent move, however. Allen had been a goalscoring hero at the club through the 1950s, had won an FA Cup winners' medal with the club in 1954 and was steeped in its history. He'd had a very successful spell as chief scout, bringing in both Cunningham and Regis in his last days in that role, and was well aware of all the footballers at the club and how best to use them. A shrewd judge, Allen could see that the side was starting to come to maturity. When an outsider might have been tempted to change things around, Allen was content to let things flow as they had under Giles.

The opening three League games brought the full hand of results – victory over Chelsea, draw at Leeds, defeat at Liverpool. Then came injury problems. David Cross was out, his obvious replacement Ally Brown struggling too, and a League Cup game with Rotherham to be fulfilled – a low-key fixture, ideal for blooding a youngster such as Cyrille Regis. 'I'd come up here from London, went in the reserves and it was hard. As an electrician in non-league, I'd trained twice a week. Suddenly you're training every day and pre-season was twice a day and I was wrecked, absolutely wrecked. And Birmingham was quiet after London, didn't know anybody so it was hard going to start with, but things worked out. Early in the season, we were playing Rotherham at home in the League Cup that night. Ronnie Allen came over and said, 'Go home, get some sleep, you're playing tonight.' You want it, you want to perform, but when reality hits and you've only played in front of four hundred people and then you've got thirteen or fourteen thousand people in a big stadium wondering who this Regis bloke is, internally the fear and excitement is incredible. Anything can happen, you don't know how you'll react in a situation. I ran on pure energy, adrenaline, I'd never had time to be taught anything professional, so it was enthusiasm and power really. I missed a couple of chances but we went 2–0 up and then we got a penalty and the crowd started chanting for me to take it. Went up, scored, never took one again after that, then I got another goal. And the crowd was unbelievable, they all just took to me straight away. I think they felt for me when I missed a couple and they were willing me to score. So then I got headlines and the negative stuff as well – what will he be like against real opposition, is he a flash in the pan? Come Saturday we had Middlesbrough at home, big Stuart Boam in defence, got picked again, and fortunately I got a classic goal, picked up the ball up halfway, turned, ran with Boam holding on to me and scored. I got five or six goals in a handful of games and I was off. That's what you need, somebody to believe in you, to give you a chance. Football is so opinionated, good players get lost because nobody believes in them at the right time. I was lucky that Ronnie Allen believed in me.'

Because of his frame, his personality and the sheer 'Roy of the Rovers' nature of his first week in the first team, there's no question that Cyrille Regis made an even bigger impact on the club than Laurie Cunningham had done. Just as Newcastle United are seemingly on a never-ending quest to find the latest in the mythical line of centre-forwards, so are West Bromwich Albion. W.G. Richardson, Ronnie Allen, Jeff Astle, the shirt was passed down from generation to generation and it took some player before the crowd would allow him to wear it. Nobody had really fitted into the shirt since Jeff Astle had hung it up. Joe Mayo and Ian Edwards were solid triers but lower division footballers. David Cross had a decent scoring record – 19 goals in 38 league games – but didn't ignite the imagination. But Regis was something else. John Trewick, who has subsequently worked alongside Regis as a coach at The Hawthorns, was able to watch him at first hand on the field. 'Cyrille just exploded onto the scene like nobody else I've ever seen. It was extraordinary. He'd played non-league for Hayes but the gap from there to the First Division is huge. Lee Hughes has made a similar impact I suppose, not as sudden because he was eased into the team, and not at such a level. Cyrille had a handful of reserve games, nobody had ever heard of him, suddenly he's here, this big, black, London lad, built like a boxer. And there weren't many black players then so he stood out even more, but he just came in and ripped everybody apart, it was startling. He'd come in for pre-season, he was very raw, we could see the pace, the strength, the power he had, though his hold-up play was a problem. We based our game on possession football and Cyrille didn't appreciate it then as he did later. We'd be playing it through to him and he'd be trying something and losing it and we'd be screaming at him "hold that bloody ball up", and Cyrille would apologise. Then five minutes later he'd get the ball on the halfway line, turn, carry Stuart Boam twenty-five yards on his back, shrug him off, go past two and slot it in the corner. Then it'd be, "Don't worry about holding the ball up Cyrille, you keep doing that!"'

As John Wile says, 'Cyrille had a refreshing style in professional terms, *Boy's Own* stuff, just got the ball and ran with it. The more he learned about the game, the more of an all-round player he became, probably the less exciting he became. He scored spectacular goals in his time here, he didn't seem to get any nudge-ins, they were all spectacular. He came in against Rotherham, then Middlesbrough, ran from the halfway line and it's a legend now, every time the story gets told there's somebody else hanging off his shirt, eventually it'll be the whole team! But he made a fantastic impact. He'd made a big impact on me in a practice game as soon as he got here. At that time not many could beat me in the air and Cyrille did it with ease. He did it once and I thought, "Right, you won't do it a second time!" I really tried the second time and he still beat me, so I knew right away we'd got something a bit useful! And then you add the fact that he's such a nice person, then he was great to have around the place and he was great for the club. Maybe if he'd been a bit more aggressive, nastier, then on a professional level he'd probably have been even more successful. But that's the man he is and on a personal level, he's a smashing bloke to have around.'

Regis made a huge physical impact. A very impressive individual off the field, there was no questioning his stature on it either. Sometimes referred to as 'Smokin' Joe' because of his resemblance to heavyweight champion Joe Frazier, the great thing about Regis was he knew how to use his physique. We've all seen countless footballers down the years who look the part physically but get brushed off the ball too easily. The years Regis had had as little more than a kid playing against fully grown men in the non-league game had toughened him up and shown him how to use his natural body strength to good advantage. Once he got the ball, it took some getting off him.

That was an attitude that ran through the club, as he remembers. 'It was a nice balance here, there were a lot of players in their early twenties or even younger, with myself or Derek Statham, then you had John Wile, Tony Brown, Ally Robertson, who were the stalwarts, learned the Giles game, keep the ball. We made an impact straight away, we came in and grabbed it, that was the kind of people we had here, we were in there and we wouldn't let go. If you're talented and you go into a talented side, it's easier, because they're doing things right. I was an individual, not a leader of the line as I became later, and there were problems with that at times. But chances were always being created, so I was always involved – miss a chance, another would come a few minutes later and you stick that away.' Within a handful of games, Regis was established, so much so that an injury coincided with a run of just one win in five games that knocked Albion off their stride.

It was a spell in which Laurie Cunningham was struggling a little too, having trouble adapting to the different demands of playing for club and country, albeit at Under-21 level. At Albion, he was never really an out-and-out winger in the mould of Willie Johnston. Cunningham would often move inside, play more centrally as an attacking midfielder, often as a straightforward striker. With the England side, his job was to provide width, pure and simple. He admitted, 'I attempted to adopt different tactics in a relatively strange position. There was no way I could give my best in these kind of circumstances. It was obvious the general overall performance would not be as good as expected because everyone was playing for themselves. This was hardly surprising when everyone is told before any game if you give a good performance you will be in line for the full international side. The outcome is you never get the kind of service from your colleagues as you would in a club side. This explains why so many players, myself included, did not play up to our club form. The restrictions imposed while I was playing for England really upset my game.' It took a pep talk from Ronnie Allen to get him back on his game again. 'Mr Allen told me to be positive in whatever moves I make on the field and I appreciate this. Being positive and taking on responsibility are things I believe in doing.'

That's an object lesson for how to deal with so many dismissed as mavericks. Because of their idiosyncrasies, they're often dismissed as difficult, as not being team players, and are shorn of responsibility. Then, because they have no obligations to the team pattern, they become increasingly individualistic and wilful – what a surprise. Handled properly and given the responsibility and status that their talents deserve, and which they often crave, they are transformed. That was true of Cunningham who began to grow in strength as he took on more and more of the side's creative burden. There's no doubt that Regis's arrival helped, not just because it meant someone to share the racial focus, someone who understood the pressure and the abuse they received, but because they were two of a kind on the field, exciting, charismatic, spontaneous. And like other double-acts of the time like Rush and Dalglish or Keegan and Brooking, they seemed to share an almost telepathic communication. Time without number Cunningham would get the ball and without bothering to look, place a ball perfectly into Regis's flight path. They were a stunning combination that, as the season wore on, began to scare the living daylights out of opposing defences.

At Christmas, Albion were rocked by the departure of manager

Ronnie Allen, who had been offered a coaching post in Saudi Arabia. John Wile held the fort as caretaker manager before a full-time appointment could be made. Ron Atkinson of Cambridge United was offered the job, having taken Cambridge United from the Fourth Division to the brink of promotion to the Second Division. As John Trewick says, he was the perfect character to take Albion to the next level. 'Ron was ideal for the time. He tried to change a few things in training, but we knew we were a decent side and had a way of doing things that was successful, so why change? And Ron had the sense to let us get on with it.' And Atkinson had other adjustments to make, even though he'd spent a lifetime in the game as Trewick remembers. 'Early on, there was one session when he wanted to get Willie Johnston to do a free kick routine, day before the game, and Willie couldn't do it. Time and again. Ron was ranting, "I had players at Cambridge who could put that ball where I wanted it" and Willie just walked off and said, "Don't worry, it'll be alright on the night." Got to the game, Willie had to produce the free kick, did it perfectly. That's the difference with the top-level players, they produce when they have to.' Atkinson did stamp his personality on the team, of course. John Wile remembers, 'John Giles liked us to keep the ball, and then when Ron came in, he upped the tempo. The '70s were quite a defensive decade, a lot of physical elements in the game. But Ron was very positive, and wanted to build on the pattern John had put in. And Ron was the right man for the club as a manager, and from the PR point of view he always had something to say, put us in the news, gave us the confidence and released players to get forward earlier. We were only allowed to do that because we had a good defence. We'd play with three or four up front, Bryan Robson and Tony Brown in the middle, who were more often up front than back in defence, Derek who loved getting forward, Brendon the same when he came in. We had an attacking side and Ron loved that.'

Atkinson took his time to look at the players he had at the club and made no premature moves into the transfer market. His first outlay was the £30,000 it took to prise Brendon Batson away from Cambridge United. Batson had ended up at Cambridge after his spell with Arsenal came to a close. 'Within four months of signing as an apprentice, I tore my cartilage and had a series of injuries, which slowed my development down. I made my debut for Arsenal as an 18-year-old and found myself in and out of the side, which was the Double-winning side. At full-back we had Peter Storey, and Bob McNab, who both played for England, and Pat Rice and Sammy Nelson, who were both Northern Ireland internationals. I had the ability to play anywhere across the back four but my debut was in midfield in place of Charlie George.' The competition at Highbury was intense and Batson was realist enough to admit that, 'I knew I was not good enough to sustain a career as a regular full-back at Arsenal at that time. Looking back, neither I nor my mum had a clue about becoming a professional footballer. I stumbled into it as a career, everything went smoothly, then suddenly I started getting injured and things weren't so bright. But I remember Bertie Mee saying, "If things don't work out, we will always find you a better club," meaning that while Arsenal might not be suited to you, another club would be. I got extremely frustrated as younger players leapfrogged me into the team. I knew I wasn't convincing enough in my performances, though ironically one of the best games I had was against West Brom. I played centre-half and had to mark Jeff Astle. We lost 1–0. At the age of 20, I could see myself making little headway, especially in such a large squad. I recall saying to my brother at the time that I didn't want to be a reserve, I wanted first-team football.'

Batson faced the dilemma that comes to so many young professionals at top clubs. By definition, the players in possession of the shirt are of the highest quality and the clubs rarely have the time or patience to bring youngsters through. If a long-term injury comes along, the temptation is always there to spend money on the finished article rather than bring in a youngster. Today that is an even bigger issue, as John Trewick, now Albion's Youth Development Officer, suggests. 'As a club in the First Division, we have to make sure we do give our kids the opportunity to progress through the ranks. I do think kids are looking at that now, thinking, "If I join that club, will they provide me with the opportunity to come through and play if I'm good enough?" Particularly in the Premier League, young boys are looking at it and thinking, "If they need a player, they'll just go and spend £5 million on an international and I'm gonna get no opportunity at all." That's an opportunity for us because we're not in the position of buying like that at the minute, so we're perhaps more attractive to the kids, but we also have to be aware that they have to be given a chance if they're up to it.'

It is a fallacy that success is easy to buy. In the short-term it may be possible, but bringing expensive players, big egos, with little real affiliation to or affection for their club rarely works over time. The biggest spenders in recent years in the top flight have been Liverpool, Newcastle and Blackburn, and it hasn't done them a lot of good. Trewick again points out the value of continuity and the team ethos. 'Sometimes you stumble on things in football, it gels, it clicks. That era where we were successful under Giles and Atkinson stemmed from the time of Ashman and Howe when there was a lot of emphasis on schoolboy recruitment. There was also a situation where a lot of those players were at the football club a long time at one level or another. Wile, Robertson, Cantello, Johnston, Ally Brown, Tony Brown – all stalwarts of the club – then people like Derek Statham, myself, Bryan Robson who came through the ranks, so we all had a lot of years at Albion. You've got that base and you add a few pieces here and there. We had the older crew, Wile, Robertson, John Osborne, a nucleus who had been here a long time, gone through a lean spell, then suddenly a few youngsters came in. We added Laurie, Cyrille, Brendon and it took off, it just clicked. A lot of the make-up of that side was the team that had got promotion. You have a feel for the club, it's not just an employer, you feel about it the way a supporter does.' Bryn Jones, sociologist and long-time Albion fan, agrees that this was a special period in the relationship between supporters and players. 'As a purist, the style and quality of football was exceptional, the attacking flair was completely unlike anything else at the time. Psychologically there was a feeling of immense potential and promise, we were taking on the best in the land and beating them, which we hadn't done really since 1954 – the 1968 team was always fallible. That panache, that optimism and all that surrounded the club made it a special era. There was a certain *bonhomie* and depth of goodwill in the crowd which certainly doesn't exist now. How much that's just about success is hard to quantify, but I'm sure it had a lot to do with the way we played as much as the results we got.'

This was perhaps the last time that there was such camaraderie between the crowd and the players. In part that's because of changing times. Even in the First Division, many first-team footballers earn the kind of money that the majority of the crowd can only dream about. While supporters scrimp and save to buy a season ticket, a fairly average player could probably buy half a dozen with a week's wages and not think twice about it. And with the attendant publicity from all sections of the media, even the most modest player has the air of the pop star about them, whether they cultivate it, welcome it or shy away from it. Equally, success is an important part of the mix. Albion supporters are, like those at many clubs, not slow to criticise the players, and results over the period since 1985 indicate there has been little to celebrate. From time to time this has flared into open hostility, but throughout much of the period there has been a sullen atmosphere existing between the two. Twenty years ago, footballers in general were more approachable than they are now and lived a life that was far closer to the lifestyle of those on the terraces. Albion were successful so fans were delighted with the players. But as Bryn Jones has suggested, Albion's style had a tremendous impact. To use a cliché, the team played with a smile on its face. They were as hard as nails when they had to be – few forwards ever fancied a one-against-one with Ally Robertson – but there was plenty of room for enjoyment too. If you went to The Hawthorns, you would see some attacking play, a team trying to play real football and you'd probably get a laugh or two from Willie or Cyrille. Like the old Labour party, a football club is nothing if it's not a crusade, and, for a brief while, everything came together to make it just that. That spirit was central to the club's success, giving the team and the crowd the same never-say-die attitude that now characterises the likes of Manchester United and Arsenal. It was also instrumental in the acceptance of black players at the club, players who were seen as 'one of us' when elsewhere black players were barely tolerated.

When Brendon Batson came to Albion, he had already done his apprenticeship in the game, gaining vital experience as a player in the lower divisions. 'Eventually, I had to ask Bertie Mee for a transfer to get away from Arsenal and get a regular game. He tried to get me to change my mind but I knew I had to go. I joined Cambridge in 1974 because their coach had seen me play in a tour game with Arsenal in Norway. They were the first club to come in for me. I was so thrilled that someone had come in for me that I signed for them. They were relatively new to the League, they were in the Third Division and struggling badly when I joined, and we got relegated. There I was within a few months of playing in the top flight and now I was at the bottom of the League ladder. I didn't have many regrets as I was always in the team. Unfortunately for the manager, Bill Levers, a giant who played with Manchester City, he got the sack. In stepped Ron Atkinson. Fortunately, I happened to be in the right place at the right time. We had our differences from time to time but his ambition was quite marked. He wheeled and dealed and managed to get a lot of young lads in at that time, all with similar ambition to Ron and I. Within a couple of years we won the Fourth Division, Ron made some brilliant signings, bought one lad for a crate of champagne! He spent £15,000 on a lad called Tom Finney, bought Steve Briggs and then Alan Biley, who got 30 goals a season for us before he went on to Everton and Derby. The following year we were second in Division Three when he left to go to West Brom. For the next game he popped into the dressing room where he was a fantastic influence. The lads were really down but his presence lifted us and we won 1–0 and went top.'

Atkinson's larger-than-life personality was central to galvanising a small town club in a city that's anything but football mad. Cambridge's crowds were small, their ambitions smaller. But Atkinson got the team to play good football, attracted both locals and football fans in exile at the university and gradually mobilised the club. Batson was an important part of the jigsaw. 'I became skipper and then we had a big falling out. Apparently it's well documented in his autobiography that he felt I had a chip on my shoulder. He suggested it was because of the racial abuse I suffered. We had a bust-up in training and he ended up leaving me out of the team. That was a huge blow to my pride, the only time in all my time at Cambridge and West Brom that I was dropped. But I got back as skipper and never looked back.' Atkinson claims it was the making of him into a mature and accomplished footballer.

Atkinson was to form a closer relationship with Cyrille Regis than with either Batson or Laurie Cunningham. Whilst Batson saw his parting from Arsenal as amicable, as well as inevitable, Atkinson suggests that there was something more untoward: 'I thought he probably felt the reason Arsenal had sold him was because of a reluctance to play coloured players.' Whereas Regis was less confrontational and more relaxed in outlook, Batson was never slow in coming forward, whether on the race issue or in seeking to protect the interests of fellow players as a PFA union representative. That prompted Atkinson to describe him as 'carrying a chip on his shoulder' and 'forever smouldering about the race question'. Is speaking your mind such an offence, given the nature of the 'offence'? But then that was an era when players were not encouraged to think, let alone speak, about such deep matters. Subservience was the clear order of the day. The pair may have had their differences over such lofty issues but a mutual respect remains. Batson acknowledges the contribution Atkinson made to his development as a player. In turn, Atkinson is gracious enough to say that Batson was deserving of an England cap and that his continuing influence in the game is thoroughly merited.

There is no question that Atkinson is sincere when it comes to tackling the 'race issue', and as a manager he has probably done more than most to assist the progression of black players, a 'committed champion of black footballers' as he calls himself. He speaks with great pride of his association with the Three Degrees and acknowledges a huge debt to them in helping him in his career as a successful manager. 'The Three Degrees became simply a part of my football history but they had already contributed to my football future – their success at WBA helped build my management reputation.' That said, what seems to be missing from the Atkinson psyche is a proper appreciation of the sensitivities and complexities associated with this issue. Atkinson was of the view that '. . . it [racism] is a matter to be resolved on the shop floor of this sporting industry', in other words, let us deal with it in the confines of the dressing-room. The familiar line 'keep politics out of sport'. If only it were that simple.

In the early days, Atkinson had to confront a few of his senior players at West Bromwich Albion who were claiming that the new black players were not contributing for the greater good of the team, citing what he describes as the 'favourite accusation that the racists so frequently aimed at the black players' – 'lack of commitment' and 'not working hard enough'. Atkinson was concerned about the threat to team harmony and the possibility of alienating his new black players and moved swiftly to stamp out this problem. 'In that era of what can only be described as widespread ignorance, there was an element of prejudice in our own dressing-room. Some players, senior pros mostly, were quite anti the Three Degrees.' Having taken those players to task, the internal race difficulties were firmly squashed on the head. It says much for Atkinson that he should choose to address this potentially difficult incident in such a way. But in doing so he made it clear that, firstly, as the boss, he was the one calling the shots and, secondly, they were all equal in his eyes.

Atkinson was also unsympathetic to those black players who refused to smile graciously in the face of racist taunts. According to Atkinson, 'It is an issue that should be approached with mellowed understanding and humour . . . And I believe that the vast majority of black players would subscribe to that philosophy.' It is highly improbable that there are too many black players, past or present, who would concur with Atkinson. He also shows himself to have no truck with black players whose actions were in his words 'politically' motivated. 'No matter how much I genuinely admire that early, pioneering generation of black footballers, I have never been happy with what came later . . . This second wave of black players – not all but dangerously enough of them – seemed to be hell bent on stirring up the whole unsavoury atmosphere once more.' Atkinson confuses their confidence and assertiveness with being 'brash', 'swaggering' and 'full of arrogance'. He also speaks of black players being 'brainwashed' and possibly 'being exploited for racist purposes by more sinister forces'. Presumably it was not acceptable for black players to articulate in an expressive way their feelings about the regular tirade of abuse and intimidation they were enduring, feelings which may have came across as emotionally charged, strident and, on the odd occasion, belligerent. Atkinson suggests that these problems were better resolved within the game, being more than a touch optimistic given that there were few managers of his mind set, belief and conviction. Images of black American civil rights activists had entered into British society and Britain was ill at ease with the possibility similar developments occurring. Given what black players had to go through is it any wonder they were angry? What was more remarkable was that they continued to conduct themselves with such dignity.

What Atkinson appears to fail to understand is that this next generation of black players were not prepared to remain silent in the way their predecessors had been forced to. Through no choice of their own that generation of pioneers endured the pain, suffering and humiliation in the knowledge that future generations would not have to suffer a similar fate. Why should people, citizens of their own country, supposedly equal in the eyes of the law, have to endure this humiliating degradation? The suggestion that a fat person or someone with ginger hair may be similarly traumatised is way off the mark. For the many strong-minded black footballers who made the grade, there were those who were unable to cope and walked away, completely disillusioned by the game and with society. Who knows what their contribution to English football could have been? People often quite rightly refer to hooliganism as the 'shame of English football'. A lost generation or two of black players may be another contender for this unwanted title.

These men played at a time before the big anti-racism drive in football, so if the football clubs and authorities were not prepared to tackle this issue then the black players had no choice but to stand up for themselves, only now it would be under another, more powerful, guise, even if that seemed threatening to those in the game. Also, listening to the stories, both inspiring and depressing, from the early pioneers, it seems that men like Cec Podd and Clyde Best had heightened their resolve. Best was genuinely concerned for both the sanity and welfare of aspirant black footballers and questioned the wisdom of young black players wanting to go into the game, proffering that advice to a few parents of black footballers. Thankfully, Best's well-meaning advice fell on stony ground and wave after wave of black footballers were prepared to take their chances, buoyed by the numbers entering the game. Within a decade one in five of all professional footballers was black, something that Brendon Batson could look upon with more than a touch of satisfaction.

Batson could be equally satisfied that, having started in the First Division and been forced to drop down to the basement, he'd had the strength of character, as well as the footballing ability, to climb all the way back up again. As has been the pattern throughout his career, Atkinson went back to his previous club to bring a familiar face with him. Batson was delighted to return to the First Division. 'I joined West Brom having watched them on TV, when I was very impressed with Cyrille. They had Laurie, Bryan Robson and a player whose like I'd never seen before – Derek Statham. As a footballing talent he was one of the best.' Batson's assessment of Statham is a good one; a natural left foot, quick and decisive to get forward, linking beautifully with Willie Johnston, lightning quick to get back into defence, strong in the tackle with a fierce shot. Ron Atkinson said of him, 'People like Leeds manager Jimmy Armfield and former Liverpool chief Bill Shankly told me Statham is the best left-back England have produced since Ray Wilson . . . when I knew I was in the running for the West Brom job I asked a friend of mine to have a look at them for a couple of weeks and let me know his views. He came back and told me they had a left-back who was so good I would lie awake at night marvelling at his skills . . . it's only a matter of time before he gets into the full England team. And once he's in, he'll give years of outstanding service to his country.' The latter stages of Statham's career were hampered by injury, but in his early years at West Brom there wasn't a better left-back in the land, even if Ron Greenwood and Bobby Robson thought otherwise at the time. Batson had plenty of opportunity to observe because he rarely got into the side in that 1977–78 season, having been bought with a view to the following season. Atkinson kept faith with established right-back Paddy Mulligan, both at the start of and towards the end of Mulligan's career. John Wile remembers, 'To be honest I thought Paddy was coming as a coach, but he was an excellent player. No pace, but he was a good user of the ball, excellent sense of timing, got by on experience, nobody gave him a hard time except Clive Whitehead for Bristol City.'

With Atkinson urging the side forward – not that players like Statham, Cunningham, Robson, Johnston and Tony Brown needed much encouraging – Albion moved into a higher gear and embarked on an excellent FA Cup run. Blackpool were brushed aside 4–1, then Manchester United were finally overcome in a pulsating Cup replay, Regis scoring twice in an epic 3–2 win. Derby were beaten by the same score at the Baseball Ground, Regis again notching two to maintain his record of scoring in every round, reminiscent of Astle in 1968. For the sixth round, Albion were at home to Nottingham Forest. In their first season back in Division One, Forest had carried all before them, Brian Clough inspiring his unlikely collection of supposed cast-offs, has-beens and, in Peter Shilton, a goalkeeper playing the greatest football of his life, to the top of the table and to the League Cup final. Forest were relentless, in the middle of an unbeaten run of 42 league games, evidence that Forest weren't the ragbag collection many dismissed them as being. They were one of the greatest English teams of all time. On the day, Albion played them off the pitch. An early goal from Mick Martin set the tone and Regis finished the job in the second half with a typically explosive shot. The team whose record proclaimed that they had the whole world in their hands dropped the FA Cup.

In hindsight, the season peaked too early. Against Forest, Albion had seemed unstoppable. Suddenly, with the semi-final looming, the rhythm went out of the side. The results remained reasonable, but the fluency was missing, very apparent when they lost 4–0 to Arsenal at Highbury. They returned there to face Ipswich in the semi-final. John Wile remembers, 'We were horrified as we sat and watched *Football Focus*. Big Ron went to Wembley and picked a Cup up, set us up good and proper. Bobby Robson didn't need to give a team talk, they just watched *Football Focus*. That was the first we knew about it but as we sat and watched it, we knew exactly what the outcome would be. I'm sure if Big Ron had his time again he would not have gone.' Cyrille Regis remembers it only too well. 'It wound Ipswich up. Apparently Bobby Robson just said to them, "Look at him, he thinks he's won it already," and that fired them up.'

In fairness to Atkinson, that wasn't the only reason Albion struggled. Injuries, loss of form and suspensions meant he started to tinker with the team. With the season coming to its climax, he left out Robson and Cunningham for the game that would define the rest of the season. John Wile admits, 'We hadn't played well in the run up to it and changes were made. We'd lost some of our fluency prior to that, and it's crucial in a big game that everybody gets a touch very early. But we'd gone from the measured build-up under John Giles to one that had a good balance between that and getting the ball forward quickly at the right time under Ron. Suddenly, as we lost form, we were getting everything forward too quickly. We'd spoken about it beforehand but on the day we played a very direct style and the likes of Willie Johnston didn't get a touch for ages. By the time they did, they'd frozen. We didn't play anywhere near the way we could and it was very disappointing. Any semi-final defeat is disappointing, but the only way you can get any satisfaction is to have given it your best, but on the day we didn't. It was a shame because we were better than that.' Brian Talbot put Ipswich ahead early on, heading the ball past Tony Godden and simultaneously smashing into Wile's forehead, leaving Wile to play the rest of the game, until his late substitution, with a bloodied bandage wrapped around his head. 'It's the only game people can remember me playing!' says Wile.

Youngsters like Statham, Trewick and Regis found themselves a goal down in a semi-final having barely touched the ball. It soon got worse when Mick Mills added another. Regis concedes, 'We just froze. After 15 minutes we were losing 2–0, you look around, we hadn't played our strongest side, Laurie was sub, John Wile was injured, it was chaos. We didn't know what to do. I froze, nothing happened.' It was a great shame for the club. According to John Trewick, 'We had a helluva chance of winning the Cup and everything went wrong on the day against Ipswich. John Wile cracked his head open, Mick Martin got sent off, Willie got injured as well and didn't play again that season, we were carrying two or three. I remember Tony Godden in the last few minutes. They had a free kick and Tony was shouting, "Come on, I want four in the wall," and I turned round and shouted at him, "We haven't got enough ****ing players to give you four in the wall." We had walking wounded everywhere. "Three's all you're getting!"' Albion rallied bravely and a Tony Brown penalty gave brief hope before Mick Martin got sent off and Ipswich sealed victory with a late third goal.

It says much for the character of that team that they returned to The Hawthorns four days later and beat Newcastle 2–0 then reeled off another three wins in four games to clinch a place in the UEFA Cup. The club achieved what it had set as its major objective before the start of the season, but the semi-final defeat was a great disappointment. The future, on the other hand, was full of promise.

FOUR

We're now used to seeing Manchester United and their ilk trotting off to the other side of the world to play a friendly or two during the close season. Back in 1978, such tours rarely ventured further than Spain or, at a time when the NASL was flourishing, they might even make it across the Atlantic to the USA. That Albion should go on a tour to China immediately after the season had ended was truly remarkable. The visit was as much a trade mission as a football tour, so it was critical that the club made a good impression on and off the field. The full squad flew out to China, minus Willie Johnston, who was on his way to Argentina with the Scotland squad for the World Cup and the drugs scandal that blighted the rest of his career.

The trip was so out of the ordinary that they were even accompanied by a BBC film crew to film a programme for 'The World About Us' series. The result was an interesting, if slightly slanted, programme, a little too keen to play up to the stereotype of the footballer as incapable of appreciating anything more taxing than a pint and a copy of the *Sun*. John Trewick, for example, will never live down one tongue in cheek comment. 'They asked me about the trip and I talked to them for a few minutes about what an eye-opener it was, how interesting the places and the people were. Then when we were talking about the Great Wall, as a joke I said, "You've seen one wall, you've seen 'em all." That was the only bit of the interview they kept in!'

Aside from Trewick's comment, Bryan Robson was heard to complain that it wasn't as enjoyable as going to Alicante where the club had been in previous years, and Bertie Mee, on the trip as an observer, said that footballers were never interested in the history of a place. In fact, a large proportion of the party went on virtually every excursion and made the most of the experience. The film highlighted the fact that the most dedicated sightseers were Brendon Batson, Laurie Cunningham and Cyrille Regis. In hindsight, it was this programme, and the Chinese tour in general, that was the genesis of the Three Degrees and all the hype that surrounded them in the following season. The BBC documentary showed them, unfairly, as a group within a group, which was never the case – there was no such clique. Nonetheless, by focusing the attention on the three of them together, it did create a certain impression in the public mind and set them apart. And it would be wrong to underestimate their impact. Here were black men having a vital impact on our national game, making up a quarter of one of the country's best, certainly the country's most exciting, team. By definition they stood out simply because of their colour – no top-flight side had three black footballers. The likes of Liverpool took another ten years to find one. Funny that.

Importantly, they were excellent role models. While Cunning-ham clearly felt a little ill at ease with the attention and shied away from much of the publicity, Batson and Regis both spoke intellig-ently and articulately and were clearly well aware of what a wonderful opportunity was being presented to them. As Regis says now, 'China was a fantastic experience. Looking back some parts were very boring. Because there was such a difference in the culture, there were lots of banquets and functions to go to that weren't too exciting. But I went everywhere, as many trips as possible. It was a great pioneering trip, a trade mission, brought the squad together, had seven games, very interesting to see that way of life.' But even at the time, with all three very new to the fame game, they conducted themselves extremely well in front of the cameras. Older hands such as John Wile knew how to say the right things at the right time, but young footballers are always potentially loose cannons. It was a credit to themselves and the club that even totally inexperienced reserves such as Kevin Summerfield and Wayne Hughes coped with the strange environment with few problems.

Regis's point about team bonding under fairly difficult conditions – at least in terms of the average westerner's experience – is a valid one. It also meant a shift in the make-up of the side and the coming together of the Three Degrees on the field. In China, Batson became first choice at right-back, supplanting Paddy Mulligan who left the club. Regis was, of course, the attacking spearhead, but Cunningham cemented his place in the team. In the absence of Willie Johnston, it was left to him to give the side width in what was effectively a three-pronged attack, which also allowed Ally Brown to come in on a regular basis and form a superb partnership with Regis. Bryan Robson became the midfield fulcrum, with the ageless Tony Brown and the intelligent skills of Len Cantello, a player who could both play the defence-splitting ball and dispense crunching tackles, alongside him. To that basic 11 was added John Trewick who was adept at the Giles school of possession football and could slot into any of the midfield roles as the need arose, sometimes even deputising for Derek Statham at left-back. But as Tony Brown pointed out at the time, a team so renowned for its attacking brilliance couldn't survive by simply going forward. 'For a side with so much emphasis on attack we must have the best back four in the country. And that's the secret. We've got the right sort of balance in each department.' Batson, Wile, Robertson and Statham across the back were as good a set-up as even Liverpool could muster and a quartet that Albion have never adequately replaced. In goal, Tony Godden took a lot of unnecessary and unfair criticism, but, if suspect on crosses, he was a shot-stopper par excellence and often kept Albion in games with some superb saves. He was unfortunate to play in an era when every goalkeeper was compared with Peter Shilton, Ray Clemence and Pat Jennings. Few in the history of the game have matched them.

How do you get a better start to a season than scoring after 21 seconds at home to one of the best teams in the country? Ally Brown set Albion on their way against Ipswich and a 2–1 win set the tone for the season. Ron Atkinson has said that Albion side was the best he ever managed, and he's right. Some of the football they produced was sublime. The 7–1 demolition of Coventry – and Coventry deserved a pasting just for wearing those dismal chocolate-coloured shirts – was just one in a series of fabulous displays. There wasn't a weak link in the side. Bryan Robson was already the finest midfielder in the country, Statham a wonderful wing-back rather than a mere full-back, but it was Regis and Cunningham and, to a lesser extent and by association, Batson, who were getting the attention. As Regis says, 'Everything was the black pearls, the black players, headlines. And the side was magnificent and the three of us, when Brendon came in, were the focus of that because it was a good story, the Three Degrees. The group came to the club, we had our pictures taken with these great pop stars, it was fantastic. Big Ron's persona, the way we played, the black players, it elevated us, it made us fashionable like Newcastle were a couple of years ago under Kevin Keegan. And Big Ron does that wherever he goes, he gets you in the press, he plays with flair and with steel, had a great back four, strength all round. We had such a side, players wanted to see all of us the way they do Manchester United now. It is such a change at the Albion, nowadays people come to see Lee or Enzo or Kevin Kilbane mainly, then they wanted to see all of us, everybody was somebody's favourite. There was always someone who could do something special, it wasn't down to one player. Derek would do a shimmy and put somebody in, Laurie would beat three, Bryan would score from 25 yards, Tony Brown was still getting goals. We were so confident, if we drew away from home the coach would be silent on the way back, we could take on anybody and beat anybody, anywhere.'

In essence, the team, the club, was living a dream, taking its place at the peak of the English game. And there were none living a dream more than the Three Degrees. But as Yeats said, 'in dreams begins responsibility', as Regis recognises. 'We were breaking new ground. Once you're in, you're not thinking about making a stand for blackness, you want to stretch your talent as far as it will go. The colour situation added another dimension because the press picked up on it, young black boys picked up on it, and you are made aware of your position, but it's not your focal point. You want to perform and on the back of that, then there's this other stuff, being a role model, destroying myths. It was difficult. Back then we'd have five and six thousand people chanting racist abuse where now that kind of thing on that scale has gone. What you do learn is to change negatives into positives. "You give me stick, OK, I'll show you how to play." You don't react, you don't go into the crowd, you don't gesture back, you get hold of the ball and stick in the net, go home with the points. That's the way to hurt the opposition. But from a black perspective, West Brom did wonders for the black community. It was radical, really radical. The real explosion started here without a doubt. A lot of the players in their 30s now, players like Ian Wright, say that we inspired them, and we helped them believe they could do it. I went to Trinidad, met some friends, and his father was full of the Three Degrees stuff. It was a radical thing, three black guys, playing well, great team, top of the league. Once we'd done it, there was never any excuse not to use black players again. And Laurie and myself were strikers, getting goals, so that makes it even more exciting, so that probably helped. Personally, we learned that football is as much a mental game, you turn things round, you use your ability to fight it. If all that racism was on the streets, affecting my kids or my wife, bricks through the window, it would have been a totally different ball game. If the racists had targeted my family away from the game, that would have been something else. But it was confined to the arena and I could handle it. You can do something about it then. You go out on the field and perform, get your goals, pocket the points, I'll show you how good I am, thanks very much. That's how you hurt them most.'

And they hurt plenty of teams. Ron Atkinson has since written that whenever Albion were preparing to play Everton, he'd get an abusive letter telling him not to use his 'monkeys', to send them back to the jungle. That Pulitzer prize winner was then forced to sit and watch as Albion turned in some of their best performances against his team. Brendon Batson remembers, 'Cyrille scoring two goals, early in my Albion career, against Everton. For one, the sheer ferocity of the shot stunned the keeper. You knew his raw power frightened the hell out of defenders. He was sometimes criticised for not fighting his weight, but when he was on song defenders were on a hiding to nothing. With Cyrille, it was his pace and power that were so impressive. He did things other players were not capable of and when he went on a run, you knew it was going to end up with a shot on goal.'

Neither the Three Degrees, their colleagues, nor the club were naïve enough not to realise the impact they had and their importance to the wider game and the wider community. As Bryn Jones points out, 'It was fortunate in terms of the black experience that Cyrille and Laurie in particular were so good. Brendon Batson was a very good footballer too, more English in style, but the other two were charismatic, exciting, they fitted into the Albion style and cut through any racism, and they immediately got that rapport.' It's an interesting point, because the Albion crowd did, in general, seem to have a different response to visiting black players. When a team came to The Hawthorns, although there were always individual idiots in the crowd who would shout abuse, there was no concerted chanting against black players, even when, like Bob Hazell and George Berry, they played for hated neighbours Wolves. Regis, Cunningham and Batson were rarely treated as well on visiting grounds, even on grounds where black players successfully plied their trade.

To conclude that there was no racism within the Albion crowd would be stupid in the extreme. It must be remembered that travelling Albion supporters at the time did sometimes indulge in racial abuse, particularly at Molineux, though even here they were less vociferous than most clubs' supporters. Perhaps that also says something about the nature of travelling support at the time, when hooliganism was still rife and a significant proportion of away fans – though never as many as the media liked to suggest – were on the lookout for trouble.

Things were a very long way from being perfect in the mid and late 1970s, as the hive of National Front activity proved. Paradoxically of course, the very desperate nature of the NF's tactics suggested that they recognised they were fighting a losing battle. Britain was slowly, too slowly, becoming a multicultural and much more integrated society. There were still many barriers, many divides economically and socially, but immigration was becoming a grudgingly accepted part of life, and the new migrants were gradually being more and more widely accepted. In the face of that, small wonder the NF became more vociferous. No wonder that they targeted football too, even leaving aside the fact that football crowds of the time did tend to provide a disproportionate number of disaffected, unemployed, young white males with remarkably few brain cells looking for easy answers that they didn't need to think about and which did not dwell on their own inadequacies. The NF's leadership was sufficiently astute to realise that the success of Viv Anderson, Laurie Cunningham, Garth Crooks et al. was chipping away at residual racism in the country, especially among the young. The more successful those players were, the more absurd racism looked. So the NF tried to minimise their success by attacking them from the terraces in the hope of driving them out of the game. Thankfully this was another of their failures. In fact, it could be argued that black footballers did, and continue to do, more for race relations than any other group.

In a sense, their success was an extension of the slowly changing attitude that had been brought about through the 1960s and 1970s by, among other things, popular music. As Bryn Jones recalls, 'In the late 1960s lots of white kids in the Smethwick and West Bromwich areas were very much into ska. I remember soul discos at places like the West Bromwich Adelphi and Thimblemill Baths, Smethwick, and the Handsworth Plaza where you could see the likes of Geno Washington, and loads of younger and more ordinary kids were suddenly getting into this stuff and ska. A group of skinhead-cropped lads from Smethwick particularly stick in my mind. Their background was probably semi-racist council-estate, but they loved ska and used to use Jamaican swear words. They also used to freak out on the Birmingham Road End, violently on occasions.

'My guess is that their parents and many peers were just as racist but the Griffiths episode at the 1964 general election was a one-off in terms of mobilising so many people to racist politics. Maybe that respect for black music and style just took the edge off incipient racism and gave the Three Degrees, as the name suggests, a little bit of potential respect from some of the crowd. Probably the black music aspect just created a bit of a chink of limited respect in part of a cohort of impressionable kids. Smethwick wouldn't have become suddenly multicultural but there was probably quite a bit of overlap between the black music fans and those who went to the Albion. Those could be the seeds of potential respect for stylish black performers, whether on stage or on the pitch?

'The average age on the Brummie Road was much lower than it is now. Now it seems to be mainly the older, greying members of those halcyon days. Blackness was a bit chic for many of that generation. Many cut their adolescent teeth on R & B, soul, Tamla Motown, ska and reggae. Obviously this doesn't make them anti-racist but I knew lots of ordinary working-class kids from West Bromwich and Smethwick who saw black folks as something other than idle, scrounging, job-pinching dumbos – as their parents probably thought. Presumably those kids would have been twenty-somethings by 1978 and still going to matches and able to exert some influence on the younger element.'

Any crowd is constantly evolving. The most vocal and influential element of a ground's crowd tends to consist of those in their late teens and early twenties. These were people who had grown up with Motown, soul music, had seen the likes of Marvin Gaye, Diana Ross and Smokey Robinson, had bought their records and been charmed by them and, later on, by reggae artists such as Bob Marley. Ska classic 'The Liquidator' was even Albion's unofficial anthem. Those youngsters had also grown up and gone to school with black kids. While for their parents and grandparents black people were exotic strangers whom they didn't understand, to these inner-city kids they were becoming a part of everyday life.

Albion's supporters did not resort to racist chanting at home. They were not angelic either, but their songs were at that level of abuse that seems acceptable within the game, singing 'where's your wife gone?' to a player who had just got divorced or 'you fat bastard' to the more rotund footballers – the general Shavian wit that characterises every crowd. Why did Albion's supporters treat black players with greater respect than most crowds? The quality of Regis, Batson and Cunningham must be a key factor. As Regis says, 'If your side had got black players in it, I think that helped. If you played a team that hadn't got any, then you were targeted. To me, the biggest thing that has helped has been the number of black players that have come into the game. And unless there's something really wrong with you, you have to ask yourself, "How can I be cheering for a black player on my team and then abusing one on the other side?" I can't give Cyrille stick when I've got George Berry in my team.' Interestingly, that didn't stop Wolves supporters, nor supporters of other clubs such as Millwall who had a number of black players in their team. The quality and the charismatic nature of Albion's players must have had some significance.

Bryn Jones adds, 'At the Wolves, for instance, they had Hazell and Berry. They were defenders, plodders, never as exciting to watch and never going to have that impact. At Albion games the Wolves supporters were vicious in their treatment of Regis, Cunningham and Batson and Moses later, but I don't think the Albion crowd chanted in the same way. There were individuals who shouted the usual rubbish, but I don't think it was the same concerted attack. I still have this view that there is some kind of cultural difference between Wolves and Albion. I don't know if it's the clubs alone, or the localities as well. The Wolves ethos has traditionally been based on strength, hardness and power, all the way back to the Major Buckley years. They used to water the pitch to make it heavy and harder for the opposition. The old Molineux was horrible – it was dark, gloomy, oppressive, down in a dip. As a kid, I used to go from there to The Hawthorns, where it was high up, there was light and the players would come out in these bright blue and white stripes while the Wolves came out in these grimy colours! Traditionally Wolves were about strength where Albion were more skilful. In terms of the locale, in strict terms, speaking as a sociologist, I have to concede there was racism in West Bromwich as there was everywhere else. But my view, which may be a bit rose-coloured, was that West Bromwich, the other end of the Black Country, was a bit more easy-going on those things, more prepared to take people on their merits. I wonder whether it's not in their nature to have the same vociferous ideological racism you get elsewhere. Although Griffiths won that seat in 1964, it was more a one-off aberration, wheras Enoch Powell held a Wolverhampton constituency for many years and possibly legitimised racism in so doing.'

In fairness, Powell's constituency contained the highly desirable and upmarket districts of Tettenhall and Compton where property prices are closer to Surrey than Smethwick. Until the 1997 general election, when Powell's successor, another right-winger, Nick Budgen, was deposed, the constituency was among the safest of Tory seats beyond the confines of the Home Counties. Essentially, whatever Powell said, it seemed to matter not one iota because this part of Wolverhampton was not ready to accept socialist representation. Nor can it be overlooked that the National Front gained significant electoral ground in a parliamentary by-election in West Bromwich in 1973 when they captured 16.2 per cent, a remarkable showing a decade on from Peter Griffiths' success in nearby Smethwick. Three years on, in another by-election in Leicester, they were still a force, taking 18.5 per cent of the vote. Equally, it is suggested by some commentators that Enoch Powell enjoyed a far greater level of sympathy, if not active support, than was manifested in the ballot box. One illustration of this was that in the aftermath of his 'rivers of blood' speech he received one hundred and ten thousand letters, of which only two thousand three hundred opposed him. This indicated a huge groundswell of support among people beyond his constituency – the fact that he represented Wolverhampton South at the time may well be less significant than is generally accepted.

What is beyond question is that Powell was a cunning politician, adept at dealing with the media. His cleverly constructed scenario of a dear old white pensioner, living in a once 'respectable' street, who had been overwhelmed by unruly and abusive black neighbours struck a chord with a nation being told that 'the country now faces the prospect of an uncontrolled flood of Asians in from

Kenya' (according to the *Daily Mirror*), in spite of the fact that that year the number of immigrants was exceeded by that of emigrants. Powell expertly used highly charged phrases and images: 'foaming with blood', 'keeping up the funeral pyre', 'whip hand over the white man', 'excreta pushed through her door'. If part of his strategy was for migrants to renounce their native cultures, he'd badly misjudged the situation. What he did do, albeit inadvertently, was to further the desire to pursue those cultures when he suggested that even if migrants were born in England, they could not become English.

So for all that Powell was a Wolverhampton MP, there's no reason to suggest that Wolverhampton was any more, or any less, inclined towards racism than West Bromwich. But, certainly in footballing terms, a difference does exist. The Wolves support is louder, for good and bad, whereas, as Bryn Jones points out, 'The situation in West Bromwich is reflected in the character of the Albion crowd. They're not a vocal crowd. Even back in the 1960s they'd be silent for long periods. It's something in the local character. There's a stoicism. They'll get a bit sullen maybe, you can push these people around a lot, but all of a sudden they'll flip, as they did at the end of the 1998–99 season with protests at the ground, the EGM and so on. But they never developed that vocal expression of emotions that you get elsewhere. And there is a lot of give and take: "he's black, he's a good player, so what?". We'd been waiting for a new Jeff Astle for years and Cyrille looked the part before he'd touched the ball.' Equally, Wolves, coming from a larger town, with a far bigger catchment area, traditionally see themselves as a bigger club. With the emergence of Regis, Cunningham, Robson, Statham, Batson, Trewick et al., they could see a period of Albion dominance stretching ahead of them and reacted aggressively to that.

There is much to be said for that theory of stoicism, inasmuch as people in the West Bromwich area are not particularly confrontational. Taken at the most basic level, local football phone-ins, Albion fans do tend to be less vociferous than those supporting Villa or Wolves, a trait they carry into the ground with them, though, as the halcyon days recede further into the past, the supporters are finally showing some signs of impatience. If there are no obvious, outward shows of emotion, it's easy to suggest that those emotions don't exist. Yet, as Jones says, there must be racism there, just as in every part of the country. Perhaps part of the issue was the loyalty of those in the area, another facet of that stoicism. When it became apparent to Albion supporters just how much abuse Regis, Cunningham and Batson were getting, the crowd closed ranks and attempted to protect their players and proclaimed ever more loudly just how great they were. Every time you went to The Hawthorns, you had a reminder of just how hated these players were. At the Woodman corner of the ground stood the Throstle Club, effectively a social club where there was live music, cheap beer, supporters club meetings and so on. On the back wall of the building was scrawled the legend 'Cunningham is a black cunt'. Imagine what kind of lowlife could write that – though how someone with such a small mind could actually write is incomprehensible. Not only was it an affront to Cunningham, Regis, Batson and to all black people, it was also an affront to decent white people. Supporters are a complex mix, but their first loyalty is to their club. The majority would consider themselves to be above prejudice. Deep down – and not so deep down in a lot of cases – a sizeable minority of Albion supporters might well have agreed with the sentiment, might even have signed up to it had it said the same about George Berry or even were it said now about Ade Akinbiyi. But nobody can say that about somebody wearing their colours and get away with it. So Albion supporters united behind Cunningham, Regis and Batson, the players who got the most stick because they were the most prominent in the land.

There is another convincing theory which says that, while many supporters in general didn't abuse black players, their acceptance of them was very grudging, at least initially. This theory puts forward the view that, while black players might be good for the team and can be accepted in that sense, the predominantly white crowd wouldn't necessarily want to socialise with them – though anyone who ever saw supporters queuing up to buy drinks for Cyrille Regis would dispute that fact. Nevertheless, the spirit of tolerance, respect and admiration was not universal among supporters. The detractors, and there were many, despite being in the minority, were vocal, motivated and organised. They belonged to an era during which the National Front was in its heyday, an organisation with a semblance of party unity that had a solid and growing membership and was well mobilised, arranged high profile marches and had a new-found electoral standing. The tide of fascism was at its highest point in England since the thuggish days of Mosley and his black shirts in the 1930s, and, in 1977, the Greater London Council elections saw the NF capture 5.3 per cent of the popular vote, that result following hard on the heels of the racist murder of young Gurdip Singh Chagger on the streets of London. Chagger's death prompted John Kingsley Read, leader of the British National Party, to comment 'one down – a million to go'. As a result, parts of London were simmering, ready to boil over, a situation repeated in other major cities and urban areas. The recent influx of Ugandan Asians into England, victims of Idi Amin's own version of ethnic cleansing, had enabled the NF to claim that the country was being swamped by immigrants and that only they could give the English back their country. They used this issue to prey upon the concerns of the indigenous population, for there are few weapons more powerful than fear, groundless or otherwise. Inner cities provided the NF with the opportunity to develop an alternative strategy, choosing candidates in sensitive, multicultural community con-stituencies, with the sole purpose of creating deep unrest and instability. In this, they were succeeding.

Many in the black and Asian communities were at their wits' end, conjuring up images of repatriation, something they thought they had put behind them ten years earlier, in the aftermath of Enoch Powell's notorious 'rivers of blood' speech. Unlike the 1968 crisis, this time certain factors emerged to dampen the anti-immigration protest. Idi Amin was unintelligent, unpredictable, part dictator, part clown. To exacerbate matters, Amin had instigated the assass-ination of several Israeli athletes in Munich in September 1972 before declaring his admiration for Adolf Hitler. Few expected anyone to wish to endure life under Amin. Progress in the area of race relations had been made, only not at the rate most had hoped for. According to former Sandwell councillor and anti-racist activist Geoff Taylor, 'By the 1970s, there was this grudging acceptance of ethnic minorities, just as long as you didn't have to live next door to one, or have one drink in your pub. It was also no problem to spout racist jokes, safe in the knowledge it was the done thing.'

The behaviour of high-profile celebrities did not help much either. Already the likes of Bernard Manning were being treated as the pathetic joke they were, but far more credible people were doing terrible damage. What greater star was there in the whole of impressionable youth culture than David Bowie? Toying with androgyny, with sexual politics, meshing black and white musical styles and presenting it all in wildly glamorous and exciting packages, Bowie was the undisputed King of the music scene in the mid-'70s. Others may have sold more records or more concert tickets, but Bowie was the star, the man who captured the imagination, who influenced a generation. Regularly reinventing himself, from the cross-dressing man who sold the world, through the red-headed glam-rock Messiah Ziggy Stardust, on to the cracked actor Aladdin Sane and the thin white duke, Bowie could never be pinned down, never tied to any movement and he never carried any baggage. In an 'apocalyptic year' as Hebdige rightly describes 1976 in his book *Subculture: The Meaning of Style*, Bowie's vision of escapism from a drab, dreary England into a world of colour, of fantasy, of no dole queues, of all the drugs you could eat, of sexual abandon and musical fervour, was a heady and seductive mix, and his role as one of the forefathers of the punk explosion of that year should never be underestimated. So in February 1976, at a time of heightened racial tension and at a time when Bowie was at the peak of his powers, we could have done without the thin white dope extolling the virtues of Adolf Hitler: 'Hitler was the first superstar. He really did it right . . . I think I might have been a bloody good Hitler'. By now Bowie's intake of hard drugs had completely divorced him from reality and, for once in his life, the arch media manipulator possibly had little idea of the effect of his words and actions. Or perhaps he was simply referring to the staging of the Nuremberg rallies, likening them to rock concerts, as U2 were to do in the 1990s, making the point that people were easily exploited by the chicanery of showbiz, that the masses were gullible – don't follow leaders and watch the parking meters. To give him an enormous slice of benefit of the doubt, perhaps his intentions were good, though considering he was detained by customs officers on the Russian–Polish border in April when Nazi books and mementoes were found in his luggage – allegedly research materials for a film on Goebbels that never made it to the screen – his motives are questionable at best. But Bowie's stock in trade was confusion; he fed on it and then fed it back to his followers who were regularly perplexed but followed anyway. And when you're dealing with fascists, ambiguity is not necessarily the best weapon. Fascism is too dangerous a force to play with. It has to be condemned in ways and by means that even the most bone-headed individual – always the target for fascist recruiting drives, after all – can understand. And sorry, Mr Bowie, but delivering Nazi salutes on your return to England at Victoria station may seem awfully witty and satirical and sharp to a pampered rock star living in isolation, but to the people in the multicultural housing estates suffering racial abuse at every turn, it's not big, it's not clever – and it was dangerous. Suddenly, David Bowie, the coolest man on earth, was on the front pages of the music press, delivering the Nazi salute. How much more legitimate could you make it?

Maybe, just maybe, Bowie was a victim of his own 'cleverness', though you might argue that if his earlier comments were misjudged, he should have at least had the wit to avoid making the same mistake twice by giving the Nazi salute. But other rock stars followed his lead, underlining just how reckless Bowie's behaviour had been. In August 1976, at a concert at the Birmingham Odeon, Eric Clapton – who had made his reputation by plundering the work of black musicians – decided to tell the world that Enoch Powell had been right. In Robin Denselow's book *When the Music's Over*, novelist and playwright Caryl Phillips recalls the evening. 'Clapton went into a rap about Enoch. His initial line was "Enoch's right – I think we should send them all back." I don't think he said "nigger", I think he said "wogs". He definitely said "Keep Britain white." Nobody cheered, but after he'd played another song, he did the same again. It was extraordinary – he stood there being overtly and offensively racist. I was completely and utterly mystified as to why this man playing black music should behave in this way.' This is the same Eric Clapton who a couple of years later was professing his undying love for the Albion, had an Albion scarf featured on an album cover and who spent interviews enthusing about the glorious play of the Three Degrees. Some might question his love of Albion, particularly in view of the fact that he hasn't been seen there in years – certainly not since they stopped being fashionable – and that in recent years when the club has been short of cash, Clapton has been conspicuous in his lack of support, refusing even to play fundraisers for the club. You might think that he saw football in general, and West Bromwich Albion and the Three Degrees in particular, as a useful vehicle for regaining lost credibility. You just might be right.

For the NF, buoyed by the free publicity that the likes of Clapton were giving them, these were hopeful days. Ironically, popular music had rarely been on their side, for all that it might be the devil's music. The 'all you need is love' mantra of the late-1960s had been the prevailing mood in music and even where violence had flared, as in Paris and the student riots of 1968, music was on the side of the angels, with The Rolling Stones' 'Street Fighting Man' becoming something of an anthem. Thereafter politics and pop had tended to go their separate ways in the 'me' decade, and prior to Bowie's unwelcome intervention, when they did mix, it was in the vein of Lennon's 'Give Peace a Chance'. Perhaps it was because music was seen as escapist, other worldly, as entertainment. Football on the other hand, was much more than entertainment; it was central to people's lives, particularly the lives of the working classes, particularly the white male. Football and music are inextricably linked – what else, other than sex, is on the mind of the average young male? And the three form a trinity – rock'n'roll offers the promise of sex, and football is there to take away your frustration when you don't get any. By its very nature, the football ground is an arena for spleen-venting, traditionally at the referee and opposition, an environment where amid the enjoyment of spectacle there is always an undercurrent of anger ready to burst through. It is, after all, the place we choose to go to let out all the frustrations of the working week. The very culture of the game is one of 'us and them', an idea that is enshrined as part of the game's traditions and its appeal. Where that's kept within bounds, that rivalry can be enjoyable, even healthy. But for those like the NF, who would prefer to foster hatred, anger and unrest, it could also offer an opportunity to unite all the white males against all those blacks out there taking their jobs, a real us and them. That's the seduction of fascism – the offer of a huge homogeneous mass where you can belong and where you can be secure in your hatred of the minority who are to blame for everything from the cost of living to the fact that you spilled your coffee that morning. At a time when the UK was in apparently terminal decline, at a time when we were at the mercy of the International Monetary Fund, at a time when there was 'no future in England's dreaming', as Johnny Rotten sang, how fortunate that it was somebody else's fault.

By its confrontational nature, football offered a fertile ground for recruitment and the distribution of propaganda material. It was also a visible environment, one in which they could guarantee themselves media attention. Those violent and hateful images lie vivid in the collective memory to this day and remain one of the reasons why still relatively few black and Asian people attend live football matches. But there were those who chose to defy the obvious dangers in support of their beloved club, among them Inderjit Bhogal. 'I had quite a detour to make to get to the ground. We lived a mile away, but I had to go in a convoluted way to avoid confronting the National Front guys.'

The presence of the Three Degrees brought a schizophrenic approach from young NF supporters. According to Inderjit, 'They didn't quite know how to respond to the black players. They took pride in wearing their red-laced Doc Martens down the match, signifying their support for the Anti-Paki League, and then they would turn round to chant Cyrille Regis's name. Once the match was over, they went Paki bashing.' Academic and football researcher Dr Les Back asserts that once the shirt is pulled on, any idea of real difference is somehow dissolved. 'The notion of "wearing the shirt" summons, in football vernacular, the deepest levels of symbolic identity and commitment.' Ignoring the race element for a moment, you can observe this phenomenon at England level. Many Spurs supporters spend their lives despising Tony Adams, until he pulls on an England shirt, at which point he has their undying support. It's not a flawless argument, as the abuse that Manchester United players often receive when playing for England at Wembley testifies, but in general, the idea holds good. Of course, at a racial level it goes far deeper than that, and such confusion had been rife for many years, notably in the skinhead movement which, tonsorial considerations aside, had, in the eyes of the majority, two defining characteristics – a love of ska, rocksteady, reggae and bluebeat music, essentially Caribbean in origin, and a propensity for violence directed, in the main, towards the immigrant population.

Like all generalisations, that merely scratches the surface of the issue. The music did, in fact, play a huge part in the process of integration, admiration for musical styles and stars leading to a greater willingness to accept black people at face, rather than skin, value. Even there, though, things were far more complicated than that; one representative of the mod movement, interviewed as early as 1964, said, 'At the moment we're hero-worshipping the Spades – they can dance and sing', at once both demeaning and celebrating black culture. The same confusion existed in the skinhead world. As Hebdige notes, the dichotomy was that skinheads stole their style from West Indian immigrants. 'It was not only by congregating on the all-white football terraces, but through consorting with West Indians at the local youth clubs and on the street corners, by copying their mannerisms, adopting their curses, dancing to their music that the skinheads "magically recovered" the lost sense of working-class community . . . even the skinhead "uniform" was profoundly ambiguous in origin . . . the boots, sta-prest and severely cropped hair: an ensemble which had been composed on the cusp of the two worlds, embodying aesthetic themes common to both.' Ironically, part of the attraction for the skinheads of the 1970s was that reggae and its attendant style was held to be more honest and more representative of the working classes than the overblown glam-rock of Bowie, music made with money in mind as far they were concerned.

As Bryn Jones points out, there is a sense that skinheads (or at least some) 'were simultaneously attracted and put off by the bits of black culture they encountered. There were claims that there were different strands to skinhead culture, some of which were tolerant and "pluralist", as we sociologists say, and some narrow and xenophobic, and that the latter tended to get the upper hand later on.' Certainly, skinheads were always portrayed as the menacing face of disaffected youth and paperback novels such as *Suedehead* from the 1970s did little to alter that view in the public mind. Equally, as the 1970s wore on, many commentators have noted that British-based reggae in particular turned inwards, became more specifically political – Hebdige refers to I-Roy's '(It's a) Black Man Time' for example – isolating the skinheads further. Having rejected white society, they were being rejected by the black culture they admired. In a nation that still considered that the world was a better place when the map of the world was pink, largely drawn from households that were, if not actively racist, then almost certainly casually so, it's little wonder that the skinheads found themselves so confused at their attraction to things they were supposed to hold in contempt. Self-loathing may well have formed a sizeable part of their make-up, the racist violence they indulged in some kind of emotional spasm. They were perfect fodder for the NF, completing a circle of kinds, for not only did the National Front recruit and disrupt football, they did the same with music. The multiracial band The Specials, kings of the revived ska movement on the Coventry-based Two-Tone label in the 1970s, often had their gigs marred by outbreaks of violence perpetrated by skinheaded NF members, skinheads who must have adored the music they were playing. But whoever gave fascists any prizes for rigorous intellectual logic?

These outbursts aside, music did bring about a greater appreciation of black culture, be it through Motown, rhythm and blues, northern soul, disco, reggae – a massive influence on punk – or the way in which white new-wave artists, such as Elvis Costello in 'Watching the Detectives', or The Police in virtually all their early work, grafted reggae onto a white rock sensibility; the way in which The Clash appropriated black rhythms, language, symbols. The Clash even toured with a reggae disco in tow, presided over by Don Letts, the film-making Rastafarian DJ who later joined The Clash's Mick Jones in the band Big Audio Dynamite. And it was rock that gave football a lead that it was far too slow to follow. Years before the Kick Racism Out of Football campaigns got underway, the music world organised itself into the Rock Against Racism movement, with most new-wave and punk artists having some involvement, appearing at benefit concerts, on protest marches, talking up the organisation in the rock press, spreading the word. As the wonderfully named Lucy Toothpaste says in Jon Savage's *England's Dreaming*, 'RAR were very good at politicising the people who came along to the gigs. There would always be leaflets, and our magazine *Temporary Hoarding*, which took up issues to do with racism, fascism and sexism. Many people who came along didn't have any political persuasion, but they responded to the statements made by musicians that it was necessary to challenge people who were putting forward racist ideas.' Thank God they did, for with football slow to act, somebody had to. Because of the tremendous cross-pollination between music and football – after all, the classic weekend double-header was always Saturday afternoon down The Hawthorns, Molineux, Highbury, Maine Road, then Saturday night at a gig or club – football supporters who hadn't thought much about racist abuse might go and see The Specials, The Ruts, The Clash, Tom Robinson, the Gang of Four or any of a host of other bands, hear what they were saying and bring that sensibility back to the terraces. RAR and music in general played a huge part in educating the football crowd, moving them towards a more tolerant stance.

Movements and groupings such as RAR and the Anti-Nazi League were crucial because the situation in the 1970s demanded a more radical response to the NF who were beginning to assert a disturbing, poisonous presence in areas that were home to growing numbers of black and Asian people. The obvious vehicle for such a response was the local Community Relations Council, a body with 120 local organisations affiliated to it. Local councillor Bob Badham was chairman of the CRC but was not convinced it was the right forum for the more direct action that was required. 'Sandwell Community Relations Council was doing a lot of good work promoting race relations. What we needed was something to combat the NF activists who took their "cause" onto the streets. Out of this came a new organisation, Sandwell Campaign Against Racism and Facism [SCARF].' SCARF took the challenge to familiar territory, beginning with The Hawthorns. 'We used to pitch ourselves opposite the NF and sell our publications.' More often than not, with the exception of some gesturing and eyeballing, things tended to pass without incident. SCARF found out that they enjoyed a far greater level of support among fans than they had initially imagined, 'To our surprise, lots of fans used to come up to us and give us support and encouragement.' The Indian Workers Association took their place alongside SCARF. By then, the IWA had a membership running into tens of thousands, with strongholds in Southall and parts of the West Midlands, notably Wolverhampton. Across the country, the IWA galvanised its growing membership to take part in rallies and demonstrations, whether for the rights of Indians, Pakistanis, West Indians or their white brothers and sisters.

The local NF's next battleground was the ballot box. Badham recalls, 'During one election, the NF held a public meeting at Cronehills School in West Bromwich. SCARF decided to enter the hall as it was a public meeting. Within a few minutes a fight broke out, leading to a local vicar and SCARF members being hit on the head with chairs.' The strain of meeting the NF head on was beginning to take its toll on Badham. His photograph appeared on the front of a *Bulldog* publication with the caption 'traitor to the white race', the Ku Klux Klan sent him threatening letters and he had to be given police protection. Given the lack of interaction with local communities, it wasn't surprising that Albion players were largely unaware of these sorts of issues. Brendon Batson says, 'We understood our presence in the team had caused a lot of interest in places like Handsworth and Smethwick among the black community. But we understood they were still reluctant to come and watch us play. That didn't surprise us, given that we were still greeted at games by monkey chants and bananas.' He acknowledges that, had circumstances been the same today, he could envisage players, black and white, coming out to lend support to an organisation like SCARF. Since becoming deputy chief executive of the PFA, Batson has been instrumental in tackling the issue of racism in the game.

On a hot summer's day in July 1999, over twenty thousand people turned up to watch a friendly between West Bromwich Albion and the Jamaican national team, a game organised as a testimonial for long-serving Albion legend Tony Brown. Brown's testimonial committee had imaginatively selected the Jamaicans as Albion's opponents, following an earlier, rather tenuous, link between the club and the national side. In the summer of 1997 West Bromwich Albion had reportedly come close to offering Jamaican 'Bad Boy [Walter] Boyd' a contract. It was during his stay with the Midlands club that Boyd had allegedly made some ill-advised remarks about the national team coach, Rene Simoes. Boyd, a renowned free spirit, both on and off the field, and a doyen idol of the Jamaican football public, was quoted as saying that Simoes wanted to 'play God in his [Boyd's] life'. Boyd's selection for France '98 remained nip and tuck until the end before he narrowly won the day. In October 1999, Walter Boyd signed for Third Division Swansea City and marked his overdue arrival into English football with three goals in his first two games.

As popular as Tony Brown remains, it's likely that only half the crowd had previously heard of him, let alone seen him play. For the other half, it was another chance to watch 'their boyz' in action. It was a journey that had begun with Jamaica's qualification for

France '98. A 0–0 draw with Mexico in the final group match had secured their right to join the world's footballing élite, a sojourn those fortunate enough to witness were never likely to forget. The team may not have met raised expectations, a 5–0 defeat against Argentina and Batistuta being the low point, a 2–1 win over the Japanese the peak. But, in so many great sporting events, it's the minnows who leave the fondest memories and so it was with the Jamaican fans. Les Back tells a fascinating story of an encounter with what turned out to be a distinguished Jamaican fan. Returning back to London, having witnessed the Argentinean drubbing, the mood was, understandably, somewhat sombre on the coach. Sitting next to Back was an older fan, keeping his thoughts very much to himself. On striking up a conversation, Back discovered he was a Jamaican High Court judge. What was remarkable was that he was just one of the fans, captivated by the sense of occasion and the significance of the event for his proud little country. This was a man in touch with ordinary folk and seemingly well disposed to serving them, unlike some of his English counterparts.

By mid morning of the Tony Brown game, the M1 was awash with cars and coaches strewn in green, gold and black as they made their way up to the Midlands. Many others had arrived the night before to descend on the wide selection of parties being thrown by their northern brothers and sisters. Once again, there would be many in the crowd who'd be entering a football ground for the first time in their lives. Party time!

As kick-off approached, Halfords Lane and the Birmingham Road, the two roads that border The Hawthorns, were a mass of black and white faces, kitted out in an assortment of Caribbean and West Bromwich Albion colours. Symbolically, one young fan was adorned in a Jamaican shirt with an Albion scarf draped around his neck, and his friend carried a Jamaican flag in one hand, the St George flag in the other. It would have been enough to send the far right into apoplexy, telling Norman Tebbit precisely where he could put his 'cricket test' and proving it is possible to have dual loyalty to one's ancestral and adopted home lands. Football, England and West Bromwich Albion seemed to have come a long way because, ironically, 20 years earlier, a similar match had taken place, one that was shrouded in controversy. Bob Badham recalls, 'Ron Atkinson had got it into his head that it would be a good idea to have a match between a black and a white team.' The idea was resisted by people like Badham, who considered it a retrograde step. 'It was a time when spectators and players were just getting used to having black players in their team and were gradually warming to the idea. We were seriously worried that such a match could turn into a confrontation between black people and white people.'

The story attracted a great deal of coverage in the local press which, according to Badham, was not always too keen on emphasising the positive side to race relations. Eventually such a match did take place, in May 1979, when a black team led by Cyrille Regis played in a testimonial for Len Cantello. The black team consisted of Derek Williams, Bob Hazell, George Berry, Mark and Neville Chamberlain, Rachid Harkouk, Garth Crooks and the Albion quartet of Regis, Cunningham, Batson and young reserve, Remi Moses. The occasion passed off without incident but Badham still maintains that the idea had been fraught with potential dangers. 'I warmly applauded Ron Atkinson for his work in developing a multiracial team and made the point of telling him so. It did a lot to improve race relations locally. My major objection centred around the proposed timing of the game. I was not convinced that local people were ready for such an event. You have got to remember the age we were in. Put it this way: most people were not as enlightened or as sympathetic as they may be today. One of the comments to me at the time was "So they want to set up their own apartheid?"'

Twenty years on, inside The Hawthorns, there were so many Jamaican fans that they were spread all round the ground. A sizeable presence congregated, appropriately enough, in the Smethwick End to sit back and watch the samba. Sadly there was no modern-day Laurie on the pitch – John Barnes in a guest appearance for the Baggies came closest – and Cyrille was now bedecked in touchline tracksuit, though he did show flashes of the old power when he scored two goals for an Albion XI against a supporters side in a warm-up game before the main event. The game took on the inevitable testimonial feel, especially when substitutions became plentiful in the second half, but that mattered little. Nor did the result, a 1–0 win to Jamaica, thanks to a Marcus Gayle goal.

As the masses departed, the Albion board, who had just seen one of the biggest crowds of the season, must have had one recurring thought: how could the club successfully reconnect with the local black community? Twenty years ago, the Baggies had been in the vanguard of a footballing revolution. Though they hadn't captured any trophies, they had been the prime movers, the spearhead of a seismic shift in English football, kicking it into a multicultural future, starting a movement that simply could not be reversed. It wasn't the glamour clubs of cosmopolitan London – though Orient must take some credit – but the barely regarded clubs of the Black Country that showed the game its future. Because of a fear of racism, the black community was unable to respond in the numbers that might have been expected. While those who passed through the Hawthorns turnstiles were few in number, the club did manage to engender a sense of goodwill within a community that previously had little cause for affiliation. Chairman Tony Hale and company were now looking out onto the children of that missed generation, the final piece in the jigsaw.

FIVE

By November 1978 it was obvious that Albion were going to have a real say in that season's Championship race. Having gone out of the League Cup at the first hurdle in a second replay against Leeds, their attention was divided between the League and the UEFA Cup. Domestically, they went on an unbeaten run of thirteen matches, winning ten including games at Leeds, Ipswich, Wolves, Arsenal and at Manchester United, where they reached something of a peak on 30 December. The 5–3 win there is a game that is still screened from time to time and certainly still discussed in reverent tones wherever Baggies supporters of a certain age are gathered together. The team worked supremely well as a unit that day, giving a perfect exposition of everything that was good about that side, playing with grace, power, flair and steel. Brendon Batson recalls Laurie Cunningham's display in particular: 'he was just gliding past people.' As John Wile says, 'We played a lot of teams off the field, there was a strong belief within the club, you have to have a degree of arrogance but there was a humility too, to the extent that you'd sometimes sacrifice your own game for the benefit of the team as a whole. That ethic was very strong. It was an exciting team; we expected to win wherever and whoever we played. We could score goals from anywhere, not just Cyrille or Ally Brown; Laurie could get them, Bryan Robson, Tony Brown always got goals, Derek Statham popped in one or two and even Brendon managed one in his whole career! There was such belief, and when you're on a run, confidence grows, it makes you better and better.' While the rest of the country was snowed off on New Year's Day, somehow Albion's home game with Bristol City was played on an icebound pitch.

Wearing boots designed for AstroTurf, Albion were surefooted while the City players spent the afternoon falling down, a perfect metaphor for the way the season was going. Twelve days later, a Regis goal gave Albion a point at Carrow Road and put them on top of the table.

By this stage, the whole Three Degrees thing had taken off, with the real Three Degrees even coming to The Hawthorns before a game while on tour in the UK. As Wile says, 'The Three Degrees were very popular at the time, and when they were in Birmingham to do a show it was natural for Big Ron to get them together with the lads. It was showbiz and he loved it, that was what Ron was all about. It was good for the club, gave us a higher profile, one we've never really attained since then.' It did pose a few problems for the players, though, as their national profile was heightened still further. Cyrille Regis remembers, 'That whole Three Degrees stuff – as young footballers you don't know how to handle it. Do you speak out against racism, or do you let your football talk for you? There were two parts to it. They tried to put you off your game, which was just laughable, but there was the more serious side because there was a lot of skinhead, NF stuff around at the time as well and that was very nasty. You'd get ten thousand people singing racist songs at you and I don't think anyone knew what to do. Imagine that now! Things have been done, thankfully, and it doesn't happen like that. But back then, you'd have thousands of people screaming "nigger, nigger lick my boots" at you. And the authorities just said "disgraceful" and did nothing. Nothing happened for years, until the late 1980s with the Kick Racism campaigns. Then laws were passed against racist chanting, but even so you don't hear about people getting kicked out of the ground for doing it, do you?'

Brendon Batson was equally uncertain how to approach the issue. 'We weren't really aware of the effect we, as black players, were having in and around West Bromwich, Smethwick, Handsworth. Because we were always travelling, I don't think we realised the impact we were having on the black community. We only learnt that a few years later. We were not aware that our success was leading to more black faces on the terraces. Instead, our understanding was that they enjoyed our success but did not feel it was safe to come to the games. I have discovered stories about black supporters of Liverpool being attacked by their "own" supporters. You've got to remember that the violence around the game at the time was about the worst it's ever been, so that didn't help.' Speaking at the time, Laurie Cunningham had a slightly different take on things. Indeed, he was happy to suggest that his new status as a role model had helped him mature as a person. 'I was a bit shy and very quiet at times when I arrived at The Hawthorns. I haven't got a fiery temper and maybe that helps because I'm able to walk away from explosive situations. It takes a lot to get me to lose my rag and so far I've been more interested in getting on with the game than looking for trouble. It's always better to keep cool and maintain your concentration, otherwise you can be a menace to yourself – and the rest of the team. It's never been my style to throw myself around the place. But certainly since arriving in the Midlands and the First Division I've been conscious of the encouragement we can generate among the black kids in the area. A lot of nonsense has been talked about black players not having enough heart for the game when the going gets tough. Well, that's a theory that has quickly been dispelled. More black players are coming into the game all the time, and that can only help others to try their luck.'

As Albion sat on top of the table in mid-January 1979, they were also looking ahead to the quarter-finals of the UEFA Cup. If anything, their European performances had been even better than the domestic ones. In the first round they won 3–1 home and away against Galatasaray, the only English team to win there until Chelsea repeated the feat in the 1999–2000 Champions League. Portugal's Sporting Braga had been seen off 3–0 on aggregate, the tie won overseas in the first leg when Regis blasted two goals. That set them up for a third-round match with Valencia of Spain, then boasting two of the world's greatest footballers – West Germany's Rainer Bonhof and the star of the 1978 World Cup, Argentina's Mario Kempes. Thanks largely to their presence, Valencia were favourites for the competition, and Albion were written off by most pundits even before they travelled to Spain. Even those few who felt they had a chance suggested their only hope would be to go out to Spain and defend in depth. Instead, the team played according to its principles, espoused by Derek Statham when he told journalists, 'We are told not to worry about the opposition. I do no go out of my way to concern myself with the winger I may face. I prefer to let him think a bit about me.' That was Albion's style in Valencia and, though the result was a 1–1 draw, Albion had scared the living daylights out of the expensively assembled Spanish team and deserved a far better reward for a bravura display.

In particular, Laurie Cunningham, Albion's goalscorer, had been irresistible. Brendon Batson says, 'My abiding memory of Laurie is that game in Valencia, which sold him to Real Madrid. That night he terrorised the whole defence. When Laurie was playing on the right he was very easy to link up with. He always wanted the ball. Sometimes you didn't know what he was going to do with it. He was playing just in front of me and I remember thinking, "Thank God I'm not facing him." It was a tragedy what happened to him, but I'm just so pleased I had the privilege to play with him. He had that grace about him, he never looked rushed. Sometimes you don't really appreciate what a good player someone is until they've gone, but in his time he was outstanding. He was insecure at times and that may have held him back, but all in all he was a fantastic talent.' Ron Atkinson noted that, 'It got to the stage where the Spanish fans were willing him to get the ball. He took them on and virtually destroyed them.' John Wile agrees. 'Laurie sold himself in Valencia. He was outstanding – along with a lot of others. He did catch the eye, he was quick, lithe, had a superb game. That was a great, great match. That and the return leg here were two of the best games I was ever involved in. Our approach in Europe was very good again. We looked on it as an adventure, not something to be frightened of. We were good pros, but we didn't let it get on top of us in terms of pressure. The atmosphere here was tremendous. It was as good as playing for anybody in the country – good side, good club, not such great divisions between clubs within the same league. We were as good as anybody. We played good football, it was good to come in to work.' Tony Brown agreed, saying at the time, 'Ron Atkinson has this tremendous enthusiasm for the game and that brings out the best in everyone. It's the same with a five-a-side game in training when he backs his team called "English Cream" against what he terms "Foreign Scum". He really gets the lads going! He knows we're a responsible bunch of professional players and that's another reason why the team spirit is good. The approach is right. I've never enjoyed myself so much in all my life.'

In the return leg, Cunningham was attended to by two, sometimes three defenders who, in the current climate, wouldn't have made it to half-time. Not that that sort of attention worried him, Atkinson saying at the time, 'He gets in at close quarters to set up chances and is not afraid when boots start to fly in and around the danger areas.' Cunningham had another excellent game and created further space for the rest of the team, as Albion went through 2–0, Tony Brown getting both goals. With Red Star Belgrade to look forward to, with Coventry seen off in the Third Round of the FA Cup and with the club at the top of the table, surely the disappointments of the previous year would be erased?

And then it snowed. And snowed. And, for good measure, it snowed a bit more. Between the game at Norwich on 13 January and a visit from Leeds on 24 February, Albion played just one game. It was a visit to Liverpool, marred for many travelling supporters by violent clashes with Liverpool supporters who infiltrated the visitors' terraces, spent the game abusing Cunningham, Regis and Batson and then, for an encore, poured through Stanley Park to wreck the coaches waiting to take the Albion supporters home. It seems Albion had inflicted the twin indignity of knocking Liverpool off the top and daring to have black players in the team. If that was showing solidarity with their team, it rather went against the Liverpool supporters' self-proclaimed reputation of being the best supporters in the land. As always, only a minority were involved, but, as usual, the damage was serious. Small wonder there were few, if any, black fans in Albion's travelling support. God only knows what would have happened to them.

Liverpool inflicted a 2–1 defeat on Albion, ending a 19-game unbeaten run, Cunningham making just about his only error in six months when he missed a golden chance to grab a late equaliser. In fairness to Liverpool – a club that had had the vision to install under-soil heating and so were able to play through the bad weather – they had a wonderful side. Having been stunned by a first-round exit in the European Cup – Cloughie was just too clever for them – winning the title was a crusade. (A note for younger readers – in those far off days you actually had to be the champions to enter the European Champions Cup. What a quaint idea.) Liverpool had a wonderful team – Dalglish, Souness, Clemence, Hansen – and were just entering that period of relentless success when they were all but unstoppable.

Could Albion have stopped them? That year, they probably could have. As Cyrille Regis says, 'We should have won the League and that weather break beat us. The effect it had on our legs to have to play so many games just finished us. We played four times in a week a couple of times. You'd think you were sprinting but you weren't. I remember going to Bristol City. I think it was Villa who'd just beaten Liverpool for us, and we were back in there. We went to Bristol and lost because we couldn't move, we were just absolutely shattered.' From 24 February to 18 May, Albion played 25 first-team games in 64 days. Little wonder the wheels came off. Such was the quality and the confidence in the team, they were still capable of reeling off six straight League wins through March to stay in with a chance, but the fluency was going and the team was running itself into the ground. David Mills had been brought in from Middlesbrough to add a fresh face, but he couldn't settle at the club. Len Cantello and Tony Brown picked up injuries that kept them out, while the rest of the side were struggling onto the field with less serious problems. Finally, as Wile recalls, 'The weather did for us, and then when we did get playing again there was a lot of flu in the club. A lot of us played when we weren't fit, and we'd gone off the boil, playing too many matches and we just couldn't pick it up to finish where we should have done, which was a great shame.' Ultimately, Albion came third, losing the runners-up slot in the final minutes of the final game of the season, when Forest won 1–0 at The Hawthorns to move a point ahead. Albion finished with fifty-nine points – two points for a win in those days – enough to have won the title in three seasons in the 1970s, certainly sufficient to come at least second in eight of those.

In Cup competitions there was further disappointment. After a huge struggle with Leeds, Albion got through in a replay in extra time. At a time when the side needed to conserve its energies, Southampton took them to a replay and extra time in the fifth round, finally putting Albion out at the Dell. Defeat in the UEFA Cup was an even greater pity, for the performance against Valencia had shown Albion had the credentials to win the trophy. They were pitted against Red Star Belgrade and as John Wile ruefully concedes, 'We learned a lot from them, in terms of gamesmanship, or professionalism if you prefer. It still happens now – it is hard to win abroad. We were honestly the better team over two legs. We were done out there, they scored from a free kick that was never a free kick and we lost 1–0 in front of 95,000. At home we created enough chances to have buried Red Star; Cyrille scored for us, it was level, and we forced them to adopt very tough tactics to keep us out and it seemed only a matter of time before they cracked. Instead they sneaked into our half late on and scrambled a fluke goal. Three of their players should have been sent off for ruthless tactics. But they got the 1–1 draw and we were out. They were the most cynical team we played; they were streetwise, and that was a learning curve for us. It was disappointing because, just as in the League, we were good enough to do better than we did, we could have gone further.' Red Star were good enough to reach the final, where, over two legs, they were narrowly beaten 2–1 on aggregate by Borussia Moenchengladbach, so it's clear how close Albion came.

Their fellow professionals recognised the quality in the team – much as they all respected Liverpool's quality and efficiency, there was a genuine sadness in all parts of the game that a side as exciting as Albion hadn't captured the title. In an end-of-year round-up in *Shoot!*, Manchester City's Mick Channon wrote, 'The Albion back four, as a unit, is organised, always knows what it intends to do and is positive at all times.' In the same piece, Tommy Hutchinson of Coventry added, 'John Wile controlled his back four skilfully and made them difficult to pass . . . Wile's experience steadied the West Brom rearguard under pressure. With his positional sense and ability in the air, John was able to prevent opposing strikers finding a way through – also good organisation on the flanks gave their defence the necessary balance. In attack, Laurie Cunningham is hard to subdue. He makes up his mind to find a path through defences, teases them and is very quick. He scored the best goal scored against Coventry last season. He collected a through ball and when our keeper, Jim Blyth, went out quickly to meet him, Laurie bent a shot over his hands to score when a goal hadn't really looked on. And the whole operation, the style and balance of Cunningham, made everything about the goal first-class.' To add to those and dozens more plaudits, Cyrille Regis was voted PFA Young Player of the Year, an award he still recalls with pride. 'To get recognition from the men you play with and against was another realisation that I had arrived as a footballer. I was sitting by Laurie and I thought he and Garry Birtles would have it between them. When Kevin Keegan called out my name, it was unbelievable.' Personal awards came in regularly throughout the side, but the failure to actually clinch a real trophy had an enormous effect on West Bromwich Albion, in both the short- and long-term. Had they got their hands on some silverware, then the next few years would surely have been different. As it was, Albion were still a 'nearly' club and Ron Atkinson and his players – all except Tony Brown – had still to win a major competition. If Albion hadn't been hampered by the weather, if the club had had the foresight to install undersoil heating, if, if, if. But if John Wile had picked up the UEFA Cup or the League Championship, then the years that followed would surely have been very different.

SIX

A season which had looked so full of potential eventually fell away at the final hurdle. Albion closed the 1978–79 campaign with a testimonial game for Len Cantello, in which his team took on an all-black side captained by Cyrille Regis. Though nobody realised it at the time, these were the final moments of a wonderful, but all too brief, era. Within days, Cantello announced he was making use of the new-found freedom of contract and leaving the club to join Bolton Wanderers. Within weeks, the club was dealt an even greater body blow with the loss of Laurie Cunningham to Real Madrid. Had Albion actually clinched a trophy in 1978–79, Cantello would almost certainly have signed a new three-year deal that would have seen him finish his career at the club. Cunningham, too, then just beginning to break into the full England side, would surely have thought a lot harder about staying in West Bromwich. Towards the end of the season, when it became clear the prizes were slipping away, he had said, 'I don't think I'm far away from establishing myself with England . . . my chance will come as long as I continue to play well for West Brom. Added to that, I believe we have a side at The Hawthorns that is close to winning a major honour. We fell victims to the weather this season in the shape of a three-week freeze-up that left us kicking our heels at a vital time. As it happened we were forced into a programme of 11 games inside a month with hardly time to breathe. But we're not complaining. It's just made us more determined to do even better. It's nice to win but it's also nice to do it in style.' Cunningham certainly did everything with style. After demoralising Valencia in that remarkable UEFA Cup game, he knew he was a hot property in Spain. At the end of the season, he got a flight out to Madrid, turned up at the Bernabeu Stadium, knocked on the door and asked if Real Madrid were interested in signing him. Journalist James Lawton described it as a 'kind of sublime cockiness. When he turned up at the offices of Real Madrid, officials were shocked and promptly delivered a stinging lecture on etiquette.' But that confidence was well placed. Because for all their surprise at Cunningham's methodology, he knew they wouldn't turn away his talent.

By the end of 1978–79, Cunningham had won three caps for the full England side, against Wales, Sweden and as a substitute against Austria, not quite the return that many had expected from such a talent. In part, that was down to the vagaries of selection policy. Football is, famously, a game of opinions, and it was Ron Greenwood's opinion that counted. To the surprise of many observers, he felt that Manchester City's talented but wildly inconsistent winger Peter Barnes offered England a better option on the left flank, while on the other Steve Coppell was understandably first choice as winger-cum-midfielder. Behind Barnes in the pecking order, Cunningham even lost out on the race to become the first black footballer to win a senior cap, that piece of history going to Nottingham Forest's right-back Viv Anderson; Anderson received a congratulatory telegram from the Cunningham family before he took to the field in his England debut against Czechoslovakia. Ironically, Anderson and Cunningham might well have created the same kind of intelligent partnership for England that Cunningham enjoyed with Brendon Batson at the Albion. Some felt that Batson himself was worthy of an England cap ahead of Anderson.

Certainly, though Cunningham had shown himself to be a prodigious talent and had done some useful things in those early England games, it would be foolish to suggest he had pushed himself to the forefront of Ron Greenwood's thinking. He'd done little more than put himself in the frame and make himself a member of the squad, but certainly not of the team. In 1979, few players in England were sampling life abroad. Kevin Keegan had famously left Liverpool for SV Hamburg in 1977, but thereafter few had followed. Centre-half Dave Watson was about to move to Werder Bremen, but, like Keegan, he was a fixture in the England side. Greenwood didn't need to monitor their form, merely to keep an eye on their fitness. Cunningham was by no means an automatic choice, so for him to move out of the country was an extremely risky move in terms of his international future, even when moving to as great a club as Real Madrid. There was clearly a chance that he would be out of sight and out of mind. Cunningham's own thinking was that playing in a different country would be a valuable part of his footballing education and would improve him as a player. 'I've thought about a move for some time and now I feel that I must learn more about the game.' Unfortunately, where the British press had followed Keegan on to the continent, filing reports, making documentaries, interviewing him at length, Cunningham's Spanish odyssey was largely ignored. His Albion colleague John Trewick says, 'He probably went abroad too early, but at the time, where else could he have gone in England that would have been better? We were as wealthy as anyone – not as big a club as an Arsenal or a Liverpool or a United but we had money and a good team. The only place worth going to here in this country would have been Liverpool. But Laurie being Laurie, the appeal of Spain was important, the game, the lifestyle, and you cannot blame him for that. If the opportunity had been there for me, it's something I would have fancied.'

Like a number of his Albion, and indeed his Midlands coll-eagues, Cunningham was frustrated by the way in which the region was ignored by the media and then, as a consequence, by the national team. As Trewick says, 'Some clubs are unfashionable and you can't change it. Even now, look at the national selections and you will see that they come from the same places. If you played here instead of at Arsenal you had to be 20 or 30 per cent more consistent to get a look-in. Bryan Robson was the same player when he was here that he was at Manchester United when he suddenly became an England regular. He played a lot of his best football here, but it's getting the opportunity. A lot rests on the

England manager being strong enough to rise above everything and pick the best players, irrespective of where they play. Generally they don't because of the level of criticism they get if it goes wrong.' Tim Beech, the head of sport at BBC Radio WM, based at the Pebble Mill studios in Birmingham, elaborates on that assessment. 'I feel that the Midlands doesn't get the publicity it deserves. Nowadays, it has got an image it's trying to shed, of an industrial area in decline with nothing to offer, but it's never been well regarded. In the early '80s there was a big campaign in the local press to get Bryan Robson in the England team. The local press and the radio stations all made a big thing of it because Bryan was very clearly worth his place in the England team. He made his debut in February 1980 but missed the European Championships, then was in and out of the side. Then, about a year later when he went to Manchester United, Greenwood said he was the first name in the squad. He hadn't transformed that quickly. He was as good 12 months before when he was at the Albion. If he'd been playing anywhere else, he would have had another 15 or 20 caps. That is a problem for the Midlands; they don't get the exposure, so they can neither get the players nor keep the players.'

In the light of this it was ironic that in moving to a truly massive club – probably the biggest Europe had to offer – Cunningham did terrible damage to his prospects of playing for England. In an era during which continental football wasn't plastered all over our screens at every opportunity, it was easy simply to forget about him. John Wile notes, 'It was a time when there weren't many players going abroad, so perhaps it was difficult in that sense for him. I don't think it would have hurt him to have had another 12 months here. He was a loner. I think he had a stable relationship, which helped, but it must have been difficult to go out there at that age and with such a big fee against his name.' As Cyrille Regis says, 'In hindsight, Laurie went too young. It was a big fee, big wages, but he wasn't mature enough – you think you are at 22, but you're not. You make decisions in life, some are good, some are bad. With some of them, you just struggle and struggle to get out from underneath and you can't do it. It was a different culture and he wasn't grounded. Suddenly, he was confronted by the pressure of performing at a huge club; he got some injuries, it all just snowballed. Again, at Real Madrid he was the first black guy so there was a lot of press and while there were three of us to deal with it here, Laurie was on his own in Madrid and couldn't share it with anybody. The whole thing was a lot to deal with. The same could have happened to me the season before. I had dual nationality – came from French Guyana, my father was a St Lucian, he had a British passport, so I was eligible to play for France as well as for England. St Etienne came in for me at the end of the 1977–78 season and offered £750,000 and there was an idea that if I did well there, I could play for France, the side that had Platini, Tigana, Tresor, Six. The main reason I didn't go was because I felt I wasn't ready. Albion had a good side, why go somewhere else? I'd only been in the game a year! I decided to stay here and got picked for the England Under-21s pretty soon after. You are at a disadvantage playing here in terms of England because you don't get the coverage. But I was happy here, no regrets. The funny thing is that though leaving Albion when he did probably hurt Laurie's career, perhaps staying hurt the likes of me and Derek Statham. However well we did, the big boys like Liverpool dominated everything and we didn't get a look in; the press covered them and the London boys. If Derek had been at Arsenal, maybe he would have had 80 caps, instead of Kenny Sansom. Laurie had such natural talent. Visually he was the best player to watch; balance, grace, style, there was nothing to touch him. On his toes, wonderful. He didn't fulfil his potential, but maybe we could all say that – me, Derek as well. Probably only Bryan really did year in, year out. It's down to circumstances, injuries, all sorts of things.'

Moving to Spain was clearly a huge decision for Cunningham to have to make and it is easy to say that maybe he should have held on for another 12 months. But playing ambitions weren't the only consideration in an era during which even top players were a long, long way from being the millionaires we know and love today. A fine player though he is, is David Ginola as good a player as Laurie Cunningham at his best? It's matter of opinion, but the answer is probably no. Yet there is no comparison between the money Ginola can command and the money Cunningham got paid. This was still an era when football was a very insecure profession, even for those players at a top club. As Cyrille Regis points out, 'Laurie would have stayed, but it was really about money in the end. He left on £120 a week – I was on more than that! He'd come from Orient, no bargaining chip, on a two-year deal, but it was not upgraded when he'd proved himself. I nearly went to St Etienne my first season here, but they didn't turn round and give me a new deal, I was on £60 a week until the end of that season and then they started to talk about new contracts!'

Just to put that figure into some sort of context – and you can't compare it with the twenty, thirty or forty thousand pounds a week that vastly inferior players are getting these days – look at it in the light of wage movement after the abolition of the maximum wage. Prior to that, footballers had been shackled to a top weekly wage of £20. When the PFA – or the players' union as it then was – finally succeeded in having that particular restrictive practice kicked into touch in 1961, clubs were fearful of a wage explosion that would put them out of business. Johnny Haynes famously became the first £100 per week footballer, but, in general, wages did not rise dramatically. They started to increase gradually through the 1960s, by which time the real footballing powers were Liverpool, Manchester United and Spurs – if you were an ambitious footballer at the top of your profession there were few other clubs that you would think of playing for. In order to avoid getting embroiled in costly auctions for a player's services, the managers of these clubs, Bill Shankly, Matt Busby and Bill Nicholson, got together and introduced an informal ceiling of £100, a figure above which none of those three clubs would go. This was around 1965. So, 14 years later, after the hyperinflation of the 1970s, West Bromwich Albion, who had finished third in the League Championship, were paying Laurie Cunningham, as gifted a player as any in the land, just £20 more.

Bryn Jones remembers, 'My father used to say that Albion were the meanest club in the West Midlands and they've always had a reputation for penny-pinching. Maybe it goes back to when they had trouble years ago, right at the turn of the century when they almost went under. You wonder if that sort of culture gets ingrained: you don't take risks, you worry about every penny and that just becomes part of the club's way of behaving. That, plus recruiting certain kinds of people, reinforces it. In the days when Laurie Cunningham was there, we had a board largely composed of solicitors, who may well be inherently conservative. Certainly, they don't need to have entrepreneurial flair to succeed as solicitors, don't need to be looking at investment to make their businesses grow in the way that industrialists or property developers do. Possibly that spilled over into the attitudes at the Albion. To an extent Jack Hayward at Wolves is like Villa's Doug Ellis in that respect, he's got a wider perspective as a businessman maybe which is why he invested so heavily in the stadium and so on. You wonder, if the Albion had had that sort of money, what the boards of directors would have done with it. You can't imagine there being any lavish architecture, like at Villa Park or Molineux! There's always been a small-time mentality at the club.'

Looking back at the summer of 1979, it is agonisingly apparent that that was the moment when West Bromwich Albion told the world they were happy to be a run-of-the-mill First Division club, rather than doing what Nottingham Forest were doing and attempting to become one of the élite. Manchester United and Arsenal both had decidedly average teams at the time, so there was a blindingly obvious window of opportunity for another club to come long and slap down a challenge to Liverpool. Albion could have done it. As Cyrille Regis explains, 'The club should never have let Laurie and Len Cantello go that summer. We had a side that could have been there for years. You add to it, not take away. We got nearly a million for Laurie and then had to spend most of that on Peter Barnes. It doesn't make sense.' Looking at it from the club's point of view, John Wile says, 'When you get an offer, you have to decide whether it's the right thing or not, whether you'll get it again. Laurie decided it was right for him to go and Ron Atkinson felt it was the right price, or he wouldn't have been a party to selling him.'

John Trewick understands the club's point of view, but, fundamentally, disagrees. 'We were attractive, great individuals; some of the games are classics still, like the win at Manchester United 5–3. We were top of the league before we got snowed off for weeks and ended up third, which was a good achievement, but maybe we were better than that and we never quite got there. I do believe the club was premature in letting players go, people like Cantello and Cunningham, then over the next year or two they lost myself, Robson, Remi Moses. We were a rich club at the time, one of the three or four wealthiest, I'd reckon, wheeling and dealing with the best. We bought the likes of David Mills, John Deehan, Peter Barnes and Gary Owen for good money, but we were selling at the same time. We accepted a million, or thereabouts, for Laurie, a big offer, but if you really want to achieve something, you've got to keep these guys together.' Trewick is right. Football clubs, especially those on the rise, those threatening the status quo, have certain players who are totemic. For all that Albion had quality throughout the side, they had three players who represented what the team might achieve, three men who represented the future and the promise it held – Bryan Robson, Cyrille Regis and Laurie Cunningham. While Albion held on to that triumvirate, they were serious players. Once they let Cunningham go, football knew that every player at the club had his price and that the club harboured no serious ambition.

When Laurie Cunningham did leave England, he did so not only as one of the very best players in the country. According to James Lawton, 'Cunningham has proved, beyond any lingering doubt, that the prejudices which lurked in the minds of so many British football coaches and managers can be assigned to history. He has liberated a whole generation of young blacks.' Sociologically, alongside Cyrille Regis and Brendon Batson, as the vanguard that came ahead of wave after wave of wonderful black footballers, Laurie Cunningham had proved himself to be one of the most significant individuals ever to tread the football fields of England. He proved that anybody who said black players couldn't make it in English football was talking out of the wrong part of their anatomy.

He proved that in football, as in life, the only thing that really matters is who you are, not what colour you are.

For all that, when Albion followers of Laurie's vintage cast their minds back, they remember a player who, when on the top of his game, could do anything he liked with a football and with the opposition. Every couple of months, some pundit will compare a fairly average player with George Best. At times like that, you can only shake your head sadly, for people like that deserve your pity rather than your contempt. In the 35 years since George Best arrived on the scene, the home nations have not produced a player who is fit to be mentioned in the same book as George Best, never mind the same sentence. You do not compare players with Bestie. You just don't. Which is a measure of how good Laurie Cunningham was throughout much of that 1978–79 season. There were days when you could look at this man and his utterly sublime gift and you would not have been surprised to see him wearing a Brazilian shirt with a number ten on the back. He was that good, he really was. The man was a magician. Where Regis was all power, a physical force that would surge in and out of games, Cunningham was artistry, deftness, thrilling trickery. If Regis merited his comparisons with Joe Frazier, then Cunningham deserved to be likened to the blessed genius of Muhammad Ali. George Petchey, Cunningham's Orient manager, said of him, as Cunningham left England for Spain, 'There isn't anything he can't achieve. He's a natural . . . He always had the talent but now he's got the right temperament to go with it. And that's a credit to himself because he's worked at getting it right.' In truth, Laurie Cunningham was such a genius that he deserved a bigger stage than English football could offer him. Laurie Cunningham deserved Real Madrid and the Bernabeu Stadium. Did they deserve him?

At the age of 22, Cunningham entered the cauldron of fire at the Santiago Bernabeu Stadium, a fully fledged conscript to the world famous Real Madrid, with clear images of that night when he had terrorised the Valencia defence shining brightly in his, and the Spanish public's, memory. The generous applause he received from the Spanish crowd had convinced him that this was the right decision. Cunningham knew this to be the ultimate move. Many of the great European and South American footballers of recent times – the most notable exceptions being perhaps Pelé, George Best and Franz Beckenbauer – have played in either Spain or Italy. The English Premier League may claim otherwise, but the irrefutable fact is that the force of European club football will always be with Italy and Spain, followed by England and Germany. The stage was set, the theatre beckoned for this outstanding performer to propel Real Madrid back to former glories. Succeed and make hay, fail and be doomed.

A new beginning was how Cunningham saw this opportunity. The last few years in England had been kind, opening up new avenues on and off the field, but in the last season or so, the football had become less challenging. The predictable lunges of bemused defenders had been mastered, the racist abuse of players and fans taken in his stride. He scented the smell of the big stage and wanted a piece of the action. Bobby Fisher, now working in the combined fields of motivational psychology and sports management, has strong memories of Laurie's time in Madrid, where he visited him on a few occasions. He is now working on a proposed documentary celebrating the life of Laurie Cunnigham. 'There is no question that his style, was better suited to Spain. In England he felt the system negated his style which is why he kept asking for a freer role. He knew that although they marked much tighter in Spain, he was clever and confident enough to beat the system.'

Moreover, the Spanish capital offered the chance to develop as a person and become part of a new culture. The Madrid lifestyle would be much more in keeping with his nocturnal habits than England ever would be. Fisher points out, 'As a player he was never one of the boys as such. After the match it is common for the lads to go on to a bar, from where the night would begin. Laurie would, on occasion, come for a couple of beers before going home to sleep until, say, midnight and then go out for the night.'

Real Madrid were desperate to recover lost ground at domestic and European level. Their monopoly of European competition in the late 1950s and 1960s was being undermined by the rise of other club sides like Ajax, Bayern Munich and Liverpool. At home, Barcelona were attacking their pre-eminence – unsurprisingly, since from 1973 to 1978 they could field a certain Johan Cruyff. It was also a lean period for the Spanish national team as the effects of the 'star-system' policy, signing foreign players, were having negative consequences. The nucleus of the legendary Real Madrid had been constructed around the Hungarian Ferenc Puskas, France's Raymond Kopa, and Alfredo Di Stefano, an Argentinean and subsequently naturalised Spaniard. Periodically, the football authorities would impose a ban on foreign players, only to see the economic power of Real Madrid and Barcelona and the political influence of the candidates for the club presidencies lead to the lifting of the ban. Real were accustomed to signing only the best and in Cunningham they knew that one of the finest emerging talents in the game had been captured.

Skill, imagination and flamboyance may have constituted the philosophy of the Puskas-inspired Real sides, but that belonged to another age. Thanks largely to the influence of one man, Helenio Herrera, a more technical, tactical and defensive style had emerged. A former manager with Atletico Madrid, whom he led to two Spanish championships, and later with Barcelona, also Spanish champions under his charge, Herrera turned the game inside out, ultimately doing the same to European football when, following his spell at Barcelona, he went on to Inter Milan to create one of the most consistently successful teams in the history of football.

Inter frequently won 1–0 and Herrera's tactical approach became known as *catenaccio*, literally 'the door-bolt'. Other Italian clubs soon followed, and for decades, Serie A had the lowest goal scoring ratio per match in Europe. During the 1970s and early 1980s, Spanish football tried to build on Herrera's legacy and take a leaf out of their Latin brothers' book. What they produced was an even harsher style – *Futbol de muerte* – that married the passion for football to another element in the sporting Spanish tradition, the *corrida* – bullfighting. The football stadium at this time was often compared to the bullfight arena and the visiting team to the bull, the *toro*, who had to die. The European Cup semi-final of 1974, between Glasgow Celtic and Atletico Madrid, shocked inter-national observers, as did the final of the European Cup-Winners' Cup in 1982, in which Barcelona beat Standard Liège 2–1 at the Nou Camp. In the first game at Parkhead, three Atletico players were sent off in a match the British football public felt to be unprecedented in its savagery. In both instances, Spanish defenders, with the apparent approval of the club's supporters, who applauded enthusiastically, used all possible means to stop their opponents. While the Italians executed their 'defensive' duties with subtle cynicism, the Spaniards were openly brutal and dangerous, and if the intention was to perform with the elegance of a toreador, they patently failed. Had Cunningham known the full extent of this new and cynical style of defending that had crept into the domestic game, would he have still gone to Spain? It was to be a decision he would regret for the remainder of his short life. Little did he suspect that the final blow to a career that had promised so much would come from the most unexpected of sources.

Quickly adjusting to life in Madrid, Cunningham exploded on the scene with a series of dazzling displays. The hugely impatient Real fans took to him instantly. He was a throwback to likes of Di Stefano and Gento, and, like the true toreador, tormented his opponents, often driving them to a state of frenzy, as he twisted this way and that way, before the final execution, a telling pass, cross or clinical finish. Within a few weeks he had charmed his way into the hearts of the home fans, which, at the outset, seemed the major challenge.

The Real Madrid club has always been seen as General Franco's team, though its a claim denied by most people associated with the club. The Santiago Bernabeu Stadium was constructed between 1944 and 1947 and is therefore seen as symbolising the Franco period. The Franco regime had permitted the Spanish Liga to resume immediately after the end of the Spanish Civil War, apparently concerned about the decline of bullfighting. Football offered the masses an important outlet for social and cultural preoccupation. In the 1950s and '60s, a period when Spain was still isolated politically in Europe, Franco sought to identify with the hugely successful and globally popular Real Madrid. Real were seen as 'ambassadors' who could assist in softening international attitudes towards a military dictatorship. Since then it has been commonly perceived that Real Madrid are a nationalist symbol, with a hardcore of right-wing followers. Leaders of that sentiment were quick to seize opportunities for bringing together mass culture and their propaganda, and a captive audience of 90,000 was a ready-made target group. Laurie Cunningham was the first black player to represent the great club and it was a prospect that, initially, caused loud mutterings of dissent among those who saw a black man's presence in the world famous all-white kit of Real Madrid as compromising the club's identity.

Fisher was one of the first people to go out to visit Cunningham. Laurie had told him that he had a big house and that he would be welcome to stay with him. 'Laurie lived in a massive complex, one of 20 houses dotted around the hills. His accommodation was a three-storey mansion. On my first visit I saw this swimming pool empty of water but full of junk. I said to Laurie, "Why don't you use the pool properly?" Typically Laurie said that the builders had never got round to finishing it and he hadn't got round to calling them back. That was over six months earlier! When we went inside the house, the first floor looked as if it had been hit by a bomb, as did the second. His living quarters consisted of an immaculate third-floor kitchen and bedroom. But that was enough for Laurie, just as long as there was somewhere for him to cook, eat his food and sleep.' Needless to say, Bobby didn't stay the night.

With supportive girlfriend Nicky Brown alongside him in Spain, Laurie focused on his dreams on and off the field. He pursued his interest in architectural design and continued to practise dance and his long-time interest in the design of clothes, something he took very seriously. As Brendon Batson says, 'If you wanted to pick a fight with Laurie, you abused his clothes!' Laurie was thinking ahead, looking to a time when football no longer paid the bills. And, as always, Laurie wanted to ensure he took control of his destiny.

Nicky Brown was 15 years old when she first met the then 17-

year-old Laurie Cunningham. Their backgrounds could not have been more polarised. She was from a middle-class background, intelligent, charming, well educated and white. According to Fisher, 'Nicky was an integral part of his character. She was his rock, always there for him.' It surprised those around Laurie when they heard he and Nicky had split up some years later. Laurie married a Spanish woman called Sylvia with whom he had one child, Sergio. Nicky spoke Spanish, and, at times, that came in more than useful given Laurie's limitations in this area. Fisher recalls, 'We once met at Madrid airport on a stopover on my way to Portugal. I happened to be carrying some clothes in a bag and two suit carriers. Laurie had suggested that we stop for coffee in the middle of Madrid. I asked him if it was safe to leave my gear on the back seat. Laurie said it would be fine because everyone knew his car and that, because of who he was, no one would dare break into it. Typical of 'Lol', this turned out to be a six-hour marathon coffee-drinking session. As we approached the car we could see glass splayed everywhere. I turned round to Lol in my panic-stricken state and asked what we should do next. He scratched his chin and said that we should perhaps have another coffee.' That relaxed and philosophical state of mind so characterised Laurie. Fisher was in no mood to share his solution, for privately he was fuming. 'At this point, I demanded he take us to the police station. I was standing there with him as this policeman talked away for about five minutes. Once or twice Laurie nods, so here am I thinking, "Well, it's all sorted." When the conversation finished, I asked Laurie what the policeman had said. Laurie replied, "To be honest Bob, I've not the slightest idea, I only understood a couple of words."'

During his first season Cunningham had silenced the critics as Real Madrid captured the Spanish league and cup double. Forever an innovator, Laurie took to taking a direct shot from corners, hitting the ball with the outside of his foot and bending it towards the goal. The fans loved it as much as opposition goalkeepers and defenders came to loathe it. Cynical defenders were left baffled by a drop of the shoulder, deftness of feet and a blinding pace. Opposition fans gave him fearful abuse, for not only did he represent the most hated club among football neutrals, the despised nationalist aristocrats, as a black player he was still a relative novelty in the Spanish domestic game. A year later he had helped Real Madrid to the European Cup final in Paris against the powerful red machine of Liverpool.

It had been a long time coming, the opportunity to recapture the most coveted prize that had once been the exclusive property of Real Madrid. Under coach Vujadin Boskov, Real had once again produced a great side. Many believed that the result would be determined by the outcome of the personal duel between midfield maestros Graeme Souness and Real's Ulrich (Uli) Stielike, with Stielike acknowledged to be the iron man of European football. Real's game plan was founded on intimidation. After winning the intimidation stakes, Cunningham would then move in for the kill. His importance to the side was shown when he made the starting line-up, despite having played only 45 minutes of first-team football since an injury the previous November. From the start, Real's tackling was X-certificate stuff and Camacho, now the national coach, showed that Real had more than one assassin in their line-up. As the game progressed, though, it was becoming clear that the clever and wily Boskov had been undone. Souness established midfield supremacy and, nine minutes from the end, the most unlikely goalscorer, full-back Alan Kennedy, clinched the game with a piece of finishing that even Laurie would have been proud of. It was a game in which Laurie struggled to get involved, his natural game being suppressed by the negative instructions of the team coach. Still, they had lost to a great team that night, a club winning its third European Cup in five years, and for Real there were at least genuine reasons to look to the future with optimism.

Cunningham was loving life in Madrid. He had developed considerably as a player, overcoming the harder man-to-man marking styles to which he had grown accustomed. Real were successful, the home fans loved him and he had won over the usually unforgiving Spanish press. Both the national daily Madrid-based sports papers, *Marca* and *As*, were praiseworthy of the 'English Toreador'. When everything pointed to a huge future for player, club and perhaps even country, fate and, some have suggested, the self-destruct button, intervened.

One night while dancing at a club, Laurie managed to break his foot. The circumstances of how this happened remain a mystery. As Laurie was not a particularly heavy drinker, the most likely source is an accident, possibly caused by an act of tomfoolery. The foot injury was far more serious than was first suggested and, as a consequence, Laurie spent virtually the whole season under treatment. With spare time on his hands, Laurie sought ways to occupy his time and energies. Inevitably that brought him back to the club scene, only this time they were proving to be all-night sessions. The Madrid grapevine was quick in informing sources inside the Bernabeu that Cunningham was abusing his status as a player of the great Real Madrid. Those stories were quick to hit the Madrid press, ever keen to fill column inches, particularly if it involved a high profile Real player. Within a few months of becoming a celebrated media star, Laurie was the scourge of gossip and rumour, most of which was ill-founded. During those dark hours, Cunningham confided in his close friend, Bobby Fisher. 'He managed to live with all the press rubbish about him being a boozer. It was total fabrication. In the early days he wanted to fight it, but in the end decided he couldn't and chose to live with it by ignoring it.'

The press had found a chink in the armour and, in customary fashion, were not going to let go. The image of an all-night party animal, not averse to drinking binges and womanising, was to remain with him until his dying day. Cunningham had never been particularly close to any one of his team mates, partly because of the language barrier and partly because of different lifestyles and cultural expectations. The Spanish footballers saw themselves as athletes first and foremost and everything else came second to serving the great Real Madrid. They began to see Laurie as someone who was besmirching the name and reputation of Real Madrid with what they considered to be his ill-advised lifestyle. Had Laurie returned from injury as the same player, possessing the same breakneck speed, then things may have turned out differently.

The legendary 'Pirri', real name Jose Martinez Sanchez, had retired from playing for Real Madrid in 1979 and came back to serve his long-standing employers as the club doctor. According to Pirri, Cunningham had lost a yard of pace, the result of his injury. His natural running style, something Ron Atkinson said was so graceful that if he 'ran on snow he wouldn't leave any footprints', had been compromised. The adjustment he was having to make to his running, allied to nature taking its inevitable toll, meant that Cunningham would never again be the same player. Given his relative youth, Cunningham could still have been a great player, but to do so he had to find something else to compensate for the loss of a prime asset. Arguably, Laurie's greatest football challenge still lay ahead of him.

He returned to an atmosphere among the players and club officials that was not recognisable as that which existed before his injury. As one of the highly paid players, and being a foreigner to boot, Cunningham found few sympathetic and supporting colleagues. All his life, Laurie had had to overcome obstacles, be they on or off the field. His response had shown him to be consistent and strong, with an incredible self-belief running through him and an 'I'll show you' attitude all pervasive. Now, for the first time, the seeds of self doubt began to emerge. The injury had taken much longer to recover from than was originally anticipated. Ask any footballer about the depression that runs through them when they are suffering with a long-term injury; in many cases, the psychological damage can be more acute than the physiological, as footballers contemplate early retirement and a decided unpreparedness for what lies ahead. Laurie Cunningham was no different. More confident and surefooted than the average player he may have been, but beneath the cool and controlled veneer was a diffident young man. And then came the *coup de grâce*.

As a natural athlete Cunningham was blessed with great recovery powers. Coupled with this, he worked hard from morning to evening to get himself back in the team. Just as he was feeling on top of his game and ready to mark his long-awaited return in style, he was crocked by an over-the-top tackle in a training match. That tackle was to set his progress back even further, by several months. Cunningham acknowledged that training was an opportunity for exuberant first team aspirants to impress the coaching staff, but, as he told Bobby Fisher, 'That tackle was premeditated. Someone went out to really hurt me.' Why anyone should want to cripple a valuable member of their own team in such a way is open to speculation, hard as it is to believe. According to Laurie certain players and some of the coaching staff had grown to resent him as an outsider and the special relationship he formed with the demanding Real supporters. Nor had the events of the previous 12 months done him or the club any favours. Laurie was never to properly recover from that training ground 'accident'. A pale imitation of the player he became during the 1979–80 season, Laurie spent most of the time on the treatment table, managing the odd, intermittent appearance. Out of the public limelight, Laurie contemplated his future. The great Real Madrid romance was now, to all intents and purposes, over, but a flame flickered and fate was ready to offer a helping hand.

Noting his situation, Ron Atkinson brought him back to England, to Manchester United, on a two-month loan deal in March 1983. Atkinson was excited at the prospect of having a Laurie Cunningham to call upon as he set about rebuilding his Manchester United team, but his opinion was tempered when he saw him in the flesh. 'I recognised the dazzling brilliance, that ability to drive defenders insane . . . What was missing was the scorched-earth pace that had planted him in a different dimension during the earlier years.' The reality was that Laurie was not up to the task of adapting to the hustle and bustle of the English league. A combination of playing in the more sedate Spanish league and injury had put an end to any prospects he may have had of playing once again in England. On the eve of the FA Cup final, Atkinson still wanted to select him as substitute, at a time when only one player could sit on the bench. Cunningham's honesty in informing Atkinson that he was not fit and if selected would only let the team down struck a chord in the manager's mind, and he later described it as an act of 'fundamental professionalism'.

Cunningham returned to Spain and a short spell with Sporting Gijon. This was followed by a year in southern France with Marseille. At this point terminal frustration with himself and those around him, including those closest to him, had set in. Marseille was not Real Madrid or Manchester United, it was a club in serious decline. Cunningham found himself despatched to the flanks in the hope he could conjure up the magic he had been previously associated with. Try as he might, and he did, it wasn't there. He moved inside, whereas before he would have gone outside the full back. He crossed from deep whereas before he would do so from the by-line. None of this ingratiated him with the Marseille coaches, who were seemingly oblivious to the scars he carried. His last game for Marseille was in an end-of-season game that they had to win in order to avoid relegation. In a fit of pique, Cunningham tore his shirt off his back when substituted as Marseille headed for defeat.

The city of Leicester beckoned. Leicester City were desperately trying to save face having sold Gary Lineker to Everton. He arrived during a state of crisis, yet another team fighting to avoid the drop. Thirteen games later he was gone. Like Marseille, Leicester City were playing with little confidence, attempting to scratch a point here and there. Laurie was a player who was always going to perform best in an outstanding team and neither of his last two postings fitted the bill. What he desperately needed was the tender loving care of a Ron Atkinson figure who would help rebuild his confidence. To do that the person would have to recognise Laurie's shortcomings and instead help to develop a new player, one whose game was based on utilising his skill, experience and vision. In a withdrawn midfield role, Cunningham still had a great deal to offer the game at the highest level. Sadly for him, no such person or opportunity ever came along. The nomadic existence also drew him to the Belgian club, Charleroi, for a short period.

There was to be one last English swansong with Wimbledon. Then Wimbledon manager Bobby Gould recalls John Fashanu bringing him to the training ground. Looking for a fresh impetus towards the end of the season, Gould and his assistant, Don Howe, decided to take the gamble. According to Gould he enjoyed his short stay. 'We were the paupers, nothing to offer him, but Laurie was happy to come in. He didn't play a lot, a few games as a sub, but I think he enjoyed it. I think he fell into an atmosphere that he'd never been in before. They were a unique breed at Wimbledon and Laurie wouldn't have been allowed to be a loner or aloof there. They always seem to bring the best out of people who are quiet. You're not allowed to be quiet, you're one of them, you go with that spirit and he enjoyed it, an opportunity he hadn't had before, perhaps. He was at the tail end of his career, in the company of people who did not give a monkey's about anything, and I think he liked that.' Observing him at close quarters, Gould was very sympathetic to the plight endured by a previously great player. 'With great players, it really hurts when you know you can't get back to the level you were at before an injury. You end up with lesser players, who are not on the same wavelength, you don't get the service, and your distribution is geared to players who think faster, so that goes astray and it becomes a frustration.' Wimbledon reached the FA Cup final that season where they defied the odds, in their inimitable way, to beat Liverpool 1–0 and deny them the double. With 30 minutes to go, onto the field of play entered Laurie Cunningham to collect his only major honour in English football. According to Gould it was a short-term arrangement that had suited both parties and they parted company, enabling Laurie to return once more to his adopted home. With the exception of 12 months in France and a few months in England and Belgium, Laurie had spent almost a decade in Spain.

Outside the top two Madrid clubs, Real and Atletico, little is known about the city's third club, Rayo Vallecano. The club has acquired a sort of yo-yo reputation, seemingly forever flitting between the top two divisions. In more recent times they have enjoyed the limelight, having stormed to the top of the Spanish Liga in 1999, albeit for a few weeks, and for the capture of former Leicester City and American goalkeeper Kasey Keller. In 1988–89, in his presence as an elder statesman, Cunningham was instrumental in helping Rayo Vallecano secure promotion to the top flight. It was fitting that Laurie Cunningham would secure the goal that clinched promotion. Once more in Madrid, accompanied by his wife and young son, it would seem that he had found peace with himself and his football, coach Felix Baderas noting, 'He is the only player I have ever known who, after being left out of the team, wished me good luck before a match.' Promotion with Rayo was a treasured achievement, not least because it offered the opportunity of returning to the Bernabeu once again. However, not all was well with Laurie Cunningham. Bobby Fisher says, 'I spoke to him not long before he died. He didn't seem very happy. At this stage, he had deeper problems, things he could not or would not say. I got the feeling he was getting into things above his head. Whatever it was he took them to his grave with him.'

On 15 July 1989, travelling in the early hours with an American companion, Mark Cafwell Latty, Laurie Cunningham met his death in a car crash. Remarkably, Latty escaped unscathed, while Laurie Cunningham was pronounced dead on arrival at hospital. It was to bring to a premature end the life of a true football genius, a hugely talented and creative presence on and off the field, an inspiration for those black players who were to follow him into English football. Yet, for all that, questions would remain, as they inevitably do when any young maverick genius goes before their time.

The tragic nature of Laurie Cunningham's death will inevitably add poignancy when people search their memories for images of him and therefore it can be difficult to analyse objectively just how good a player he was. The words 'great' and 'genius' are much overused in modern football. Players who excel in the English Premier League are bestowed greatness even before they have achieved anything of note on the international stage. There may be those who question whether a player can be labelled 'great' if he only ever performed at the top domestic level for a few years. In Laurie Cunningham's case, he had a total of only five full seasons with West Bromwich Albion and Real Madrid. Remember also that Cunningham managed only a handful of England caps, in which there was barely a performance of any note. As far as Laurie

Cunningham is concerned it has to be a case of 'never mind the quantity, feel the quality'.

When leading and still highly respected people in the game eulogise Cunningham in a way we hadn't seen in this country since the days of George Best, then we have to stand up and take notice. The obituaries speak for themselves. He may have been a flawed genius, most tend to be, that somehow goes with the territory. Many people believe that when in his prime he never received the credit and press coverage he deserved and point to his racial identity. It is difficult to think of another English player of his generation who would have gone to Real Madrid and created the impact he did. Around the same period, Kevin Keegan went to Germany to play for SV Hamburg where he enjoyed great success, winning the European Player of the Year twice, a quite fantastic achievement. Yet it is debatable whether Keegan could have made a similar impact at Real Madrid. While there is no shortage of press archive material on Keegan there is comparatively little on Cunningham. Understandably, it begs the question why?

Laurie Cunningham enjoyed a good press in Spain but that rarely found its way through to England. How ironic that the English press go to town on the arrival of Steve McManaman at Real Madrid and yet chose largely to overlook Laurie Cunningham's time at the same club. Did we not take Spanish football very seriously, were not Real Madrid one, if not the, great clubs of Europe? Admittedly Real Madrid were reluctant on occasions to release him for international duty, but can this really explain why Laurie Cunningham was regularly overlooked in preference to Peter Barnes? As good a player in English domestic football as he was, Peter Barnes in most peoples' eyes was not in Laurie Cunningham's class. Once again, the 'system' and those charged with making best use of it had failed England's football fans. During the late 1970s and early '80s, the English game was in a parlous state as groups like the National Front and British National Party assumed the nationalistic mantle. Laurie Cunningham was such a good player he did not need any form of preferential treatment in selection policy, but it is worth thinking about the effect an England side containing Laurie and his old teammate, Cyrille Regis, may have had in tackling racism in the game. Bobby Fisher provides an interesting theory on the lack of press coverage and resulting interest from England managers. 'He became incredibly misunderstood by the media and those in the game. They simply did not know how to take him, nor where to place him. Because he was different, he frightened people. To them his attitude suggested that he didn't care and did not display passion.' But just because you don't have the clenched fist and blood-stained shirt of an Ince or a Butcher, it doesn't mean you don't care just as much. Ron Atkinson refers to an incident after the England–Switzerland game when he chided Laurie Cunningham for not playing his natural game, taking on opposition defenders. Cunningham replied that he had been told to play to a system which put the emphasis on pass and move, stifling dribbling. In the end one is not sure who was more exasperated, Atkinson or Cunningham.

In the absence of English football giving Laurie Cunningham an appropriate send-off it was left largely to his family, those friends closest to him and those who were spiritually close to him – members of the black community. The occasion is remembered by some as an event hijacked by black extremists. Reference is made to a hostile, almost anti-white atmosphere, though this is more because of a cultural misunderstanding rather than anything sinister or untoward. Ask anyone, be they Jew, Sikh, Hindu, Muslim or anything else, and they'll tell you that funerals are occasions when people outside that particular community can feel excluded, because funerals do give rise to strong cultural identity. Laurie Cunningham's death had raised questions within the community and the sense of injustice was running high, understandably so.

Laurie Cunningham was never an angel, but geniuses tend not to be. Occasionally he managed to drive managers and teammates round the bend, but they made allowances for the wayward genius, knowing that he would produce the magic to salvage a lost cause. He was an exceptionally talented footballer who shone brightly, albeit for too brief a period. But during those years with Leyton

Orient, West Bromwich Albion and Real Madrid, he produced football of a quality we continue to yearn for, particularly in this age of the modern, somewhat predictable, footballer. He went to a hugely sceptical and critical Madrid audience and won them over with his flashes of brilliance, by no means a feat within the realms of mere mortals. A succession of injuries led to a premature end for Laurie Cunningham, 'drowning in his own opera' to quote Sartre. However, thanks to people like Bobby Fisher and many others in the black, as well as wider, community, the memories live on, as does the debate. 'Genius or not?' – there can only be one answer.

SEVEN

The sale of Laurie Cunningham was the beginning of the end for that great Albion side, a side still loved by those who watched them regularly, despite their ultimate failure to deliver the glittering prizes they deserved.

In fairness, Albion were able to stay in touch with the top sides for several years to come, continuing to play adventurous football, attracting some top-quality footballers, but somehow, with the departure of Cunningham, a spark left them. It wasn't simply that Albion missed his ability and his presence on the field. It was what he and his going represented in symbolic terms. It was as if the team, supporters and all, recognised that a special moment had come and gone and that it had been let slip too easily. Put simply, a bit of the club died.

Cunningham and Cantello were replaced by good footballers, the Manchester City pair of Peter Barnes and Gary Owen coming to the club. Owen was an excellent midfielder with a great range of passing, slotting in neatly alongside Bryan Robson. Had he not had such a slight figure, then surely he would have carved out an even more successful career for himself, but he was often subject to injury. Peter Barnes was the archetypal enigma, a winger blessed with great close control and all the skills he needed, but who was infuriatingly inconsistent in utilising his gifts. He didn't have an easy ride at Albion, as John Wile concedes. 'It was always going to be difficult for him because Laurie and, before him, Willie Johnston, had been superb players. It was a blow to lose two players who could win a game for you in such a short space of time. Peter struggled to live up to their standard. He was a good player but a different type. Although he had the pace and ability to go past people, he tended to jink and hold up more than those two; he had a slower way of playing and that was a bit frustrating for the crowd after the pace of the other two. It gets people up off their seats to see people flying down the wing and hurdling tackles. So Peter didn't have the easiest of rides here. He had a good shot, scored a lot of goals, was top scorer in his first season. But it must be a trait among wingers – you do wonder if they're all there! Peter had his own views about how the game should be played and how coaches should work. He missed team-talks, he'd stroll in after they were over; it got to the point where Ron Atkinson preferred that because if he wasn't involved, the team-talk was more readily understood by everybody. If Peter got involved, you could guarantee it would go wrong!'

The 1979–80 season was a nightmare. Not only had there been the changes in personnel, but Cyrille Regis was missing until mid-November with injury, Derek Statham managed just 16 games, Ally Brown only 12, and it inevitably took Owen and Barnes time to find their feet. To replace Regis, Atkinson bought John Deehan from Aston Villa, a player who never settled in at the club and who was asked to play alongside Regis once he returned to fitness, in an unbalanced combination that was never going to work. As John Trewick points out, 'Ron had that flamboyant personality and I think sometimes he felt he had to be in the transfer market, even when there was no need. It did upset the balance of the team a bit.' Even the introduction of a tigerish little midfielder, Remi Moses, who restored the Degrees to their full complement of three, could not fully lift the gloom.

Albion won just one of the first nine League games, were hammered 5–1 at home by Forest, went out of the League Cup in the fourth round at Norwich, stumbled out of the UEFA Cup at the first hurdle, losing 4–1 on aggregate to Carl Zeiss Jena, then in January went out of the FA Cup at the first attempt to eventual winners West Ham after goalkeeper Phil Parkes played a blinder at The Hawthorns. From mid-January, they then lost just two of eighteen games to stave off any threat of relegation, ending in comfortable mid-table security, but after the heady days of the previous year, it was a season to forget. Yet, in spite of their poor form, especially in the early part of the year, that side had plenty of players worthy of England recognition, notably Bryan Robson, who began to win the occasional cap at a time when he was playing as well as anyone in the country. Cyrille Regis was also making his presence felt, albeit at Under-21 level, but no Albion players made the big breakthrough that would have sent them to the European Championships in Italy.

The team learned from that adversity and in 1980–81, they were once again a force to be reckoned with, playing the fluent football that had been their hallmark a couple of years earlier. Benefiting from a settled side that saw Regis and Ally Brown back in tandem and Bryan Robson scoring ten goals from midfield, Albion were in the hunt for the title for much of the season, though never in such close contention as they had been in 1979. Ironically, the final outcome to that title chase was heavily shaped by Albion's results: within four days, they thumped Ipswich 3–1 at home, Brendon Batson getting his only League goal for the club, then went to Villa Park and, in front of 47,998 supporters, lost a frenetic derby 1–0. Villa took the Championship from Ipswich by four points, and were on their way to winning the European Cup the following season. Albion's fortunes looked to be in the ascendancy, though, finishing fourth, eight points behind Villa, but securing the all-important UEFA Cup place.

Success for a club outside the real élite – Liverpool and Manchester United at the time – is a double-edged sword. Every club, every player, every supporter wants it, but with success comes attention, and once you've grabbed the attention of the wider public, the big clubs start fishing around, partly because they're always on the lookout for good players, partly because it's in their interests to destroy any pretenders to the throne. It had happened with Cunningham two years before. This time, events at Manchester United would conspire to rip the heart out of West Bromwich Albion and leave it in a state from which it has never recovered. United were in the midst of that lengthy period without a League Championship, a period then stretching to 14 years. Dave Sexton's side reeled off seven straight wins to end the 1980–81 campaign in eighth, but they were a colourless outfit, certainly not the sort of successors to Law, Best and Charlton that the Old Trafford fans demanded. So, in the close season, Sexton went.

United went through a difficult process in trying to replace him. Bobby Robson was approached but had no intention of leaving Ipswich, well aware that Ron Greenwood would leave the England job after the 1982 World Cup campaign and preferring to stick with what he knew lest he blot his copybook in uncharted waters. (Interestingly, Ipswich have followed a similar pattern to Albion, regularly losing players – Talbot, Mariner, Wark, Muhren, Butcher – to bigger clubs, and their manger, too, in their case to England. Like Albion, Ipswich have never recovered from this butchery, though they did not fall so far, nor so fast.) Lawrie McMenemy was another on the United shortlist, but he was content with life on the south coast at Southampton. Inexorably, Manchester United's search was heading in one direction, as John Wile recalls. 'It was inevitable Ron would go. We were in America on tour when the United job came up. Among the players we talked about it and said that if ever there was an ideal candidate, it was Ron – he was made for it, the personality, the style of play. You could see the candidates falling away and it was obvious that Ron was going to get it. So much so, he never left the hotel in America, which was not like Ron, he used to like to get about! But in Florida he never left the hotel, he was waiting for the call!'

The call duly came and, amid some acrimony, Atkinson walked out on West Bromwich Albion, not for the last time. Predictably, the supporters were disappointed with his decision, particularly as Albion had a far better side than United at the time. But United were a far bigger club, always will be, and it is that that clubs in the rest of the country are constantly fighting. Deep down, few Albion fans would quarrel with Atkinson's decision – which of them would have turned down a better job, more money, a greater challenge? What did turn the supporters against Atkinson, unfairly perhaps, was his behaviour once he was installed at Old Trafford. He took his assistant, Mick Brown, and coach Brian Whitehouse with him and then started to decimate the playing staff. Cyrille Regis recalls, 'Big Ron left and he said he'd come back for Bryan, me and Derek. He got Bryan and Remi in the one deal and there was so much fuss. It was a bitter, acrimonious deal and there was no way Albion would let us go as well. Bryan had sorted out a new deal with the club, but it got into the press about how much he was getting and that rubbed Bryan up the wrong way. He'd just had enough and went.' As Bobby Gould, who spent much of his playing career in the Midlands says, 'It's not a glamorous area, there is an apathy there and the Midland clubs never take off like Liverpool did, or United have done recently. We didn't have the flamboyancy as an area, even though the likes of Big Ron gave it that for a while. When players reach a certain level, they outgrow the area. It's unfortunate, but it's a fact of life. Cyrille would have relished being on the big stage, it was ideal for him, he was that kind of player, that kind of man. I think he suffered at the hands of the media when he was younger and then he came back to be a very impressive man.'

Whatever the rights and wrongs – and Atkinson had a responsibility to do the best job he could for his new employers – from his office in Manchester, Fatkinson, as the Albion fans now called him, undermined Albion in his hunt for players. Scarcely a day went by after his departure that United weren't linked with an Albion star, particularly Bryan Robson. It created a poisonous atmosphere around the club which new manager Ronnie Allen, back from Saudi Arabia, struggled to cope with. Early season results were poor, and there was soon a rumour circulating that, once Albion were out of Europe, Robson would be on his way. He didn't have to wait long. On 30 September they were bundled out of the UEFA Cup by Grasshoppers Zurich and Robbo was on his way.

If Laurie Cunningham was the most supremely talented player to wear the stripes in the last 30 years, Robson was, without doubt, the best all-round footballer to do the same. Year in, year out, Robson was simply the best in the country, a truly marvellous footballer, Captain Marvel as Bobby Robson was to term him.

Perfect balance, lightning feet, vivid imagination, superb close control.
Laurie Cunningham graced English football like few others have
ever done. (Photograph © Laurie Rampling)

Cyrille Regis leads out an all-black side in Len Cantello's testimonial game
at The Hawthorns in May 1979. Albion are led out by former manager
Johnny Giles. (Photograph © Laurie Rampling)

Brian Little, Laurie Cunningham, Dennis Mortimer and John Trewick
in a frantic Albion–Villa derby at The Hawthorns, 22 April 1978.
(Photograph © Laurie Rampling)

Albion's FA Cup fourth-round replay with Leeds, 1 March 1979. Left to
right: Laurie Cunningham, Ron Atkinson, Bryan Robson, George Wright
(trainer), Ally Robertson, Brendon Batson, Tony Godden, Derek Statham,
Ally Brown, John Wile, Cyrille Regis. (Photograph © Laurie Rampling)

ABOVE: Albion on the attack in a Black Country derby in the top flight at The Hawthorns, April 1980. Helping out with defensive duties is Andy Gray as John Wile looks for another goal. (Photograph © Laurie Rampling)

RIGHT: Regis at his elemental best, against Leeds United, FA Cup fifth round, The Hawthorns, 26 February 1979. (Photograph © Laurie Rampling)

Substitute Laurie Cunningham helps Cyrille Regis prepare for the
sixth-round FA Cup tie with Nottingham Forest at The Hawthorns,
11 March 1978. (Photograph © Laurie Rampling)

FACING PAGE TOP: Cyrille Regis accepts congratulations from Brendon Batson and Remi Moses after scoring Albion's winner in a 1–0 victory against Crystal Palace at Selhurst Park, 4 October 1980.
(Photograph © Laurie Rampling)

CENTRE: Albion's first-team coach Cyrille Regis and Youth Development Manager John Trewick point the way ahead. (Photograph © Dave Hewitt)

BOTTOM: Enzo Maresca, perhaps the greatest talent seen in an Albion shirt since the halcyon days of the Three Degrees. (Photograph © Dave Hewitt)

ABOVE: Adam Oliver, a highly promising product of Albion's youth policy, gets an early taste of first-team action against Fulham at The Hawthorns, 30 August 1999. (Photograph © Dave Hewitt)

Cyrille Regis at The Hawthorns, where he belongs.

(Photograph © Laurie Rampling)

Liverpool were also in the hunt for his signature once it became clear he was leaving The Hawthorns, and it's as well for the rest of the country that he didn't go to Anfield, because if he had, they would have won treble after treble. Nothing would have stopped them. But, like Cunningham before him, he should not have been allowed to leave. John Trewick says, 'We could have kept players, because contractually the clubs held the cards. Now it's gone full circle and players can be on contract and not even play if they don't want to, it's ridiculous. But then if the club had you under contract and wanted you, you stayed. Looking back, players left too soon and too easily. The club made a few quid, but if you let good players go, you have to replace them, and when you're at the top and you let players go, they are good players. It's not easy to replace Bryan Robson – there aren't many who've done it at that level.' John Wile agrees. 'Perhaps when Bryan went to Manchester United that wasn't the right time for the club to sell him, and in saying that I've no doubt he'd still have gone to United a couple of years later. But once the lure of Manchester United comes, there aren't many people who can refuse it. And the package took Remi there too, and it meant we lost two very strong players from the midfield, strong being the operative word. They were both very competitive and they were hard to replace. How do you replace Bryan Robson? England haven't.' The package deal was valued at around £2.2 million. The Albion mantra ever since has been 'where did it go?' Who came in? Andy King and the Dutch pairing of Romeo Zondervan and Martin Jol, very good players both, but never likely to repeat the success of Thijssen and Muhren at Ipswich, let alone replace Robson. Zondervan was, like Owen, too slight, and Jol too – how shall we put it? – aggressive, spending most of his time suspended. With John Trewick gone too, with Peter Barnes having already left in the summer for £900,000 and Steve MacKenzie the only significant signing during the close season, the club had pocketed a great deal of money, but at what cost? A team had been murdered.

Ronnie Allen did his best to find a pattern in the chaos, and wasn't helped by a terrible run of injuries. But where in the previous season ten players played more than thirty League games, this time around just seven did. Where Albion had used 19 players in Atkinson's last year – Cross appearing only as a sub, Benjamin getting just one game – in 1981–82, Albion went through 28 players. The fear of relegation haunted the club throughout the season, ten defeats in eleven games through April and May taking things to the wire. And yet as they struggled in the First Division, in both cup competitions, Albion were on a roll. In the League Cup, they overcame Shrewsbury, West Ham, Crystal Palace and Villa to arrive at a two-legged semi-final with Spurs. Just one goal came in three hours of football, from Spurs's Micky Hazard, and so, once again, a Wembley appearance went begging. But it wasn't the end of the world – the FA Cup was still there for the taking. Blackburn, Gillingham, Norwich and Coventry fell by the wayside as Albion strode towards a semi-final appointment with Second Division Queens Park Rangers, played at Highbury, scene of the Ipswich defeat four years earlier. Surely this time Albion would make it to a final? No. In a dismal, dismal game, Clive Allen did the job in which he was so successful for so long – the most anonymous player on the pitch popped up when it mattered most and scored the winner.

That was the latest hammer blow to afflict the club – Ipswich '78, the bad weather of '79, the loss of Cunningham, Atkinson, Robson, now two semi-final defeats inside two months. It was that game at Highbury which sent the club spiralling towards relegation with that wretched run of defeats, as though it had sucked the last spirit from the players. If any one of those events had turned in the club's favour – if they'd kept Robson, if they'd captured a trophy in '79 – then the club's history would surely have been very, very different. As it was, they seemed destined never to achieve the final breakthrough. Ironically, as Albion were struggling, the return of Ronnie Allen meant that Cyrille Regis was playing perhaps the best football of his career, his 17 goals in 37 games keeping Albion up. 'Ronnie Allen realised my stamina wasn't my strong point so he told me not to defend. At Coventry John Sillett called me a Rolls-Royce with a Mini engine.' Eventually, after several years in and around the England Under-21 side, Regis finally won promotion to the full squad. 'With the Under-21s we travelled with the full side. It was a great experience to be with players like Keegan, Shilton, those boys. But then you had to wait your turn. It was very rare you'd get in after a year playing well. The senior pros were in, playing well, Ron Greenwood was very loyal. I didn't get a full cap until 1981–82, which was nearly five years after my Albion debut. I'd been playing well pretty much throughout that period. Football is about opinions, the coach in charge makes the decisions, there were plenty of forwards about. Some players get a run without playing well, and grow into it, some don't get the chance. It's opinions. Now, as a coach, I can see it from the other side! To get a cap, against Northern Ireland, was incredible. To think that five years before I was on a building site and playing part-time in the Athenian League, and now I was at Wembley; it was a great climb. I was very proud to reach that level. I got on for 20 minutes, couple of half chances against Pat Jennings, and thought I did okay. To get in the set-up is totally different, you do need five or six games. The mentality's different, the football's different. If you can get your toe in, you get confidence, you see what's needed. You can't come in and pick it up straight away. You play one way with your club and then you have to change to play with England. You have to keep the ball, you can't give it away. So for England I had to learn to pace myself, pick my runs, retain the ball or I'd be running round all day. But you need time to adapt to that.'

Under Ron Greenwood, England were hardly a freescoring outfit and, much as Midlanders had puzzled over Bryan Robson's continued omission from the side – oddly rectified now he was at Old Trafford – few could work out why Cyrille wasn't given a run in the team. With the World Cup in the offing, Greenwood belatedly introduced him to the fold, but again fate played its hand. 'I had a very good season and it's probably my biggest disappointment that I missed the World Cup. I think I'd have gone, but we played Leeds in the last home game to stay up. We won 2–0, which basically sent them down instead – they wrecked the ground afterwards. I scored but, late on, I pulled a hamstring. I tried to get fit and went out with the England squad to Iceland to play a friendly before the final squad was announced. I played 20 minutes and pulled it again. That made up Greenwood's mind for him – he couldn't risk me.'

Missing the World Cup was a bitter blow to Regis and the start of a run of misfortune that took him a long way from the peak of the English game before his strength of character enabled him to climb back up again. He wasn't helped by events at Albion during the summer of 1982. Despite reaching two semi-finals, Albion's league form wasn't good enough for the board of directors, and Ronnie Allen was moved upstairs to the post of General Manager, basically an honorary appointment with no real significance or control over the club's playing affairs. At this stage, Albion were still looked upon as one of the better playing sides in the country, despite their problems the previous year, which could easily be ascribed to the Atkinson upheavals. But still the club had players like Regis, Batson, Statham, Wile, Robertson, Owen, Jol, Zondervan, MacKenzie, Whitehead, Godden – men who had shown they could play at the top level. That should have been enough to attract a manager of proven quality. Instead, the board appointed Ron Wylie, then the youth coach at Coventry, a move that had to be a gamble given that he had no track record. Then the decline really set in.

Wylie wasn't lucky with injuries, it must be said. Steve Mac-Kenzie managed only one game, Regis played 26, missing most of the second half of the season after he fractured his cheekbone at West Ham, and Brendon Batson managed only 12 games. But, even with these problems, Albion should have done better than mid-table obscurity. John Wile had been playing in Vancouver during the summer in order to maintain his fitness. 'We got in the play-offs, so I didn't get back until the season had started, and the manager didn't say hello. His first words to me were, "Don't think you're getting back in the team." So he set his stall out but it just seemed a very premeditated attitude towards me and the other senior players. It gave me a great deal of satisfaction that he had to come back in a couple of weeks and put me in the team. That was my last season. They were very conscious of us. Alastair Robertson was coming to the end; he was a very strong character and he needed strong characters around him and after I left, he took on the mantle of being the main spokesman, but he was isolated and he was seen as being a problem when he wasn't. The club missed a big opportunity there; we had it within us to continue the success that we'd had and to take it on, and who knows where we would have been now? I felt there was a big opportunity here in the early '80s to build a Liverpool-style coaching set-up. It might not have worked, but I thought it was a massive opportunity that we missed. It's not often you get a group of people with that ability and who are of a similar age at a club at one time, and I just felt that the management was very suspicious of the players. I left in '83 and I felt that the team was broken up too quickly. You always think you can carry on, but when I left, I have no doubts I could have done at least another season and brought on my replacement at the same time. Ally Robertson was coming to the end of his career, Brendon was starting to get injuries, so was Derek Statham; Martyn Bennett who was the obvious replacement for myself or Alastair was having problems, we sold Bryan and Remi. So a lot of influential players were coming out of the side. I think it was weak management that allowed players to leave too early. The management saw senior players as a threat to their authority, which was a nonsense. If they'd had any sense, they'd have sat back and let the senior players maintain the development. And I think we could have helped our successors to bed in. Once that little group of players went, then Cyrille a little later – and I don't think he'd have gone had those other players still been at the club – we've been chasing our tails, trying to replace those people and spending atrocious amounts of money on people who weren't good enough. That became a vicious circle, spending more money on poorer players to the point where the club suffered. We've recognised you can't keep doing that. If you're going to spend money, it has to be on the right player and if you can't find him, you have to bite the bullet and not waste your money. I know it's not what people want to hear, but we've had 15 years of doing that and it hasn't worked, so there has to be another way.'

One of the great losses of the Wylie era was that of Brendon Batson. Seriously injured at Portman Road on 30 October 1982, Batson never played again. Eighteen years later, Albion have yet to adequately replace him. John Wile says of Batson, 'He had a lot of pace, was very good in the air, attack-minded, suited Ron Atkinson's style down to the ground. At one point there was the thought he'd take over from me at centre-half, but my career kept going and Brendon was very comfortable at right-back, excellent player. And then, as I was finishing, Brendon got injured.' Batson was more fortunate than many of his colleagues in that at least he had an alternative career to follow. Years of service on the PFA Union Management Committee had already put Brendon in line for the position of chairman when Steve Coppell announced his retirement from the game. The position of chairman was always held by a current player, so, as Batson says, 'I could have taken the position, but it was at a time when I was also struggling with injuries and it didn't feel right to step in. In the back of my mind I knew I was heading for retirement. Had I been in a position where I was able to play out the rest of my career in the lower divisions, then I may have accepted the challenge.' Severe cartilage damage required a series of operations that led to retirement in 1984. Although he applied for the vacant manager's job back at Cambridge United, he didn't feel quite up to the challenge at that stage. Shortly thereafter he was offered the position of assistant secretary at the PFA, number two to Gordon Taylor and a position for which he was ideally equipped.

It was clear from his first involvement in the professional game that Brendon would be destined for an advocacy and campaigning role. He had acquired a reputation at his clubs for having a natural tendency to speak his mind, something that didn't go down well with some managers, who at times regarded him as 'bolshie', an epithet too easily attached to those ready to stand up for those whom the establishment would rather keep in a subservient role.

Batson also acknowledges the influence of others in guiding him during his time in the game. 'Growing up as a London lad, you've always got something to say for yourself. I remember always speaking up for the younger lads. At Arsenal, Bob Wilson was the players' rep and I was always picking his brain. My interest heightened when I left Arsenal and I decided I wanted to know more about contracts. At Cambridge, I used to talk to the rep and told him I wouldn't mind taking over his duties if he didn't fancy it any more. Looking back, I chuckle now about travelling up to Manchester for the Union Management Committee meetings and getting lost around the city centre. I think back and ask how I got where I am today. It has not been through design as such, more a case of people guiding and supporting me.'

Today, the PFA is consulted by government departments and parliamentary committees, clubs, chairmen, managers and Football Task Forces. In the words of Gordon Taylor, 'the PFA can no longer be ignored in any matter affecting the game.' While many see Taylor as the principal architect, his long-standing colleague and able deputy, who confesses to 'clinging on for dear life' in his first year, has gone on to make his own, not inconsiderable, contribution to the PFA and to the game as a whole.

By the mid-1980s the PFA had evolved considerably as an organisation. Its pre-eminence coincided with a time when the game was suffering from the absence of clear and decisive leadership. The PFA was arguably the only footballing body able to speak with a common voice, an opportunity which it seized to stamp its growing footprint across the game. It was not only the absence of leadership that was seriously undermining the game. Attendances had fallen from 24 million in 1980 to 17.8 million in 1985, hooliganism was rampant, stadiums were crumbling, and the country was in a state of severe economic recession, led by a government who were at best indifferent to the 'people's game'. Margaret Thatcher had no time for the game, national sport or not, and let it be known with her ludicrous and, ultimately, highly dangerous identity card scheme, a scheme that might have created disaster after disaster on the scale of Hillsborough.

These factors combined to take their toll on club finances and, in turn, on players, whose livelihoods were being threatened. The Football League and club chairman apportioned blame to 'greedy' players who had exploited their freedom of contract rather than examining the inadequacies of their own poorly run administrations. The situation pointed to the inevitable rationalisation of football clubs and the prospect of a 'Super League'. Thankfully, the PFA had a different agenda on this issue. From a selfish angle, it was understandably worried that if there were fewer clubs this would mean fewer members. More importantly, and for the good of the game, it also spoke out about the impact such changes would have on ordinary supporters and the towns that hosted these clubs. Championing the cause of ordinary football fans was an astute move, particularly at a time when such interests were being overlooked by football's governing bodies.

In 1984 Gordon Taylor, realising the growing role and responsibilities of the PFA, recommended the appointment of an assistant to help share his workload. 'I invited Brendon to come and work for the PFA when he was considering his options post football career. He had been a delegate at West Bromwich Albion and member of the PFA Management Committee and I had been impressed with his contribution.' And so began an association which has continued into the new century. The new responsibilities had a profound effect on Batson in the early days as he made the adjustment from spending a few hours of doing this sort of work every week to doing it full time. 'During the first year in particular I wondered what I had let myself in for.' It was now a case of hundreds of players screaming down the telephone as opposed to the two dozen he had become accustomed to. 'At times I questioned my suitability for the job but I stuck at it, in the knowledge that here was a growing and ambitious organisation.' The work brought with it a great deal of variety. One of Batson's early tasks was to observe the development of the PFA's educational role.

The PFA were keen that young recruits entering the game should serve a proper apprenticeship and not have to endure the customary abuses then associated with Youth Training Scheme programmes. As Batson notes, there were wider repercussions of their actions for the game. 'In the climate of financial hardship, clubs were taking the soft option of cutting back on youth development programmes. If they had carried on like that the production line of good players we see today may not have materialised.' Thanks to the PFA's intervention the YTS programme survived, leaving a strong legacy. John Harding, PFA historian, argues with strong justification that, 'The ultimate impact of YTS can be regarded as one of the most significant developments in the game.'

The crisis that was taking place in the game had brought about a growing alienation between clubs and local communities. Batson says, 'We took the view that something needed to be done and went ahead with a pilot regional programme in the north-west.' The scheme quickly expanded, but not without difficulties for the PFA, who were accused of using the scheme to create jobs for former players. Its critics argued that footballers without any formal community development training were ill-equipped to do this work. The suggestion was not denied by Micky Burns, the scheme architect, or by Batson, who concedes, 'The primary concern was that this scheme would improve relations between clubs and women, ethnic minorities and the disabled, but we can't deny that the welfare of our members was not a consideration.'

Whether ex-professional footballers, most without any formal community development skills and experience, are best suited to this area of work will remain a bone of contention, as will the perceived reluctance of the PFA to recruit from outside its ranks, though there are a few exceptions, such as Neil Watson at Leyton Orient, who coincidentally runs the best Football in the Community programme in the country. What is not in dispute is that at a time when the game was calling out for some interface with local communities it was the PFA that stepped into the breach, thereby making another significant contribution to football's future.

In 1988 it was rumoured that Batson would succeed Taylor, who was said to be on his way to the Football League. Taylor resisted the overtures. By then he and Batson were seen very much as a team, never more so than when they were called in to mediate in a row over a threatened break-up of the Football League. Taylor is warm in his assessment of Batson's gifts. 'As a colleague and as a person he is extremely trustworthy and reliable and has great ability to negotiate with all types of people in differing situations. He reflects a kind and considerate nature and is a man of integrity.' It was these qualities which prompted the PFA to install Batson at the helm of PFA Financial Management Limited. Batson recalls, 'The PFA had this joint venture with an established insurance company. However, we found ourselves having to sort out unresolved matters. We therefore decided to do the whole thing ourselves and bought out the partners.' The newly formed company offers a comprehensive package, ranging from personal and legal help with everything from contracts to private pensions, private medical insurance packages, a non-contributory cash benefit scheme that ensures every player a substantial lump sum on retirement, severance pay when a player is not offered a new contract, death benefit to dependants and a programme of educational assistance. Once again, critics may say that the PFA have managed to create job opportunities for ex-players. Batson contends that it is important to have well qualified ex-professional players selling products to modern-day players. 'Knowing that you can relate to the players' circumstances is invaluable.'

The PFA were prominent in tackling other evils that afflicted football. Hooliganism had brought with it racism. Black players were subjected to abuse and intimidation. While players had no choice but to subject themselves to these hostile environments every week, black supporters exercised their right by not attending. Once again, the game's chief governing bodies had largely ignored the problem of racism. The PFA, led by Batson and ably supported by Taylor and the wider membership, was determined to address this issue head on. Batson says, 'Ten years on from when I had retired I had not expected the next generation to suffer from the same problems I encountered.'

By galvanising the support of its high profile members, black and white, the PFA successfully popularised their campaign, ably supported by the Commission for Racial Equality. Slowly, the FA and Football League, which had thus far shown only tacit approval for the campaign, came on board. Sir Herman Ouseley, chairman of the CRE, says, 'Brendon and the PFA deserve great credit for their work on the campaign.' Gordon Taylor similarly pays tribute to his black members, saying, 'The likes of Brendon Batson, Garth Crooks, George Berry, Oshor Williams and Alex Williams have done themselves and the PFA proud in their work on the anti-racism campaign.'

Batson's progress at the PFA is a microcosm of the organisation he represents. His sound, accomplished and tenacious on-the-field performances have been the hallmarks which have so clearly distinguished his career in football administration. So what does the future hold for one of the game's most respected administration figures? Eventually he may succeed Gordon Taylor but that is unlikely to be for a decade or so. A few years ago it was rumoured that Batson was offered the newly created post of chief executive at his former club West Bromwich Albion, only to see a divided boardroom turn instead to former teammate and captain, John Wile. The possibility of assuming a similar post at another club remains. In doing so he would break a mould and open up opportunities for other black players keen to work on this side of the game. Access to senior jobs, whether they be chief executive or manager, remains a barrier for black players. It is an issue over which Batson is prepared to take up the cudgels. 'There is some-thing amiss when you see former black players with good coaching qualifications, great ideas, who are enthusiastic and who enjoy respect within the game struggling to get interviews for jobs, never mind being appointed.' Somebody who is gradually working his way up the coaching ladder is former teammate Cyrille Regis. But even for Regis it has not been without a struggle as he has watched former white players of his generation breeze in and out of jobs. As Regis says, 'There are plenty of footballers out there who want a shot. It's what you know, you're comfortable in the environment, but it's getting a break.' But once again, just as when Regis was plying his trade on the field, the bar is set that much higher for black managers. Any failure is met by 'oh, black managers can't cut it'. Only great success will do, but that's no new challenge for

Regis. Given the opportunity, he will succeed, just as Brendon Batson has in his chosen field. They will come through because of the men they are, not the colour they are.

When Batson finally had to admit defeat as a player and set off on a career with the PFA, football's gain was incalculably Albion's loss. The departure of Batson – who had been seen as a possible successor to John Wile in central defence – further undermined a rapidly declining club. Ron Wylie lasted a little over a year, his major contribution to the club being the signing of Coventry's Garry Thompson and Aston Villa's Ken McNaught. But there was no coherent policy and the team was a mere shadow of its former self. By February 1984, relegation was threatening again and Wylie had to go. In replacing him, this time the board seemed to have got it right, bringing Johnny Giles back to the club. Perhaps everyone should have paid a little more attention to the adage that you should never go back, for this time around, success proved elusive. There were a couple of astute purchases – Steve Hunt and Tony Grealish – and relegation was staved off, but things barely improved. Hopes were put on an improvement for 1984–85, after Giles had had time to work with the players in the summer. After a promising start – two wins in three games – things quickly slipped away. And then Giles decided to relinquish whatever goodwill he still had by taking a gamble that was never likely to work. He sold Cyrille Regis, the last link with the Three Degrees. The symbol of the glory days the club were trying to repeat, and he sold him. The King was dead, so were the Albion.

EIGHT

In October 1984, just a couple of years after injury had denied him a role in the England squad at the Spanish World Cup, Cyrille Regis was deemed not good enough to get a game in an Albion side that was destined for relegation 18 months later. It was an extraordinary turnaround, one in which injury played its part, as did a certain staleness, as Regis is big enough to admit. 'From a career point of view, I should have gone in 1982, when I was playing well. I was in the England squad, loads of goals, flying, then after a good start the next year, I smashed my cheekbone at West Ham, and I was out for nine months. Then it was a struggle for a couple of years and at times I played when I shouldn't have, just because the manager was desperate to get me on the pitch. The idea was that if I was out there, it lifted the crowd, lifted the team, because I was the goalscorer. Andy Gray had the same happen to him at Villa and Wolves. And I was just picking up more injuries because I wasn't fully fit anyway. And you can't perform properly in the First Division if you're only half fit. Then that affects your confidence and by the time you are fit, your confidence has gone and you're not playing well, so it became a vicious circle. And later on, I was stale, nobody was pushing me. Maybe I'd been at the Albion too long, maybe I'd got a bit lazy. It was a massive learning curve because I'd never been criticised before and then suddenly people were having a go. When Johnny Giles got here, he decided he didn't want me to play with Gary Thompson, wanted to change it round.' Regis was replaced by David Cross – who Regis had seen off as the main striker back in 1977 – and then by a reserve called Nicky Cross who, with the best will in the world, was not of Cyrille Regis's stature and, hard though he tried, never would be.

Regis's final rejection at The Hawthorns came after a discouraging period in his professional career. After the World Cup in 1982, Ron Greenwood stepped down and Bobby Robson took the helm. If Regis had hoped this would push him forward, he soon was to be disappointed. 'Bobby Robson came in and I was back in the Under-21s against Denmark. I was a bit disappointed, but it was good to be involved, great to be captain. You have to be professional and make the most of it. It was John Barnes's first game and once again racism reared its ugly head; John came on and the England fans started giving him stick and you wonder what's going on. When England fans give you stick, you have to remember it's the minority – the majority is on your side. As a black person, you've grown up with it all your life, it's nothing strange, nothing new, you just deal with it. We won 4–1; Garth Crooks played, I think he got a hat trick but he never got a full cap and he really should have when he was at Spurs.' This comment might equally apply to Regis, Ian Wright, Les Ferdinand and a number of other black strikers down the years, making you wonder if there is some institutionalised racism within the Football Association. Regis did make it back into the England side for the friendly against West Germany in October 1982 at Wembley and recalls, 'They were the World Cup runners-up, I played 80 minutes and I thought I'd done enough to get another chance. Ron Atkinson is my biggest fan and critic and he thought the same, but that was it for five years.'

One opportunity to impress against possibly the best side in the world doesn't seem a lot really, but it was symptomatic of the misfortune that afflicted his career at the time. A fractured cheekbone interrupted his progress, as did playing in an Albion side that was self-destructing. On a personal level, and though it didn't seem like that at the time, getting away from West Bromwich was probably the best thing he could have done. 'In some ways it was probably a mistake, I should have stayed. Should have stayed and fought for my place or waited for the right club to come in for me. But I was 26, I'd been here all my career and you take that rejection emotionally. I was hurt and I just thought "right, I'll show you" and I went to the first club that came along which was Coventry City. I didn't realise how poor they were, nor what a low status they had in the game. I was still a big name when I went there and people in football were saying "what is he doing there?" People couldn't believe it. I should have stayed, but it hurt. After seven years in the game, it was painful to know that nobody else came in when I was available for £250,000. This was only five years after I could have gone to St Etienne for £750,000! I would have thought that, with my record, better clubs would have come in for me, but they didn't and that slaughtered my ego. We're all proud, we all believe in our ability, and when all that was after me was Coventry, that hurt. I reacted immaturely, let my heart rule my head and I made a decision to go: stuff it, I'll show 'em.'

The manager who bought Regis for Coventry was Bobby Gould. 'I bought Cyrille for £250,000, which must be one of the best investments Coventry ever made. I'd been through a spell where I'd had to have free transfers. I'd had Bob Latchford, Martin Jol and Kenny Hibbitt and I just needed substance behind it. The chairman asked me who I should buy and I wanted Cyrille and Peter Barnes because I thought they'd work together – they had done at Albion – and because I thought they'd excite people. Cyrille was the spearhead through the best period Coventry have ever had. And it was the death knell for the Albion in a way. Cyrille always gave a club a lift. Cyrille has a presence about him, a quiet presence. When John Charles was at his height, he'd walk into a room and he had an aura, and I think Cyrille gives that impression too. Maybe his career hadn't gone as far as people anticipated, but the change was good for him in the end, got him another cap, an FA Cup medal.'

Things didn't look quite so rosy a few weeks after Regis arrived at Highfield Road, though. 'I signed for Bobby Gould and within two months he'd got the sack! Don Mackay and Frank Upton came in and it was a nightmare for two years. I was a big fish in a small pond, we were a really bad team, we were fighting relegation every year. I started losing my hair because of the stress, seriously! The thing was, I was the only name that people could talk about and everything was about me because I was the only name people outside Coventry knew – "Coventry lost today and Regis had a poor game". But, having said that, it was incredibly character-building. That's part of life; you're trying to attain some kind of wisdom all your life. Then there's another level, applying that wisdom, incorporating it in your life, which is a totally different ball game! This is what makes life difficult, makes it rich; but I was low. They tried to get rid of me to Wolves in exchange for a full-back for about £40,000! I heard it through the back door, they denied it, but I was playing that badly! I even went out to PSV Eindhoven for a three-day trial when Gullit was there, during the pre-season, but it didn't work out and I came home. But, character-wise, you have to still believe in yourself, despite everything. You'd have a good game and think "yeah, it's back", then you fail again and you're miserable.' In Regis's first season there, Coventry escaped relegation by a point. The next season, 1985–86, was much more comfortable and they stayed up with two points to spare as Albion finished bottom and were relegated by a country mile.

Gradually, things began to improve at Coventry. In 1986 George Curtis took over as manager and formed a partnership with John Sillett that basically transformed Coventry's fortunes. At a small club, with no money to spend and in a town that, with all due respect, is no footballing hotbed even now, the management team is so crucial. Because of Sillett's outgoing personality and the way he got Coventry playing a lot of attacking football, the whole mood of the club was lifted overnight. So many struggling clubs can't see beyond a war of attrition as being the only method of salvation, unimaginative thinking that might see them hanging on for years, yet entertaining nobody and energising nobody, inspiring nobody, until, eventually, the euthanasia of relegation almost comes as a blessed relief. Over the years, though, it has become clear that supernatural forces make relegation for Coventry an impossibility. If they went down, it would be like the ravens leaving the Tower of London, maybe even a sign of impending Apocalypse.

Sillett and Curtis might not have been master tacticians in the

Ramsey vein, but they knew how to make it fun for the players to go to work, knew how to put on a show for an increasing number of supporters, knew that a football club has to have a soul if it's to work. They were fortunate that Cyrille Regis had remained at the club, for he was the kind of man they could build a team around. 'John came in, asked me how I wanted to play. I told him I wanted it to feet, and I became the fulcrum, held the ball up, linked the play. I had to lead the line, link up the play, become less of a goalscorer and create more, and that kept me in the game for 19 years.' Instead of humping long, hopeful, hopeless balls upfield and watching them come straight back, the Coventry back four were told to look for Regis. They could knock the ball into him with his back to goal and, more often than not, it would stick. He'd bring the likes of Mickey Gynn and Dave Bennett into the game, giving the defenders breathing space, allowing midfielders like Lloyd McGrath to support the forwards, and suddenly they were a team transformed. They were never going to push the likes of Liverpool in the way Albion had done, but they weren't going to be struggling so desperately either. And even if they were in the bottom six, the spirit of the club was so much better that they all believed they'd get out of trouble, rather than hoping they might. As Regis says, 'That was the best team spirit I ever had in football, even when we had such a great team at the Albion. We had good players, nothing great, but we had character because of the relegation thing – the first year we had to win the last three to stay up! So we had the strength of character to dig in.'

With scarce resources at their disposal, Coventry had to make the most of all they had. Sillett and Curtis – who, after his first season, took on the role of managing director, leaving Sillett as manager – recognised that the atmosphere in the dressing-room was the key to Coventry's chances of surviving and prospering, and they spent what little money they had on maintaining and building on that. Regis recalls, 'Under John Sillett and George Curtis things looked up. They changed the philosophy of the club, had a stark effect on how the players went about their football, thought about themselves and then, in 1987, we won the FA Cup and my career was back on an even path. It had been a really rough two or three years for me, but, in the end, I think it made me a better person, you learn from those difficult times.' As Bobby Gould says, 'Cyrille had the mental strength to get himself back up from those bad times, which Laurie Cunningham maybe hadn't. It's a very important part of the game, having that inner strength.'

Life at Coventry was never going to be plain sailing, as Cyrille points out. 'We couldn't compete on transfers or wages, but we fought and fought for each other. They threw a bit of money at team spirit instead of on players. We'd go away to Bournemouth for a week three or four times a year, we'd have leery tie competitions, little fining systems, it was real fun, we were tight, a really tight little group. We played some good stuff, but it was the spirit, we had a great time.' That spirit took them all the way to Wembley, overcoming Leeds in a monumental semi-final tie and then coming back from going a goal down to Spurs in the opening moments of the final to eventually win it 3–2. As Regis says, 'That Cup final epitomised what that team was about – we kept going and going. To be part of Coventry then was awesome.' Ironically, after all the hype that had surrounded his years at West Bromwich Albion, after all the potential and quality that that side had shown, Regis finally got his hands on a medal at Coventry City, just 12 months before Laurie Cunningham repeated the trick, winning his only domestic honour as a substitute for Wimbledon in the 1988 final against Liverpool.

Such was the renaissance that Regis was enjoying, he returned to the England fold once again, to play for the national side as a substitute against Turkey at Wembley in October 1987, five months after winning his medal. That was his fifth cap and, despite having little chance to shine in his few minutes on the field, he was not offered any further opportunities. It's not simply Regis who has suffered this way; countless players have been given ten or fifteen minutes to make their mark and then never been seen again, a bizarre selection policy that has, as results prove, done England no good at all down the years. If you're good enough to get in the squad once, you do nothing wrong when you're there, why aren't you offered further opportunities? As any good professional must, in the absence of any other answers, Regis analyses his own performances. From the distance of a dozen years, he says, 'You have to look at yourself. Were you committed enough? Were there better players? Should I have been more consistent? Could I have been fitter? Should I have had a few less beers, done a bit more in training? The England thing – in retrospect, it was great to have five caps, but in reality it was disappointing because you know there could have been more. Potential's a massive word. You think back and think about what you might have done. If I could have polished it all up, what could I have done? But you live with the decisions you make.'

That self-analysis, along with the changing role he enjoyed at Coventry, turned Regis into a more complete, if sometimes less explosive, footballer. John Sillett picked up on his excellent footballing brain. 'John made me and Trevor Peake coaches. He thought we had the potential. It was in name only, really, we didn't do a lot. It's something that's a natural progression for a lot of players who've been around the game.' Regis continued to be a vital presence in the Coventry set-up, but given Coventry's situation as perennial strugglers, paupers in First Division terms, any manager, however successful, can only succeed for a short period of time. When all depends on team spirit and morale, on the ability of the manager to motivate a collection of largely ordinary players to play above themselves, there comes a point of diminishing returns, when it's all been said and done a hundred times. As players age and need to be replaced, it's hard to replace them with the right kind of player with the right kind of character. John Sillett was replaced as Coventry manager in 1990. Terry Butcher came in and, inevitably, wanted to build his own side. Cyrille Regis didn't fit the plan and was released on a free transfer in recognition of almost seven years excellent service. At the age of 33, at a time when most centre-forwards are thinking of hanging up the boots, or at least dropping down the divisions, Regis got the call from Ron Atkinson, newly installed as Aston Villa's manager, to help him rebuild a side that had only just escaped relegation the previous season under Dr Josef Venglos. Regis admits, 'It was a good move for me at that time, a real increase in pressure, in the demands that are made on you. Going from Coventry, whose only ambition was to stay up, to Villa who have a different mentality and want success and good Cup runs, you have to handle expectancy.'

After two successful seasons with Villa, the time had come to move down the scale and, amid rumours of a possible return to The Hawthorns, Cyrille continued to collect Midlands clubs by moving to Molineux, where, as a perennial substitute under Graham Turner, he had to play second fiddle to Steve Bull. Still loving the game, Regis took another free move at the end of the 1993–94 season and moved to Wycombe Wanderers, managed by Martin O'Neill and then looking to establish themselves in the Second Division, having won promotion from the Third in their first season in the Football League. With Regis the ideal elder statesman, Wycombe had a wonderful season, finishing sixth and only missing out on promotion in the play-offs. A couple more years followed, with struggling Chester at the wrong end of the Football League. Some might consider that to be something of a comedown for a man who had represented England, had played in European competition, had won a Cup winners' medal and been one of the most important figures of his footballing generation. To think that is to misunderstand the man completely.

Regis loved football as much at the end of his career as he ever did and was happy to be enjoying his game without the excessive pressure, without the media spotlight, simultaneously giving something back to the grassroots of the game and still performing well, at a higher level than when he began his journey, with Hayes more than twenty years earlier. As he says, 'I had a long career, which was great, because you have to keep performing. Mentally it gets easier as you get older because you've been there and done it at the top, and then you're at Wycombe or Chester at the end of your career, a second or third division match, a training game, there's no pressure. But you still need self-motivation; for Wycombe against Rochdale you have to have your pride to make sure you do well. And it was enjoyable; I used to train a couple of times a week. Play Saturday, two days off, play or train on Tuesday, two days off, come in Friday, five-a-side, stretching, play Saturday. If the manager trusts you, that's fine; if he trusts you to give him 75 minutes on Saturday before you're too knackered to carry on, that's great!'

Reflecting on a playing career, the most important advice he has for any young player is straightforward: 'you've only got a career in football when it's all over and you can look back on it. Things can be going well, you go out on Saturday, break your leg and never be the same again, never play again, maybe. Look at Laurie. The last couple of years he was here, there and everywhere. He didn't perform, he'd had injuries. I don't know, maybe he lost a bit of interest in the game; he never really got anywhere near his potential, and that has happened to other talented players – Peter Barnes, David Rocastle, plenty of others. Laurie was a shadow of what he could have been. I say that to the kids here all the time. It's the next month, then next month and suddenly you've had ten years. You get judged on those 90 minutes, week after week. Everything in football is performance. You can look like a star in training but if you don't do it on Saturday and affect the game, you're nobody. Can you score, unsettle the defence, put somebody in, change the game? If you've been playing a couple of years and you get complacent – bang, that's it, you're finished. That's when you need mental strength and if you haven't got it, you're lost, you can't get back up there. The average pro gets eight or ten years, nothing, so you have to make the most of it. For me, the 19 years I had as a player, I look back and think that I really enjoyed it. And that's the most important thing.' Anyone who saw Cyrille make any of his 740 senior appearances and score any of his 205 goals at club level would have enjoyed it too.

NINE

By now, it's apparent that West Bromwich Albion, as a club, committed error after error through the early part of the 1980s. Some of the problems could have been deferred, though Cunningham and Robson would have left eventually. There was misfortune alongside the mistakes; injuries to Batson and Statham in particular were devastating blows. There were some decisions that looked good at the time but didn't work out – the second coming of Johnny Giles, for example. But, in general, the leadership of the club was woefully lacking in ambition, content merely to exist in the First Division, with the hope of a Cup run every now and again to add spice. Once you set your sights that low, if you fail to reach them, you leave yourself no margin for error. Too many good players were allowed to leave too soon, when they didn't want to or could have been kept – Cantello, Trewick, Wile, Robertson and, in particular, Cyrille Regis. Teams need a totem, a symbol, particularly in difficult times. A player like Regis gives a side a focus to rally around, knowing he's always likely to get them out of a hole. Fans need someone like big Cyrille to give them hope, to remind them of the good times just past and to suggest that the current times aren't so terrible after all – 'if we can keep Cyrille, we can't be that bad.' But too many players came and went in too short a time, brought in by managers who weren't good enough, were in the wrong place at the wrong time, or simply weren't given time. Albion were left with an unwieldy squad that lacked quality. Larry Canning, a player with Aston Villa in the 1950s and a commentator on the Midlands game after his retirement, draws a comparison between Albion in the 1980s and

Villa in the 1960s. 'At Villa, I told the manager, "If you keep buying Third Division players and keep on putting them in your team, where do you think you'll end up?" Villa eventually dropped into the Third Division. So many of the managers in the Midlands have done that, or have had to do that, so it's no surprise that the clubs are where they are.'

After Regis's departure, 1984–85 was quintessential Albion, veering from the sublime to the ridiculous. Starting in November, they won seven League games out of nine, suggesting Giles's rebuilding was on the right lines. As if to deliberately dispute that, they then embarked on a run of six defeats in seven matches, contriving to lose in the third round of the FA Cup at Orient in the process – due revenge for having stolen Laurie Cunningham almost a decade before. Twelfth place marked some kind of improvement, although relegation was avoided by just six points and Giles was not fooled. He flashed a little cash in the summer, bringing in Garth Crooks and Imre Varadi to try to bolster a lacklustre attack, a job Regis might have done given the chance. The season opened with a dreary draw at home to newly promoted Oxford United, followed by nine straight defeats as Albion endured a massive injury crisis – they used twenty players in those ten games. After a 3–0 defeat at Coventry, Giles quit, to be replaced by Nobby Stiles as caretaker manager. Stiles didn't want to take on the job, but held on to it for four months until Ron Saunders was brought in. By that time, Albion were relegated in all but name, having managed just two wins up to the end of January, against a similarly doomed Birmingham City and against Graham Taylor's Watford.

When Albion and Blues dropped through the trapdoor, they were following the precedent set by Wolverhampton Wanderers two years earlier. If Villa had dropped three more points, they'd have joined Albion and Birmingham in making the drop and the Midlands' humiliation would have been complete. In 1981, Villa won the Championship, Albion were fourth and Blues thirteenth. Wolves came eighteenth but were FA Cup semi-finalists, having won the League Cup the year before and still sporting British transfer record man Andy Gray in their ranks. Five years on, the Midlands was a footballing wasteland and has remained the same ever since. How was the entire area brought to its knees?

There is no simple answer, no unifying thread that runs through this era of discontent, no blindingly obvious reason why the Midlands clubs should suffer so grievously. But surely it's more than just a coincidence that Albion, Blues and Wolves should all be so far off the pace and that even Villa have achieved comparatively little given their potential for success – sole top-flight club in England's second city certainly offers plenty of scope for expansion. As Brendon Batson suggests, it's not surprising that Villa have remained pre-eminent in the area. 'The commercialisation of the game has had a big impact. Those who had, or have, the right structures in place have profited most. Villa have been well geared up for years, something Doug Ellis makes public with some justification. On the other side, Wolves, for example, have spent most of the £40 million injected into the club on the stadium, player fees and contracts. Generally, Villa are streets ahead. All clubs have that commercial department to some degree, but it needs to be greater the bigger the club and the greater your ambition. Generally, West Midland clubs haven't done well commercially, not if you look at the way they've developed retail outlets. Those at the top with great ambitions, when they travel abroad, they take their mobile merchandising operations with them – look at Manchester United's visits to Hong Kong, for example. I don't think it's too late for our clubs to join the gravy train, but every year represents a missed opportunity, which multiplies in terms of its effect.'

Certainly, this area was very slow to grasp the importance of marketing, of the unique branding opportunities presented to a football club and of the vital role that off-the-field activities play in funding the playing operation. Maybe China in 1978 wasn't ready for a marketing onslaught on the United scale, but Bryn Jones isn't entirely joking when he mourns the loss of 'those billions of potential fans!' As the first Western club to visit the country, Albion should have left some kind of legacy, but they left nothing. That's symptomatic of their operations on a local level. Indeed, rather than improving as the '70s wore on, they got progressively worse. Even in the 1960s Albion had tried to involve local supporters in the club, as Bryn Jones points out. 'Okay, they weren't corporate strategists, but the Throstle Club scheme was a brilliant way of extending the club's influence throughout the Black Country. The Throstle Clubs were social clubs that provided live music, cheap beer and, of course, access to Albion info and personnel. This was part of a big push, a "plan" to develop West Bromwich Albion's image as an integral part of the Black Country. At first, these clubs, or at least the one in Tipton, were very popular, but, whether through subsequent poor administration, changing leisure patterns, or just the general decline in the club, they were gradually closed down.'

This tale is symptomatic of the decline of the clubs in the area. Ironically, the loyalty of the supporters has allowed clubs to get away with neglectful, negligent management. As Larry Canning points out, 'There have been too many times when the clubs here have been run or managed by people who don't know the game, who are in it for prestige. And supporters around here have been very loyal – Villa got massive crowds in the old Third Division, Wolves, Birmingham, Albion still get pretty good support, and that allows those at the top to get away with it. They probably don't even think there's anything wrong as long as fifteen or twenty thousand people are coming in.'

Mismanagement has been rife at all the clubs, with both Birmingham and Wolves on the verge of extinction and Albion coming much closer than many ever suspected. Why was the Midlands such a magnet for poor business practice? Larry Canning suggests, 'We attract abysmal chairmen because the Midlands is full of business people who have sprung up through hard work, mainly in industry. They're up there and have to do something with their money to get some glory and power, so they take over a club. You get a guy like Doug Ellis who thinks he knows the game, but he doesn't. That's the sad thing about the Midlands in general. Directors are heavily influenced by the press and in this area the

153

press reporting has been poor for a long time. The press is too powerful. In the 1998–99 season, John Gregory had incredible luck in the run of fixtures at the start that let Villa stay top of the League for so long and the press were painting him as the Messiah! Then when they lose a few games, the same people are saying "Gregory out"! It certainly has a big effect on this region's football because it's only in the local papers that our clubs get real coverage, so you don't get a broader picture.' This is a charge that Bobby Gould echoes. Gould had two separate spells as a player with the Wolves, scoring 31 goals in 74 games. Sandwiched between those days at Molineux was a spell at the Albion, where he scored 18 times in 52 games. He returned to The Hawthorns as manager in 1991, so he has an interesting and informed view of the issue. 'The media in the Midlands had a very damning effect on personnel, the local phone-ins were very important there. Before then, you had the *Sports Argus*, your reporter from the local paper who followed the team as a reporter, not as a fan. I went on George Gavin's radio programme at BRMB when I was at Albion and asked him if he'd seen us play and he said "once". So how could he give opinions? They were very aggressive and the boards became very aware of it, and where phone-ins had been a bit of fun, they suddenly became poisonous, very critical. That was a new dimension you had to handle, and the papers took that lead. We went top of the division, having beaten Chester, but instead of celebrating the fact that the area had a team top of its division, in the Birmingham *Evening Mail* Steve Tudghedt wrote a pack of lies on the lead page about us. Then they got the knife into Jo Venglos at Villa, with "For God's Sake Go Now" across the back page. You didn't want to work with them and that venom does nobody any good, it becomes a vicious circle. When you're the butt of it, it's very nasty. Criticism – that's fair, we can all take it; we might not like it, but we all get things wrong, part of the game. But when attacks are lies, when they're personal, when they're deliberately nasty to sell newspapers, that's something else. And you then find people get very defensive and scared to do anything in case they get criticised and that doesn't bring the best out of people. The press like to move managers on and so they incite "sack the manager". The board react because they know that if they don't, pretty soon it will be "sack the board" and you end up with a situation like that at Albion, where Gary Megson is the seventeenth manager in just over twenty years. You get no stability, and that's a problem all over the Midlands.'

There is some truth in what Gould says, but media speculation, concentration and manipulation is just as rife in Liverpool, Manchester and on Tyneside. Tim Beech of BBC Radio WM says, 'People have an insatiable appetite for news about their club. That has grown and some clubs deal with it better than others. Football has been catapulted into this new status. I'm not making excuses because if there are problems with PR, we in the media are on the receiving end! But clubs have found it hard to transform from being small, closed businesses with almost no scrutiny. In the 1950s, for instance, most supporters would never listen to or read a player interview. Now the top players are film stars, football is front page and back page. Clubs have had to respond and there are many who are struggling to come to terms; there are still the vestiges of dealing with things as they did years ago. But it's a new age; the media and supporters will ask questions considered impertinent or intrusive in the past and they have to come to terms with it. There have been improvements, but too slowly, and that paints the clubs in a bad light.'

There are undeniable problems with PR at all the Midlands clubs, and, while Beech is right to point out that improvements have been made, they've been nothing like fast enough or good enough. It's a little unfair to keep comparing Midlands clubs with Manchester United, a club which had inherent advantages even before their current success. But United are, like it or not, the benchmark in English football, and, back in 1981, were no more impressive on the field than any of the Midlands teams. Certainly they have the wealth to employ the best people, to innovate and push the boundaries further and further, but you don't have to be the biggest, the richest or the best to take a quantum leap forward. Derby County were certainly no bigger than Albion or Wolves, but in recent years they've been transformed. They've had the benefit of a certain cash injection from Lionel Pickering, but not one that has massively outstripped the money pumped into Blues or Wolves. Yet they've used their money far, far better and built a new stadium into the bargain. As Brendon Batson notes, 'Derby County have been transformed in recent years and a lot is down to commercial activities. They appear to be a supremely aggressive marketing outfit. Pride Park is custom built, fabulous facilities, they host everything imaginable, and that is necessary for clubs to survive.'

Wherever you look, at whichever facet of the footballing business, you seem to be faced with the same conclusion: the Midlands teams, and most notably Albion and Wolves, have spent a very long time making bad decision after bad decision. Some of those decisions were so calamitous and timed so incredibly badly that the clubs have still not recovered from them. Just as it is an extremely happy accident that Albion, Wolves and Villa were founder members of the Football League, its inception coming at precisely the time the three clubs were flexing their muscles most powerfully, it is equally unfortunate that, just as the gravy train that is the Premiership came into being, Wolves, Albion and Birmingham were each enduring the worst periods of their existence and missed out on the indecent wads of cash that have been floating around the upper echelons of the game ever since.

Albion's failings have already been discussed at some length. At the other end of the Black Country, Wolves were collapsing yet more spectacularly, felled by a combination of dismal planning and over-reaching ambition. John Richards is now chief executive at the club, but in the 1970s he was the club's goalscoring folk hero. Richards's contribution to the old gold and black marks him down as an all-time Wolves great. Until his goal-scoring record was surpassed by Steve Bull, John Richards was the most prolific scorer in Wolves history. His successful partnership with Derek Dougan and the mercurial David Wagstaffe was the cornerstone of much of the success the club enjoyed in the '70s. Sadly, Richards the player was to suffer an ignominious departure at the hands of former teammate and mentor, Derek Dougan, chief executive of the then controlling Molineux administration. Following the death of Billy

Wright, Richards was appointed to the board of directors before taking up the post of managing director in 1997.

Richards was the symbol of a successful decade for the club. They reached the UEFA Cup final in 1972, losing to Spurs in the only all-English final of a European competition. In the early rounds, Portuguese side Academica Coimbra and Den Haag from Holland were both swept aside 7–1 on aggregate. East German outfit Carl Zeiss Jena went the same way. Then came the much-feared Italian giants Juventus, led by the indomitable German Helmut Haller. Having drawn 1–1 in Turin, the Wolves won 2–1 at home. A remarkable set of penalty saves by Phil Parkes in both home and away legs saw off the Hungarian team of Ferencvaros 4–3 in the semi-final. Surely Spurs would do the honourable thing and allow Wolves to take their 'rightful' place as holders of a European title? It was a question of destiny.

Sixteen years previously the national papers had screamed 'Champions of the World' when Honved had come to town complete with Puskas and half the Hungarian national team, smug from that famous 6–3 drubbing of England at Wembley. Wolves, 2–0 down after 14 minutes stormed back to win 3–2. Honved were joined by other illustrious names: Spartak Moscow, Moscow Dynamo, Racing Club of Buenos Aires, Borussia Dortmund, Valencia and, in 1957, Real Madrid, who were soon to dominate the European Cup. At a local level, Wolverhampton Wanderers gave the town and its inhabitants immeasurable pride. Given the national context of these high profile televised friendlies, this sense of pride in the team's achievements rippled well beyond the town. A growing legion of followers, most without any real association with the town, were won over as lifetime supporters. Thanks to a combination of swashbuckling, morale-boosting performances captured on the nation's television screens, Wolverhampton Wanderers became perhaps the first 'national' club, a forerunner to the likes of Liverpool and Manchester United. Alas, there were to be no similar nation-grabbing headlines in 1972, as Spurs ran out 3–2 winners on aggregate. It was rough justice for a club that had done so much to fly the flag for a nation whose innate sense of footballing superiority had been rudely shattered. That said, the memories will live on, captured on television footage.

To that excellent UEFA Cup run they added the League Cup in 1974 and then again in 1980, when that symbol of the newly resurgent, confident club, Andy Gray, scored the winner to beat Cloughie's Nottingham Forest. The signing of Gray from Aston Villa smashed the British transfer record in October 1979, showing that Wolves meant business. To buy Gray, one of the finest goalscorers in the country, from Villa surely showed that Wolves were a club with bigger ambitions. John Richards recalls, 'They were exciting times, but I don't know if we necessarily appreciated it here for what it was, because we were always compared with the team of the 1950s, which was only fifteen or twenty years in the past. That Billy Wright era had such a fantastic team, nobody could live up to it. But apart from one poor year when we were relegated, we were in the top flight, had good players, UEFA Cup final, League Cup winners twice, semi-finals, we had a good period. Bit of luck, good management – probably the second most successful period we ever had at this club.'

Driving the club with steely determination and vision in the latter stages of that period was John Barnwell, the former Arsenal, Sheffield United and Nottingham Forest player, who had worked managerial wonders at Peterborough United, arriving at Molineux in 1978. Barnwell, a successful entrepreneur, demonstrated his astuteness in the marketplace with the capture of Emlyn Hughes for a bargain £90,000. He followed this with an audacious move that involved selling Steve Daley to Manchester City for £1.43 million and using those proceeds to sign Andy Gray. Had his next two prospective purchases come off, who knows whether the club would have had to endure the traumas that were lying in wait for them.

It was an era in which English clubs still retained major reservations about signing foreign players. Ardiles and Villa and Thijjsen and Muhren had managed to make strong cases for more such captures but clubs remained unconvinced. In France, a young midfield player was winning rave reviews for his performances and had broken into the French national Under-21 team. Outside

France he was largely unknown, but it was rumoured that both Juventus and Real Madrid were closely monitoring his developments. Undeterred by such interest, John Barnwell set off to Nantes to meet this young man and his representative, who happened to be his father. The idea of playing football in England appealed to both father and son, and negotiations began in earnest. Within a few weeks of that first meeting, the young Michel Platini broke his ankle, an incident that was to bring to a close the negotiations. But, at the same time as negotiating with Platini, Barnwell was in hot pursuit of another young player who also went on to become another huge success at international and club level – Zbigniew Boniek. It was reported that a fee for the transfer of Boniek from Legia Warsaw had been agreed. However, before the deal could materialise, Poland was plunged into turmoil as the old Communist regime was toppled by Lech Walesa. The new regime immediately put on hold the exit of all Polish nationals from the country.

The arrival of Platini and Boniek might just have been the impetus the club needed to get onto the next level. Instead, the pair came together at Juventus, where they were to play a major role in the revival of that other sleeping giant. Overridingly, what these events did reveal was that the club was determined to push the boat out in a bid to restore former glories. Yet by the midpoint of the 1981–82 season, Barnwell had departed, the victim of a poor start to the campaign, a combination of some less-than-inspirational signings, an ageing team and the inevitable restless natives. Less than two years after winning the League Cup against Nottingham Forest, the club was witnessing demonstrations out on the pitch after home games. Action groups were formed and the club itself received a lot of bad publicity. In a moment of combined inspiration and desperation, chairman Harry Marshall turned to the brightest young managerial talent in Britain – Alex Ferguson. With Aberdeen, Ferguson had broken the Glasgow hegemony and taken the Premier League title to the north-east of Scotland. It was apparent that a move to a bigger stage was only a matter of time. Ferguson was suitably impressed by the stature of Wolves and by the challenge offered. In his autobiography *Managing My Life*, Ferguson confirms that whilst still manager of Aberdeen he turned down a serious offer from Wolverhampton Wanderers. Ferguson sensed the club had deep-rooted problems and decided that going to Wolverhampton would not be a good career move. A decade on another member of the Ferguson family was to find himself at Molineux, though the impact that his son Darren made was nothing like what Alex Ferguson himself could have made. Darren Ferguson, with his lightweight midfield presence, found himself the butt of the fans' criticism and was shown the door, given a free transfer.

The extent of Wolves's financial problems finally came to light on 6 June 1982 when it was announced that the club was some £2.6 million in debt. Panic and anger hit the town as a largely bemused public sought answers. Chief among the opinions offered by the townsfolk was that the board had pillaged club funds, the standard first response from all fans when their clubs encounter such a situation. That panic and anger turned to helpless despair on 2 July when news that the official receiver was being called in became public. Within hours, hundreds of the disconsolate faithful had converged on Molineux ready to pay their last respects. By now, they had resigned themselves to their loss.

On 16 June, Harry Marshall resigned, bizarrely opening the way for former Aston Villa chairman Doug Ellis to step into the breach. Ellis took one look at the situation and within a few days took his place in Wolves history as having held the shortest ever tenure as a serving chairman – by recommending that the club should go into liquidation. What made this decision all the more strange was that shortly afterwards it was revealed that the club's assets would easily cover their outstanding debts. Among some Wolves supporters a conspiracy theory was proffered, suggesting that Ellis saw Wolves as the biggest local threat to Aston Villa and therefore wanted to see them eliminated from the competition. In defence of Ellis, he did attempt a takeover bid following the appointment of the official receiver and there was no guarantee then that he would ever return to Villa Park.

Throughout the summer of 1982 it had been touch and go as to whether Wolves would begin the next campaign. With time running out fast and the first League game imminent, up popped Derek Dougan to save his beloved club. Only three minutes remained before the deadline set by the receivers, when Dougan came up with a successful takeover package worth £2.3 million, which saved the club from extinction. A successful season saw the club return to the top flight, for what remains today its last season in the élite division. During that season, and much to the disappointment of the fans, John Richards went out on loan to Derby County before signing for Madeira-based Portuguese League side Maritimo. Promotion could not gloss over the shortcomings of a very limited squad and, true to the fans' misgivings about the season that lay ahead, the club were relegated, having won only six games and losing twenty-five. Worse still, the promises of the new owners never materialised. In fact, the Bhattis never made a public appearance, leaving their position to be explained by Derek Dougan. Dougan, himself a Wolves legend, soon began to incur the wrath of those who had once hero-worshipped him. The following season, Tommy Docherty, looking for new after-dinner-speaking material post managerial retirement, was brought in. Suffice to say the comings and goings at Molineux did not disappoint him in this regard, as the place took on a permanently shambolic existence. Players of the most ordinary standard, some patently not even good enough for league football, were now being asked to wear the once proud shirt. Among Docherty's charges was a player Wolves had signed from non-league football, Mark Buckland. Buckland, in fairness not a bad player and certainly better than many he played with, was from the gypsy community, leading a nomadic existence both as a player and in his personal life. During one half-time interval, Docherty was said to be berating his charges when he asked where Buckland was. A few minutes later, in a scenario that would not be out of place in a Sunday League pub team, in walked Buckland with hamburger in one hand a plastic ketchup bottle in the other. He had even queued up to make his purchase. By now even Dougan had seen the owners for what they were and resigned his position.

Wolves had spent heavily in the late 1970s and early 1980s because, like Albion and Villa, they took comfort from the perceived wisdom that, even when they had dipped into the Second Division on occasion, the bad times would be short-lived and that promotion would be virtually inevitabile within a season or two. Simply put, Albion, Wolves and Villa were just too damned big ever to fall from grace for long, and even Birmingham were approaching that level. Just as the natural order said that Liverpool and Everton, Manchester United and City, Arsenal and Spurs were, to all intents and purposes, permanent members of the élite, so too were the West Midland quartet. As Richards concedes, that bred a degree of over-confidence. 'The late 1970s coincided with the need to improve the stadium and we invested in the John Ireland stand, which was finished in 1978. We might have over-stretched ourselves, but it's a no-win situation; you have to have both the team and the stadium. There were plans to continue that, but we didn't do that well in the League, despite winning the League Cup, and so we weren't getting fabulous crowds. Then we got relegated and that set off the financial spiral that led to receivership.' Ambitious forays into the transfer market had brought relative success, but the famous old stadium was in urgent need of modernisation; the ground had remained largely untouched since 1932. Matters were exacerbated in 1978 with the introduction of the Safety of Sports Grounds Act, which revealed that the Molineux Street stand (now John Ireland stand) would not pass the required safety regulations. A year later, the club bought the terraced houses on Molineux Street to make way for a new £2 million, specially designed, 9,343 all-seater grandstand equipped with 42 executive boxes. The cost of the new stand proved to be beyond the club's means and creditors, led by Lloyds bank, began to knock on the door. In attempting to restore the past by looking to the future, the club had lost sight of the present.

It was now in apparently terminal decline. The infamous Bhatti brothers, fronted by Derek Dougan, some would say naïvely, had, within four years brought, the club to its knees. The once great and famous Wolverhampton Wanderers plummeted from the First Division to the Fourth Division, becoming a subject of pity, bemusement and amusement in equal measure. In doing so they became only the second club, after Bristol City, to be relegated in successive seasons. English football had lost the likes of Accrington Stanley and Bradford Park Avenue in the past, but never before had such a major club, one of the game's most famous and illustrious clubs, been put to the sword in such a way. By now, the Bhattis had been removed in a high court order as Wolves were given a ten-day stay-of-execution. It was 1982 all over again. The turnover of players continued, as did that of managers. Bill McGarry returned to occupy his former seat for 61 days before realising that this was no longer the club he once knew and loved, departing to coach in Africa with more than a lump in his throat.

After five successive seasons of doubt and uncertainty regarding the future of the club, a deal was struck to bring about a measure of longer-term stability. The leader of Wolverhampton Council, the late John Bird, a Wolves devotee, persuaded the Council to purchase the ground and the adjoining land and property developers, the Birmingham-based Gallaghers and the Asda supermarket chain, to pay off the club's debts, which they did on condition that they would receive planning permission to build a new superstore behind the old North Bank End. The deal contained a covenant which meant that Molineux could never again be used for anything other than sporting and recreational purposes. This would put to an end any ambitions speculative property developers may have had about turning Molineux into a housing site, an allegation that had been levelled at the Bhatti's company, Allied Properties. Bird played a major part in the revival of Wolverhampton Wanderers, something he rarely gets credit for. Hayward's millions may have taken the club to another level but were it not for John Bird it is debatable whether the club could have survived. No one is more aware of that than Sir Jack, who played the most glowing funeral tribute to John Bird for his role in saving their beloved club. 'Like myself, John loved Wolverhampton Wanderers with his heart and soul. His role in securing the future of Wolverhampton Wanderers was testimony of his commitment to the town and the football club.'

Although the millstone of the great Wolves team of the 1950s hangs around the necks of all their successors, Charles Ross, editor of the Wolves fanzine *A Load of Bull*, acknowledges their influence in pulling the club through the crisis-ridden '80s: 'That era was crucial in giving town and club the will to live and pull through from the brink of oblivion in the mid-'80s. Its legacy is an underlying level of passion and support which sees relatively huge gates to this day and drives a belief even among the younger generation that our status is that of a major force in the top echelon of English football.' Wolves were perhaps unfortunate that the timing was wrong and, in a region where football has been suffocated by its refusal to plan for the future, it's perhaps a little harsh to criticise the club for at least trying to be progressive. But it was that ambition which caused the demise of the club, as Tim Beech points out. 'Wolves were in essentially the same position as Chelsea who also struggled for several years after they'd spent money on a very expensive new stand. But Chelsea came through it, partly because of where they are. They're in a really fashionable area, fantastically high prices, able to generate money to regenerate the club. Wolves couldn't really do that. Wolves failed by trying to do the right thing. Blues, on the other hand, did what their supporters wanted, spent money on players, but on the wrong ones, and then suffered. Football finances have never been sane and people make decisions they wouldn't make elsewhere in business.' For the club's survival, it was just as well that insanity or, to put it more kindly, sentimentality, persisted. Had Wolverhampton Wanderers been in any other industry, the club would have been quietly liquidated. Because it was the town's football club, it survived. In the words of John Dryden, 'there is a pleasure sure, in being mad, which none but madmen know'.

TEN

In their varying ways, by the summer of 1986, Albion, Wolves, Blues and, to a lesser extent, Villa, had done a fabulous job of squandering what promised to be a golden future. Though we didn't know it at the time, the region, a footballing powerhouse just five years earlier, was consigning itself to a decade and more of underachievement, appalling football and patronising features in the media about 'sleeping giants'. These clubs have slept so soundly you'd be forgiven for thinking they were in a coma.

In an odd way, they parallelled football's decline through the early 1980s, as hooliganism, an era of dismal football ruled by an obsession with the long-ball game, steadily inflating prices and increasing irritation with woeful facilities conspired to turn many fans away from the game. The fire that claimed 56 lives at Bradford's Valley Parade, a young fan crushed at Birmingham's St Andrews ground by out-of-control hooligans, and the 39 deaths at Heysel before the European Cup final, all in three terrible weeks at the end of the 1984–85 season, symbolised a sordid, soured game that was dying on its feet. Perhaps that grim day at Heysel marked the nadir. The spectre of Heysel made it clear that the game needed to put its house in order and slowly, very slowly, campaigns to weed out the hooligan element bore fruit. Organisations such as Let's Kick Racism Out of Football helped to improve the poisonous atmosphere that engulfed our stadiums and, in what seemed its darkest hour, football began the long, slow climb back into the nation's affections. Things continued for a while to look bleak, but football was gradually repositioning itself so that when the upturn came, when the Taylor report demanded that clubs give their supporters safe stadiums with better facilities, when Gazza's tears alerted Middle England to football's emotional power, when Murdoch and his millions arrived, the game in general, and certain clubs in particular, were ready to take advantage.

Money was coming into the game from new sources: shirt sponsorship was still a relative novelty, but becoming increasingly valuable; the Football League Cup attracted sponsorship; executive boxes continued to spring up in many grounds. Whether many supporters viewed these as positive developments is a moot point, but at least these developments provided evidence that there was still an interest in the game and that, in future, money might be prised from business in greater quantity and with greater regularity. Most significant of all, the effective cartel between the BBC and ITV was breaking down. Where previously they'd worked together to get the greatest amount of football for the smallest amount of money, now they fought one another to gain exclusive rights, pushing prices up. And on the horizon was this new idea, satellite television. The forward-looking clubs saw the possibilities of satellite TV, saw how it had transformed sports in the USA and in Europe and recognised what it might do for clubs in England. They began to ready themselves for the challenge, began to look at marketing operations, started to look at how baseball and gridiron teams worked, started to pick up tips from multimillion-dollar operations. In the '80s it was axiomatic that almost all our football clubs ran at a loss, a situation that was not allowed to happen, at least for any length of time, across the Atlantic. How did they do that? A few of the sharper types went out and had a look and saw that the future was television. Many clubs decided that satellite TV would never catch on, that the rest of the world had nothing to teach us and that they knew best. And into which category did Albion, Wolves and Blues fall? Good guess. As John Trewick, now Albion's Youth Development manager, says, 'Football started to change in the mid-'80s. People often try to resist change, and a few try to get ahead of the game. Clubs round this area in general didn't have the foresight to do that. Now the game is changing every year, it's frightening. Unless you stay ahead of it with your ideas, it will pass you by and the club gets left behind. That's the same for any club.'

It's a reasonable assumption that the sight of the Wolves in free fall had a salutary effect on the other clubs. If it could happen at the now empty Molineux, it could happen at The Hawthorns. When relegation was inevitable, very early in the 1985–86 season, the board sought out a strict disciplinarian, an enforcer to restore order at the club and to address the reduction of a squad of quite unmanageable proportions. Another monumental error of judgement. Crowds at Wolves had collapsed because the team was completely hopeless. A few years before, the supporters had had the chance to watch John Richards, Derek Dougan, Kenny Hibbitt, Dave Wagstaffe, Andy Gray et al. playing massive League and cup games against top-class opposition. Now Wolves were hosting Rochdale and, with all due respect, to a crowd brought up on richer fare Rochdale are not an attraction guaranteed to set the pulse racing. That's why the crowds collapse, that was the lesson to be learned. The antidote? Play your football at a higher level. It's not exactly brain surgery, is it? As Bryn Jones says, 'People talk about the competing attractions for football, but what are they? There seems to be lots of choice but nothing worth having. And where the clubs are successful, you can't get in! Our clubs aren't losing supporters because they want to go shopping or play PC games, they're losing them because they play badly.'

Ron Saunders was appointed by the Albion board as a hatchet man. He's taken a lot of abuse down the years from Albion fans who point to him as the guilty party, the man who not only destroyed Albion but, an ever more heinous crime, saved Wolves, by selling them Robbie Dennison, Andy Thompson and their record goalscorer Steve Bull, the man who almost single-handedly dragged Wolves from Fourth Division to Second. As the tale goes in West Bromwich, Saunders reckoned Bull 'had no first touch'. What he failed to notice was that his second tended to stick the ball in the back of the net. Whether Bull was ever a Premiership quality player is a moot point, but he was certainly good enough to have scored Albion a hatful of goals and carried them back to the top flight.

For all that Saunders seemed to be operating to a pre-planned agenda, he was not the first choice to take the job. Typical of the time, Albion made a complete mess of replacing Johnny Giles. The first choice was John Wile. Club captain in the great days under Ron Atkinson, he'd served an 18-month apprenticeship as a manager at Peterborough United. He represented an interesting choice, almost a Liverpool boot-room-style philosophy. At the very least, Wile was a man who was Albion through and through, who knew, loved and understood the club, credentials that Saunders could never match as a former boss at both Villa and Birmingham. Wile recalls, 'I was offered the job as manager, but in the end I couldn't pursue it. I was offered it when John Giles left and I was manager of Peterborough. Because of the delay in being offered the job by the chairman, Syd Lucas, and actually getting the contract sorted out, I felt it put me in an unfair position with my employers and I withdrew. I suppose I was too keen and didn't handle it right. Albion wanted me to come for an interview and I didn't feel that was right – I'd been at Albion for 15 years, only been gone 18 months, they knew me very well. I couldn't see any benefit and I felt it was unfair to me and to Peterborough. In hindsight perhaps I should have come and talked to them, but I felt it was wrong at the time.' So Ron Saunders it was who was eventually handed the poisoned chalice that the Albion manager's job had become.

History shows that if you want to get promoted back to the division that's just thrown you out, your best chance of doing so is within the next couple of seasons following demotion. Generally speaking, a relegated side has a nucleus of players who can cope at a higher level and who should, in theory, be of better quality than the majority of those in the lower division. If a club can keep hold of them, overcome the disappointment of relegation, regroup, re-organise and get stuck into the task at hand, immediate promotion should be a very real possibility. The Albion squad that Saunders inherited in February 1986 included Garth Crooks, Imre Varadi, Steve MacKenzie, Tony Grealish, Clive Whitehead, Derek Statham and Steve Hunt. It might not have been quite the blend of the Regis, Robson, Cunningham side a few years before, but these were all still top-flight footballers capable of doing a decent job for the club, more than capable of holding their own in the First Division. Sure the squad had to be trimmed, but there were plenty of poor footballers who could have been removed from The Hawthorns. But the bad players were cheap, while the quality of Crooks and company came at a slightly higher price. So the good players were sacrificed to keep the bad. As Cyrille Regis, by now an onlooker from Coventry, said, 'Ron Saunders took over and got rid of a bunch of very good players overnight. They bought players for £100,000 to replace them and you're not going to get that same quality. Quality attracts quality and if you haven't got it, you won't get it and you can't compete.' Tim Beech agrees and makes a telling point. 'The biggest indictment of the Albion is to look at the squad they had in 1979 and put it into the transfer values of today, then look at the value of the current squad. The asset value of that club has diminished massively and if that happens, there must have been some very bad decisions made. You must have sold good players and bought in comparatively bad.' In today's market, Bryan Robson and Cyrille Regis would probably cost more than the current Albion squad put together.

There were stories that Saunders transferred players like Crooks out of the club because they wouldn't move house to live nearer to the ground. Others suggest he was simply told to cut the wage bill by the board. At this distance, it makes no difference exactly who was to blame for the policy. What is an issue, and remains one, is the prices at which the players were sold. At least when the likes of Laurie Cunningham and Bryan Robson moved on, Albion got the market value for them. But players like Garth Crooks were still top-class players, more than capable of playing in Division One. Crooks wasn't sold to Charlton, he was virtually donated, so low was the fee.

Such panic measures – get the high earners out of here as quickly as possible and don't worry about the returns – indicates a board running scared. Wolves's plight contributed to that, but the decline in the club's fortunes was played out against a wider backdrop of social distress, scripted by that doyenne of the economic disaster movie, Margaret Thatcher. Although the region had had its economic ups and downs since close of play in the Second World War, by and large, the Black Country, like the wider West Midland region, had escaped real economic trauma, certainly at the level that had at times engulfed the north of England. Demand for steel, for metal-based products in general, had kept the area's factories busy, while the car industry, notably British Leyland, was a major factor in keeping the attendant component industry in work.

At the start of the 1980s, worldwide demand for steel in particular was falling; there's no hiding that. But rather than introducing a sensible, planned policy, encouraging a movement away from the traditional industries into newer ones with a brighter future, the Conservative government's savage deflationary measures, their high interest rates and their removal of aid from the motor industry, meant that almost overnight the region's economy collapsed. Wednesbury, just outside West Bromwich, saw its two major employers, a British Steel plant and the Patent Shaft, close within months of one another, all but closing the town. As the big factories closed their gates, so too did the smaller companies who relied on them. Add to that the demise of the motor industry and you had an economy in free fall. It was a pattern repeated across the area – the Round Oak steelworks, now the site of the massive Merry Hill shopping complex, closed down, decimating Brierley Hill and Dudley for example. The region hadn't seen anything like it in fifty years, not since the Depression, and it had no strategy in place to cope. Thatcher's recession inflicted a blow to business confidence in the area, a blow from which it is still only gradually recovering. John Richards at Wolves agrees. 'This area went through massive change in the '80s. It's an industrial area and it suffered. A lot of engineering went and much of it has been replaced by service and leisure industries, which has meant a major cultural change in society. That is a big adjustment for the people and we're in the middle of it; it's impacted on us, we were caught up in it, football was going through a massive change as well and we weren't ready to deal with it. This area as a whole has taken a long time to get itself together and it's only now that we're moving forward.'

The shocking blow of the recession, and it was genuinely shocking in every sense, forced the region into a lengthy period of introspection. Ludicrous interest rates all but prohibited new investment anyway, but there was little appetite for it. As businesses and individuals alike saw a lifetime of work swept away on a tide of political dogma, what little money remained in the region was jealously guarded. It certainly wasn't going to be spent on football clubs, some of which might well go to the wall in the new slimmed-down, rationalised, atavistic England envisioned by Thatcher. And good riddance – if you can't pay your way, if you have no economic rationale, what right had you to exist? Football was just a business like any other, as we were being perpetually reminded. Of course football is a business. But it is *not* like any other. Bryn Jones echoes the point. 'I see the decline of football as related to the economic changes. Clubs are run by business people and West Midlands business has tended to be backward, traditionalist, resistant to new ideas. The clubs worked the same, resting on their laurels, trading on tradition and not looking ahead. "We know how to run a car factory, you can't tell us anything." There was complacency, a resistance to change and they just lost out. People with businesses were reluctant to spend money on anything except themselves and possibly, since the recession, which was a huge shock in that region, they've lacked the confidence to do anything but look out for themselves, except in the cases of the super-rich like Hayward at Wolves and Sullivan and the Golds at Birmingham. Like everything else, the economy went haywire; those clubs that had their houses in order survived and those that were badly run suffered.'

So, in the mid and late 1980s, as football was gradually crawling out of its slump, slowly investing in itself and in the possible future that TV promised, the clubs in the Midlands were reining in their spending, cutting costs. At a time when, with Wolves and Birmingham on the brink of extinction, Villa and Albion could have established themselves for evermore as *the* clubs in the region, neither had the foresight to make the big push. Villa had some small success, but never built a solid platform, veering from the upper reaches of the top flight one year to a relegation battle the next. Admittedly, teams in the First Division were on a more level footing with one another in those pre-Premiership days, but if Villa had seized the moment, seized the initiative, made investments in players and a top-class manager as Manchester United did, they could have been consistently successful. As it is, the chance was missed and has probably gone for good. Bobby Gould was in the region, managing Coventry at the time, and recalls, 'When I went there in '83, the people in the area weren't prepared to release the reins. They wanted the responsibility, but not the power, didn't put the financial collateral in, maybe didn't have the financial substance to take it forward. Then I went to work with Sam Hammam at Wimbledon and he ran the club as a business. Before, clubs had been the hobby of the butcher or the solicitor, now it was becoming big business and those clubs were too slow to see it. There had been family set-ups, the Coombs at Birmingham, the Silks, the solicitors at Albion. Perhaps Tom Silk, who was killed in an air crash, might have taken it forward at the Albion, because he was very sharp. But, in general, there wasn't the business orientation at the clubs at the time it needed it and so they couldn't generate the money they needed to be successful.'

At least Villa have been able to enjoy a largely uninterrupted life in the top division, a year in Division Two in 1987–88 being the only blip. Albion, on the other hand, wanted the impossible. They wanted to get rid of good players, cut the wage bill, bring in inferior players on less money and get promotion. Just a thought. If that were possible, wouldn't Manchester United be replacing Dwight Yorke with a fat bloke from the Conference? Had the Albion board of the time shown just a little foresight, just a little imagination, then promotion back to the top flight could have been secured at the first attempt, gates would have returned to healthier levels and money would have been generated. In fairness, nobody could have foreseen the magnitude of the Premiership gravy train, but it didn't take too much to work out that in the First Division attendances would collapse. Once a team has played at the top level, if it has a history of belonging there and, if just seven years earlier, it produced the most exciting football in the country, supporters aren't going to put up with second-class fare indefinitely. You're certainly not going to attract new, young supporters when they could go a couple of miles down the road to Villa Park to watch Liverpool and Arsenal instead. Not for the first time, nor the last, Black Country management took the wrong lesson from the facts presented to them.

Why have these four clubs, even Villa, failed so badly? Didn't Liverpool suffer recession? It did, but it came at a time when both Liverpool and Everton were already very, very strong, better able to cope with the blows. Merseyside was no stranger to economic deprivation, so when Thatcherism descended upon it, it wasn't as bewildered as the Midlands, it wasn't psychologically traumatised by the hammer blows of mass unemployment, bankruptcies, economic collapse. As Bobby Gould says, 'The Midlands had never suffered from a recession and didn't know what to do with it, whereas up north, perhaps they had suffered before and knew how to ride it out, weren't put off investing. The Midlands clubs were all negligent on youth policies, they didn't have the facilities. Albion, for instance, sold Spring Road, which was such a short-sighted move. Blues never had an established training ground and there was no forward thinking, which I think covers all those clubs. In 1962, Jimmy Hill bought the Ryton ground's three pitches for Coventry City, made one into an all-weather pitch, and Coventry have been up there for thirty years or more now. They were a very progressive club.'

Manchester also had an idea of how to see out a recession, though in some ways, Manchester City are a northern equivalent of Albion, Wolves and Blues. Manchester United had the charismatic name, a degree of infrastructure and, most important, probably the best club manager of the last 20 years at the helm. Manchester City, on the other hand, had a chairman with delusions of competence, a fixation on chasing a team they could not compete with, and a board who made decisions every bit as catastrophic as those made in and around the second city. But at the time of writing, Manchester City are top of the First Division and look to be on the way back to the big time. Then you have the north-east: Middlesbrough, Sunderland and Newcastle. In many ways, their version of the 1980s was every bit as dismal. Recession hit the region hard, Middlesbrough went to the brink of extinction before a new club was born in 1986, Newcastle were on the verge of Third Division football before Sir John Hall injected millions and brought Kevin Keegan on board, and Sunderland looked to be another comatose giant whose time would never come again. Now all three are fixtures in the Premiership with impressive stadiums and bright futures.

We have the stadiums in the Midlands, but the futures for our clubs sometimes look so black that we have to carry a torch. Perhaps that's unfair, because Albion, Wolves and Birmingham have made gradual progress in recent years, yet it's so gradual that impatient supporters barely notice it. As John Richards says, 'There have been significant improvements – there's no comparison between the grounds as they are now and how they were in 1989, but people tend to ignore that.' Having returned to the club as its chief executive, John Wile underlines the point that progress has been made. 'In 1995, this club was near bankrupt, partly as a result of chasing the glories of that team. They never replaced those players with equal quality, but spent a fortune and gave lots of money to players who weren't good enough. It was only through good management by the board that the club survived and now has a future.' Results are still the be-all and end-all, but that's an attitude which, particularly when coupled with nostalgia for a wonderful past, creates its own problems, as John Trewick points out. 'We are not ready to compete with some of the better, bigger clubs in this division. Now, a lot of people might say "we are one of the better, bigger clubs". But the facts of the last dozen years don't prove that. I'm afraid we live in the present, not the past, so we really need to take stock, get away from this impatient attitude. Nobody would want promotion more than the current manager, the current board, the current staff; everybody would like us to step up. But we have to be realistic and ask if we are at the stage where we can do that. We've got to make decisions based on that and improve over a period of time, until we get to a situation where we are like Charlton were two or three years ago: knocking on the door every year, then one year stepping through that door and into the Premier League. I'm a realist, my own view is we need a strategy and need to work to that to achieve what we all want, but recognise it won't happen tomorrow. We have players who are trying very, very hard, they're doing their best, but we need to pull together, to improve over time. Perhaps some of our players need more time to produce their best. They are playing under very difficult circumstances because everybody is so impatient to do something which, in my opinion, is hardly achievable at this moment. There have to be realistic targets because otherwise you just end up with frustration, and that becomes a vicious circle: everybody gets deflated, even though they might have made some progress, because they feel they haven't made enough quick enough.'

That's a perfectly valid comment on the plight that Albion and, to a slightly lesser degree, Wolves and Birmingham find themselves in. Wolves and Birmingham are in a little better shape, buoyed by injections of private cash from Sir Jack Hayward and the Gold brothers respectively, though it's money that has not always been used wisely. Back in 1986, the possibilities, the potential, were still good. Albion dropped into the Second Division to join Leeds, Ipswich, Bradford, Barnsley, Blackburn, Sunderland – all teams who were genuinely afraid of meeting Albion, and all teams who have left Albion behind. A little judicious investment and Albion could have walked back into the First Division. But because of economically induced fear, the money was never forthcoming. You can throw a grievous lack of ambition into the equation, too, something Scotsman Larry Canning points out. 'We are small-time compared with London, Liverpool, Manchester. I've been in Birmingham since 1941, been happy here, I owe a lot to the city, but, as an outsider, I can see things a bit clearer, perhaps. The area has a village mentality, even when you're talking about local politics and business. There's a huge fuss made about the Convention Centre, the work they've done in the Gas Street Basin and on Broad Street. And that's it! That's supposed to attract the world, but it means nothing to anyone outside Birmingham! They shout and shout but it's only when you're not very good that you have to make a noise!' Bryn Jones agrees, and adds, 'I think there are narrow horizons and a willingness to make do and mend instead of striving for the best in the Midlands. That might be changing, but it's a slow process.'

Wolves's demise had been swift and traumatic. Albion's was a more gradual affair. Never establishing themselves as promotion contenders, playing some miserable football, Saunders's tenure was inevitably short-lived. The first season in the division ended in fifteenth place, just three points away from relegation. A woeful start to the next term, 1987–88, saw Saunders sacked, as much down to style as results. To remedy that, Ron Atkinson returned to the club, keen to rebuild his reputation after his sacking at Manchester United. When Atkinson was at the club the first time round, he'd been able to spend big money. Now, the financial situation was closer to that he'd endured at Cambridge. Using his contacts in the game and the fact that players were still keen to play for him, Atkinson was able to bring in Andy Gray and Brian Talbot, their experience proving essential in a season-long battle with relegation that was only won on the final day with a draw at home to Barnsley.

Nobody was naïve enough to imagine that Atkinson's stay would be anything but brief. Within weeks of the start of the next season, he was off to Atletico Madrid. He has since written that he would have been willing to stay at the club had the financial position been healthier and had the board been more ambitious, but, in fairness to the club, it's unlikely that he could ever have resisted the lure of trying his managerial hand on the continent. He certainly left the playing side in better shape than he'd found it. Although Gray was soon off to Rangers, Talbot was a tremendously influential figure in midfield, Stacey North and Chris Whyte had been brought in to form the best central defensive pairing since the heyday of Wile and Robertson, Arthur Albiston was a sound left-back, and Don Goodman was beginning to get among the goals.

With Atkinson gone, Brian Talbot took over as caretaker boss and took the side on a run of five straight wins to secure the job for himself. In what remains probably Albion's best season since their relegation from the top division, they briefly headed the Second Division at Christmas and looked certainties to at least reach the play-offs as they scored goals seemingly at will. They were paired with Everton in the third round of the FA Cup and had them seriously worried at The Hawthorns, Everton delighted to escape with a draw. By then, Everton had worked out that the threat came from Goodman, and, unsurprisingly, he didn't finish the game at Goodison and failed to regain full fitness for the rest of the season. Similarly crocked was Colin Anderson, who had been in outstanding form in midfield. Everton won the game 1–0 but, more importantly, the injuries badly disrupted Albion's rhythm. They gradually slid down the table and ended in ninth place. Perhaps more significant, symbolically at least, was the sale of two of Albion's brightest youngsters, David Burrows and Carlton Palmer. It signified that things were now so bad at the Albion, they had become a selling club, further proof that any lingering ambition had been extinguished.

The following season, Talbot effectively finished his playing career to concentrate on management full-time. The great problem he faced, and one which he never really resolved, was how to replace himself on the field. Talbot had been the lynchpin of improved Albion performances, controlling the play, displaying a good range of passing and stamping his authority on games. Without his playing influence, and without adequate funds to replace him, Albion again struggled and 1989–90 was another long, hard struggle against relegation, a struggle ultimately won by just three points. The team now seemed incapable of playing the passing game that Atkinson had reintroduced and, in desperation, Talbot started bypassing the midfield, relying solely on Goodman's pace to get goals, a tactic which was flawed anyway, and which eventually collapsed when Goodman got injured. By January,

Albion were in deep trouble, but at least had the consolation of a home tie against Woking in the FA Cup and the prospect of a Cup run to improve the atmosphere. Wrong. It's now a legendary game in the annals of Albion history. Despite taking the lead, Albion somehow contrived to lose 4–2. And this was no one-off Cup upset where the non-leaguers weathered the storm and got a lucky break. Woking were the better team and fully deserved their victory. Inevitably, Brian Talbot did the decent thing and disappeared into the drawing room with the revolver – Albion were looking for a new manager again.

Stuart Pearson took over as caretaker for a short while and did a reasonable job and certainly had the fans on his side. Albion were still out of the relegation zone, they played some bright football and got a couple of good wins, but the board had decided to look outside, unwilling to appoint the caretaker as they had done with Talbot. After two months of uncertainty, Bobby Gould was appointed in March 1991 in a move that, in many ways, echoed the appointment of Ron Saunders. Gould was never accepted by fans, who feared he would abandon Albion's cherished footballing values for the long ball game he had utilised at Wimbledon, a strategy which helped them win the FA Cup. But Gould was just the wrong man at the wrong time, though, in hindsight, it's hard to imagine just who the right man might have been at a club that had a death wish. In an extremely unhealthy atmosphere, Albion strung together seven straight league defeats, and though they then responded to that by going nine games unbeaten to the end of the season, only two of those nine were won. Relegation to the Third Division for the first time in the club's history was finally sealed on the last day when they drew 1–1 at Bristol Rovers, Albion taking the drop instead of Leicester City.

Bobby Gould found a club in a state of utter collapse, where the decline in gates and in the general interest in the club had had a terrible effect on finances. Relegation certainly didn't help and, repeating the mistakes made when the club was relegated from the First Division, Albion decided they had to cut the wage bill. Gould was charged with the responsibility and became a convenient fall guy. As he says, 'There had been too much movement of players. Some works, some doesn't. I had to sell Don Goodman, which I didn't want to do, but then bought in Bob Taylor and made a profit of eight-hundred thousand pounds or so on it. But if I'd been allowed to buy Bob and keep Don, we'd have got promotion that first year and might have got promotion the year after as well. That would have been a superb goalscoring duo! Instead I had to play Gary Robson up front, and he was a good little player, but he wasn't a goalscorer. I bought Paul Williams and got slaughtered over him – I thought we needed a big back-post merchant, but he couldn't handle it. And then we couldn't provide the service, no wingers. They've had Kilbane since then, but who was the last winger they had before that? When you're down there, you buy potential – maybe good footballers, but not men yet, and you expect them to turn it on from day one. You have to let them mature. You've a better chance if they come through the ranks, if they understand the football club. That supply has dried up in recent years, a problem which goes back to the youth cutbacks. Take Lee Hughes – okay, he didn't come through the ranks, but he's a supporter, he knows the club, knows what's required. That goes back to the time when they were successful in the 1970s. I think Albion, and probably Wolves, too, got carried away. They could suddenly buy players – Andy Gray, Peter Barnes, Gary Owen – and they neglected the youth policy, which was silly, because you always need to bring through the ranks. Buying in players sounds out a message to the kids that they're not going to get a chance.'

Gould was never going to get a chance, either. As Tim Beech points out, 'Albion have always wanted to play with style and that accounted for Ron Saunders and Bobby Gould, who were never accepted by the crowd. Now, it's been so long since they had any success, most of the crowd would trade that in style for results. Under Ray Harford they played some very dour, uninteresting, very defensive football, but they were doing well and he was accepted because they were in the top three. Denis Smith played a free-flowing game, some excellent football, extremely good to watch at times, but they didn't win enough and the fans were very unhappy! They've been down too long for style to matter to the majority, and it will only really become an issue again when they start winning, and then people will want style as well.' The first season in the Third Division started well enough, a 6–3 win over Exeter on the opening day suggesting there would be goals a-plenty. Albion were strongly positioned until the sale of Don Goodman in December, when the goals started to dry up. Although Bob Taylor was an instant hit with the crowd, the team began to betray its inadequacies and other signings failed – an occupational hazard when a manager is having to gamble on cut-price transfers – and, yet again, too many footballers were used – 34 in the League. As John Trewick says, that was a stark contrast with affairs a decade before. 'When Ron Atkinson left the club to go to Manchester United, we had a very good side. When we were relegated four or five years later, hardly any of those players were left at the club and that says it all. In 1978–79, we probably only used 15 players and that was the case for three years or so. If you weren't good enough, you didn't get a sniff – it was very, very close knit. When we struggled, there were dozens who came through, in and out of the team, getting a few games and leaving. A club needs consistency of players and of management to be successful.' By season's end, Albion had slumped so badly that they didn't even make the play-offs, a situation made all the more galling by Birmingham's automatic promotion. Albion were now the lowest of the big four Midland sides, and Gould was on his way.

Recognising the demand for football played in the Albion tradition, Ossie Ardiles was appointed, Albion's most forward-looking move in years. Sadly there wasn't sufficient foresight to get him to actually sign a contract and after one excellent season in which promotion was gained at Wembley in an emotional play-off final against Port Vale, Ossie was off to 'Tottingham'. At least he left the club back in what is now the First Division, rubbing shoulders with Wolves and Birmingham once again, which is pretty much where we all find ourselves seven years later. Given the resources poured into the clubs, why are we still there? Bad decisions play a part. Wolves employed Graham Taylor then sacked him too early, then picked the wrong replacement in Mark McGhee before sacking him and employing his assistant, Colin Lee. Birmingham were seduced by the larger-than-life Barry Fry who bought and sold players at a bewildering rate before turning to the former boy wonder, Trevor Francis. Albion employed Keith Burkinshaw at a time when the club was teetering on bankruptcy, gave him little or no money and blamed him for the failings. They then employed the distinctly small-time Alan Buckley, watched him lose eleven straight League games but rewarded him with a new contract before sacking him. Ray Harford was employed without signing a contract and then walked away to be replaced by Denis Smith, who was fiercely committed to the club, but no more imposing a figure than Buckley had been. As Larry Canning says, 'You look at great managers, like Bill Shankly: they'd go to Third Division matches, see a lad and think, "He'll become Kevin Keegan." That's the difference. That's what good managers do. And we haven't had many here. The board and the managers in general aren't good enough, haven't been for a long time, and have served the fans ill. That filters down the club. The scouts pay homage to the manager to keep their jobs, you get bad players coming in, it goes on.' Even given that the clubs have not attracted the greatest managerial talents, in a decade when clubs with far less potential, such as Bradford, Barnsley, Watford, Crystal Palace and Oldham, have all had spells in the top flight, when Wimbledon and Southampton still survive in the Premiership, it's hard to understand why not one of the three has ever really threatened promotion. Is there some deeper malaise, some fundamental structural problem afflicting the region's clubs?

As a footballing purist, Canning questions the tastes of the region. 'In this area, people in general equate success with power, with strength. Perhaps it's to do with being so connected with heavy industry. Midlanders like hard work, industry; they don't have the same regard for intelligent football. It's got to be something to do with, "I have to work for a living, why aren't the players running about?" Working hard in that sense has nothing to do with football, and people don't realise that. Trying is no good, you've got to be doing! Steve Bull was a basher, but he suited the style of play that's been prevalent here too long – hoof it as far as you can, expect him to break his neck, get kicked to pieces and get on the end of it. But to say he was a great player, a Billy Wright of a footballer, that's such an insult to Billy Wright it's not true. Bull was an honest, hardworking player. You can see the same at Villa. John Gregory bought Watson from Newcastle. Watson cannot play at the top level, but what Gregory loves about him is that he suffers from sweat rash! He runs about all the time. But it's bad players who run about. Good players don't have to. Then Gregory set his sights on Juninho, an artist. How do you reconcile a Clydesdale horse with him? You cannot. You cannot replace technique with effort, and that's a mistake that has been made in this region for too long. When Albion were successful under Ron Atkinson, they were lovely to watch, played good football, played the right way. Doesn't that tell you something? Look at the teams doing well now: Leeds, Manchester United – good players playing good football. Over a period of time, that's the only way to do it.'

One issue which regularly raises its head is that of the number of teams in a small area. Could such a small area sustain four Premiership sides? London is clearly an exception to the rule. Such is its metropolitan sprawl, the generally healthier economic situation in the south-east and its huge population, it can clearly sustain a greater number of clubs, and even they are pretty well spread across the wider capital. But elsewhere, regions fall into the hands of one or two big clubs. In the north-east there are three teams, Newcastle, Sunderland and Middlesbrough, but they are spread over a wider distance. Merseyside has Liverpool and Everton. The Greater Manchester area has only United in the top flight at present as others, such as City, Blackburn, Bolton and Oldham, have come and gone. In Yorkshire there's the same situation – Leeds are pre-eminent, while Sheffield Wednesday, Bradford and Barnsley are all transient pretenders to the throne. Certainly, having Albion, Wolves, Blues and now Walsall all in the same division, with all those local derbies, cannot be helpful to the individual clubs' aspirations. In the opening weeks of the

1999–2000 season, Walsall beat all three of their more illustrious neighbours and, with all due respect to the Saddlers, judging by their other results in early season, that has to be something to do with the 'derby effect'. If Gillingham had been the opposition instead, it's hard to imagine all three going to defeat against them.

Of course, the idea that each region should only have one 'super club' that magnetically attracts all available resources is one that holds enormous appeal for businessmen and shareholders. You can just see the likes of Doug Ellis and Martin Edwards rubbing their hands at the thought of their club being the sole survivor in their city, but what kind of a future is that? The rape of the national game for the good of a few? God forbid, as Bryn Jones explains. 'If your perspective is that which formed the Premiership, that you've got to have an élite of a few big clubs because only then would the game generate the income to get the players to be successful in Europe, then of course you should be arguing for one big club in each area. But most real supporters wouldn't accept that – that's not the logic of football in England. It's the scenario that's being forced upon the population but, personally, I don't believe in that determinism, that just because somebody says it's the way forward we have to accept it. The danger is that some of these are self-fulfilling prophecies. The Premiership was structured in such a way as to deliver that. The classic of the model is Scotland, which is now a complete joke. In Scotland, you barely have two clubs. Rangers qualified for the Champions League and the commentators were talking about a great day for Scotland! A great day for Scotland with a team almost exclusively foreign, managed by a Dutchman? The only thing that's Scottish about them is where they play! But if you see that as a model, there is no room for four top Midlands teams. The most you can hope for now, unless you are the top four or five big clubs, is to hang on in the Premiership, a good Cup run maybe.'

For better or worse, the football business is barely recognisable from the way it was when the three dropped out of the First Division. That's no surprise. As Larry Canning says, 'The whole situation of living has changed in 20 years and so have people's ideas of football. Because the local clubs have struggled in this recent period, they're almost consigned to First Division football because they missed out when the big money was starting to come in. Clubs like the Albion stretch themselves to the limit to pay people like Lee Hughes good money, yet the money he's getting is only a fraction of what they're paying most players in the Premiership, so they can't compete.' And it isn't simply a question of money. Villa can, broadly speaking, compete on an equal financial footing with all but Manchester United. But, as Tim Beech says, they face a different problem. 'Salaries are one issue, but a big thing for footballers now is lifestyle. With the best will in the world, London may be a more attractive place for them. There's a lot happening here in the Midlands now, but it's a lot harder to sell it. If Villa are competing for a player with Spurs or Arsenal, Villa are behind before they start. Birmingham has a great deal to offer, but it is a hard sell. And it's not the reality of the area, it's the perception of it. At First Division level, you have Albion who are without a training ground. So what do they show prospective players? If they're competing with a club that has got a good facility, what chance do they have?'

As ever, the root of the evils that currently afflict the clubs is money. John Richards points out, 'Even before the Premiership, it was hard simply because of where we are. It's not been the wealthiest of areas, so it is hard to compete with London, and it hasn't had the coverage that Liverpool, Newcastle, Manchester get, both as footballing areas and in general, so we've always been catching up. The Midlands has never been looked on as an exciting area in the way those others have and that impacts on the football. A lot of players round here would have played many more times for England over the years if they'd played at Arsenal or Spurs. Even Derby and Forest were, and still are, disregarded when successful. That's not just football, it's everything. Comparisons are unfair, but inevitable. There is more pressure simply because we're not in the Premiership. Wolves and Albion have high expectations, the fans have long memories and can be very critical. Nobody likes to be on the end of that and it makes things harder. At least when I played and we were compared with the Billy Wright years, we were in the top division, so there was consolation in that and we were able to have good Cup runs. There's been such growth in football in the last ten years, such a lot of money involved, a lot of clubs growing very quickly. We've missed out on that and we're struggling to catch up. So we have a squad here at Molineux that isn't Premiership quality – some are but not all. We can't afford them at the moment and a lot wouldn't drop down a Division even if we could. We have to get up with the big boys first before we can get a squad that good. The Premiership has just magnified that gap between the divisions.'

With every year, the gap grows, the likelihood of resurrection becomes more remote. Christ rose on the third day. If he'd been asleep for twenty years, even he might have been hard pushed to rise again.

ELEVEN

Clubs being charged with a lack of 'ambition' has become a by-product of a football era in which fans have grown frustrated at the inability of their teams to achieve. Ambition is, of course, relative but the charge remains whether the club is in the Premier League or the Third Division. It's the sign of the demanding and greedy times we find ourselves in, the enduring Thatcherite legacy.

There are similarities between both Black Country clubs – poor and misguided investment and inept management being among the more damning indictments – but there are, nonetheless, significant differences that help to define the singular identities of Wolverhampton Wanderers and West Bromwich Albion. Whereas Albion have continually failed to spend big when the occasion has demanded that type of investment, preferring instead to 'make do', even before Sir Jack Hayward took control of Wolves the club had shown itself to be more imaginative and adventurous. The staging of midweek floodlit, high profile European games in the '50s showed the club to be progressive in its thinking. Signing Andy Gray in 1979 for a record transfer fee showed a boldness that sent a positive message about the club throughout the football world.

Chairman Harry Marshall will unfortunately go down in Wolves history as the man who triggered the club's demise in the '80s, a situation from which the club has never properly recovered. Yet Marshall showed no lack of ambition when he backed John Barnwell in signing top-class, high-profile international players. He clearly got his sums wrong but there is no denying Marshall sought the best. A decade of hand-to-mouth existence followed before a launch pad was established for Sir Jack to throw in his millions.

Within five years, Hayward had spent an estimated £35 million on developing a stadium that football grounds expert Simon Inglis has described as one of the best small to medium-sized stadiums in Europe. It has seemingly proved to have been a good investment, coming at a time when new stadiums were beginning to crop up across the country. The new Molineux is a comfortable environment which encourages home fans to take pride in their new 'home'. Allied to the main stadium are integrated facilities which enable the club to offer a 24-hours-a-day-seven-days-a-week service to a wide variety of customers. Wolves's operation covers corporate types hosting dinners, those wanting to have a pie and pint, keep-fit enthusiasts and pensioner groups, all of whom help the club make generous commercial profits. Managing director John Richards says, 'All the clubs have to look at revenue from non-footballing activities; we couldn't survive without them. Twenty-five years ago, it was a case of football club and nothing else. The football manager was the club manager. The manager, the chairman, the secretary, that was all you needed. Now we've got more staff on the non-football side than on the playing side, and that's not unusual now. We can no longer just survive on gate money.' His counterpart at West Brom, John Wile, is frustrated at the club's inability to capitalise on the use of all the ground for similar commercial generating possibilities. 'The difficulty we have is that to rebuild the Rainbow Stand would cost £8 million. To do that, that expenditure would be at the expense of the playing side or the proposed training ground. However, if we went down that route the club would reap the longer-term dividends of a strong flow of commercial income. At the moment, with the ground as it is we cannot compete commercially with Wolves, Villa or Birmingham.'

While Hayward's money built a solid ground and commercial infrastructure, half his injection of cash went into purchasing mediocre players. The Hayward millions should have given Wolves a leading edge over their competitors. It should have bridged the gap between First Division and Premiership, the gulf that the likes of Charlton, Bolton and Crystal Palace have found so difficult to manage as they have yo-yo'd between the top flight and the next tier of football. Charles Ross of *A Load Of Bull* says, 'In one very obvious sense, the money once spent couldn't be replaced. Money spent on the stadium would have a lasting benefit, but not necessarily the money that was often frittered away on inadequate and under-performing players.' Under both the Graham Taylor and Mark McGhee regimes, it was not only a question of spending money on mediocre players, it was also the impact their high salaries had on the club's balance sheets. And, even though Sir Jack had once said, 'I'll keep spending until the men in their white coats come to take me away,' it was inevitable that the spending, bordering on the reckless, had to come to a halt. However, when that decision came it was a bolt out of the blue. It was a defining moment in the modern-day history of Wolverhampton Wanderers.

In Mark McGhee's first full season in charge, 1996–97, an automatic promotion spot beckoned, until Barnsley laid to rest that hope. Still, Wolves were seen to be a good bet for the play-offs, until handing Crystal Palace two late goals in the first leg at Selhurst Park. At Molineux, the huff and puff in a highly charged and frenzied atmosphere proved inadequate as Palace held out for a 4–3 aggregate victory. As fans were coming to terms with yet another bitterly disappointing campaign, one which promised so much but had failed to deliver yet again, few could have expected Sir Jack's comments in what amounted to a soul-searching outburst. No one could have predicted the deep sense of rage, anger and disappointment running through him. Above all else he felt the fans, his constituency, had been betrayed, that they deserved Premiership football. The failure to deliver that was something he elected to take personal responsibility for. 'There has been too much sloppiness and disregard for money. They thought the Golden Tit, me, would go on forever.' He then went on to speak about being 'blackmailed' by his son Jonathan and the club's managers, as they sought that final piece in the jigsaw with yet another expensive purchase. He launched a blistering assault on his highly paid players, accusing them of not having shown 'commitment'. The departure of Jonathan and his own hands-on involvement was inevitable once he went on to say, ' . . . we have to have better management behind the scenes. Someone has to take the club by the scruff of the neck.'

On acquiring the club, Sir Jack had installed son Jonathan as Chairman. A successful cattle breeding, Northumberland-based farmer, Jonathan had no previous experience of running a football club. Sir Jack left his son to his own devices, retaining a distant interest in club affairs from his home in the Bahamas. He presumed that with his millions, even an inexperienced young chairman in charge of the club would achieve promotion. Every time Jonathan approached his father, Sir Jack would write out a cheque for another player. Jonathan Hayward operated on the basis of spending about half the week running club affairs from Molineux before returning to his Northumberland home. In his absence, running of the club was delegated to the joint auspices of club secretary and commercial director. To many, this seemed to be an odd way to run a business by now turning over in excess of ten million pounds per annum, and, for some supporters, it seemed to reinforce the view that daddy had given over the club as a plaything for his son. Jonathan Hayward's inexperience was particularly highlighted in transfer business. Stories of Wolves paying way over the odds for players are legendary in footballing circles. Sir Jack once commented that Leicester City's promotion to the Premier had been funded on the basis of generous donations from Wolves, £2.5 million deposited for Iwan Roberts, Steve Corica and Steve Claridge, none of whom ever remotely looked as if they would repay their fees. This was followed by the £250,000 capture of a goalkeeper that never was. This incident typified the 'sloppiness' that Sir Jack was referring to. Allegedly Mark McGhee had come to an arrangement with Leicester's manager and chairman that the Australian goalkeeper, Kalac, would sign for Wolves for an agreed sum of £250,000 on completion of a trial period. Following the trial Wolves sent Kalac back. Leicester City reported the matter to the Football League accusing Wolves of reneging on an agreed transfer. On appeal, the Football League awarded against Wolves and asked that the club pay £250,000 in compensation to Leicester and, to rub salt into the wound, Leicester were told that they should retain Kalac's player registration. In the end, the issue had come down to Mark McGhee's word and that of his Leicester City counterpart. A combination of poor judgements of this kind and indifferent results prompted Sir Jack to take control of affairs.

On Sir Jack assuming control, McGhee was infomed that there would be no new money for players. He would have to generate his own funds and, at the same time, start to prune the outlandish wage bill. Within 18 months, McGhee had sold £5 million worth of players and had spent around half of that on new players. Fans demanded to know why McGhee had not spent all the proceeds on replacements. The fact that the remaining proceeds from transfers were going to meet budget deficits was not particularly well communicated to the fans. By now, McGhee, with no significant upturn in results, was treading water, was a condemned man. In a final act of defiance he managed to convey the impression of being an obedient employee who had met his master's every command, only for the master to deny him his promised reward. It was an astute stroke from a man schooled by the master himself, Sir Alex Ferguson.

Having stated that he would not put another penny of his money into the club, Sir Jack's first action was to write a cheque for £8 million to clear the club's overdraft. He convened a meeting with all the staff and informed them that from now on the club would have to become a self-financing operation. His comments were particularly targeted at the players. 'The wage bill is at the source of our problems and that is why stringent measures are being taken so that Wolves can be assured of a long-term future.' Sir Jack had set the trend for things to come. The absence of a single executive in overall charge of club affairs was long overdue. Surprisingly, Hayward turned to someone with very little experience of running a multimillion-pound operation, certainly in the commercial sector. The placing of an advert in the broadsheets and specialist trade journals had suggested the successful candidate would come from a 'blue-chip' background. Whatever John Richards may have lacked in business expertise he more than compensated for with his passion for the club and a deep understanding of the club's inner workings, fans' expectations and the relationship the club has with the town. As Charles Ross says, 'Wolverhampton is wedded to football and Wolverhampton Wanderers remains its best loved institution.'

A restructuring of the club boardroom followed. With Jonathan removed, Sir Jack invited his other son, Rick, to serve as a fellow director. Like his father, Rick Hayward is a Bahamas-based businessman and is seen to have more of his father's business qualities than Jonathan. The difference in the two brothers is telling. Whereas Jonathan spoke of his dreams to see Wolves promoted, Rick speaks of the same aim but qualifies it by saying he hopes also to see the club operating in the black. Next followed the appointment of Derek Harrington, a long-time business partner of Sir Jack, as vice-chairman. Harrington was brought in to help restructure the financial side of the club. The final piece in the jigsaw saw the arrival of City financier, Paul Manduca. Sir Jack has spoken of his desire to give the club 'back to the fans'. With the club's finances in sounder order, the issuing of some form of shares rights is not far away. It would seem that Manduca, chief executive of the highly successful Rothschild Asset Management Group, is well placed to assist with this task.

Within 12 months of taking direct control, Sir Jack was able to comment on the progress that had been made. 'We have in place the most stringent of financial plans, which are being met. The excesses of the past have been curtailed and a realistic monetary strategy, which is vital for the future stability of the club, is being carried out.' That said, the club is seen by some as not being sufficiently aggressive or proactive when it comes to promoting the Wolves brand name. According to Dr Sean Perkins at the Sir Norman Chester Centre for Football Research, University of Leicester, 'Wolves have a fantastic tradition and with it a major appeal in the United Kingdom and overseas. For example, despite being out of the Premier for almost 20 years they have one of the biggest followings in Scandanavia. They were the first big English club to go to America and to this day enjoy a following out there, likewise in other parts of the world. The Centre's research shows that Wolves are among the few clubs who could turn pay-per-view into a serious earner. People in the City of London, as was evidenced at a national seminar held last year, see Wolves as being very marketable. Yet, for all that, the club appears to have little idea or serious intent when it comes to promoting the Wolves brand.' Charles Ross concurs and adds, 'The club's commercial competence remains in the dark ages. How many businesses turning over £15 million don't have a sales or marketing director on board? With Sir Jack no longer throwing millions at Wolves, we have to stand on our own two feet, and not try to do it blindfolded.'

The names Sir Jack Hayward and Steve Bull have become synonymous with the recent history of Wolverhampton Wanderers. Their respective roles have been huge in helping restore the lost status and respect of the club. Arguably the name of Chris Evans, the club's Director of Youth, should be placed alongside that of Bull and Hayward. Evans is the architect of a youth development programme that is widely admired and respected across the game. In the last twelve months alone three of his graduates have gone on to win senior international honours, and, to cap it all, Robbie Keane has become the most expensive teenager in British football history following his £6 million transfer to Coventry City. Things were a lot different when Evans arrived at Wolves nine years ago, when he found the vestiges of a much neglected youth policy. Motivated by the challenge and 'a desire to see this once famous club restored to former glories', Evans, ably assisted by others, among them former Welsh national team manager Mike Smith, set about painstakingly and meticulously assembling what has now become an impressive infrastructure. 'We continue to develop and expand into historical hotbeds of football and I feel we now have one of the largest and most successful networks in the country.' The fact that Wolves can compete favourably with the likes of Manchester United, Leeds and Arsenal in North and South Ireland and across Wales speaks for itself. Further testimony to his efforts is the report of the Football League's youth development programme monitors: 'The Centre of Excellence operation is of a high standard and when fully enhanced will be a set-up few, if any, will match. Everything about the Centre is of an excellent standard.'

Having scrambled around for facilities in the early days, Evans has access to excellent training pitches at the club's main Compton training headquarters and at the state-of-the-art, £8.5 million indoor facility at Aldersley Leisure Village, once home to Britain's finest athletes. Furthermore, a £3 million sports complex is under construction at the Compton site. The most satisfying aspect of Evans's work is to produce future players for the first team. During the last two seasons, Robbie Keane, Carl Robinson and Lee Naylor have gone on to establish themselves at first-team level. Ryan Green, Colin Larkin – a 17-year-old goalscoring first-team debutant – Shane Tudor, Matt Murray, Adam Proudlock, Gordon Simms, Seamus Crowe and Keith Andrews have featured in first-team squads. Behind these 18-year-olds are a host of others who Evans has great hopes for for the future, among them central defender Joselyn Lescott, already being talked about as a future England international. Evans has calculated that Wolves are among the top seven clubs in the country for giving youth-team players experience of first-team action, a must for clubs like Wolves. 'We do not have the attractive benefit of Premier League status, and are not investing the amounts of money into youth programmes that top academy clubs are, and therefore opportunities in the first team become our most attractive proposition.'

The drop-out rate for young players between 18 and 21 in the game is alarming. Wolves have addressed this issue with the appointment of former Leeds United and Bristol City striker Terry Connor. 'Many times in the past, younger players at Wolves and elsewhere have been allowed to escape from the net. All too often players grow too old for the youth team and find themselves playing perhaps half a dozen reserve games a season. They then lose heart and lose form and find themselves on the soccer scrapheap.' This is another significant piece in the Chris Evans development programme. Without rich handouts from BSkyB television money, those clubs outside the Premier have had to moderate their ambitions for the setting up of youth academies. The cost of a properly developed youth academy can run to several million pounds, a prospect which has forced most clubs nation wide either to develop on an incremental basis, a 'building block' process as Evans puts it, or to attempt to rush something through, knowing that it does not meet the required specification. During its first year of operation, Birmingham City's youth academy was criticised by Premier League inspectors for the poor quality of certain facilities. According to Evans, 'When we seek academy status, rest assured ours will be sustainable and highly professional.'

While most Wolves fans were horrified when Robbie Keane was sold to Coventry City, Evans remained philosophical. As Wolves fans begin to come to terms with the fact that they may have become a 'selling club', something that they previously only associated with smaller and lower division clubs, Evans can take comfort from the fact that in the last two seasons, two of his prodigys (Keane and Jimmy Smith) have realised £7 million in transfer income. He is also only too aware that the first team can only be strengthened if money is generated from the sale of players. That said, he confessed to more than a touch of sadness in his heart when it was announced that Robbie Keane, a young boy he had persuaded to sign for Wolves in the face of stiff Premier League opposition, was leaving to join Coventry City. Clearly in an attempt to comfort Wolves fans, Evans boldly pronounced that the future of Wolverhampton Wanderers was bright because the club had 'other Robbie Keanes in the making'. That remains to be seen, but there is no doubting the sheer belief Evans has in his ability to emulate the likes of Liverpool and Leeds when it comes to youth development. In those moments when Wolves fans are clinging on to crumbs of comfort it is to Chris Evans that they look.

Evans is unlikely to receive the testimonial he so richly deserves. It is difficult to see how the club can repay its indebtedness to a man who has almost single-handedly transformed the club's programme for the development of young players and, in doing so, raised a multimillion-pound bonus into the bargain. Wolverhampton Wanderers are extremely fortunate to have such a committed, dedicated and talented person on their payroll. Hunted by a number of Premier League clubs to direct their newly formed youth academies, Chris Evans won't be distracted from his goal. 'I have witnessed this club being bulldozed to the ground. I have witnessed major investment, colossal diligence and an army of fans who deserve success.' Evans may be building the cornerstone of future success, yet, even with the best will in the world, his endeavours won't bear the fruits of promotion overnight. As each season outside the Premier League passes the wider the gap grows between the 'haves' and 'have-nots', even for clubs the size of Wolverhampton Wanderers.

The prospect of Wolverhampton restoring former glories, winning League Championships and FA Cups and challenging the best in Europe, is now a pipe dream. Too much ground has been lost to the bigger clubs in the Premiership, who have since capitalised on the generous handouts from TV deals, sponsorship and increased attendance income. Even 'smaller' clubs, that is, those with fewer supporters and the absence of a benefactor but aided by TV money, have become richer than Wolves. At best Wolves could conceivably achieve middle-ranking Premier status among the likes of Everton, Newcastle and Leicester, good enough to avoid the relegation zone, maybe the odd cup run but not serious challengers. Even that would be a Godsend for fans who have become increasingly beleaguered and frustrated at the lack of progress made. One suspects there are those who may even have resigned themselves to Football League status for the foreseeable future. Black Country folk are nothing if not pragmatic and will have worked out that their best chance may have escaped them. If Sir Jack's millions and Steve Bull's three hundred-plus goals can't do it, then what will?

In what has effectively become a Premier League II, Wolves are now pitting their wits against clubs who may have considerably smaller turnovers but who understand the working environment and have acquired the invaluable knack of knowing how to achieve results. No longer are they intimidated when the so-called 'big boys' arrive on their doorsteps. Instead, they comfort themselves with the knowledge that aspirations towards the Premier are not the preserve of the bigger clubs. Although Charlton and Barnsley have quickly returned from whence they came, both clubs have been able to regroup, aided by 'parachute' money, and relaunch another assault on the Premier. Other clubs of similar size and stature have been inspired by their efforts and are all the time asking searching questions of themselves and the so-called bigger clubs. That leaves the half-a-dozen or so stragglers at the bottom end of the table, the perennial strugglers, seemingly always destined to remain so. Many of the longer-serving First Division managers, like Bruce Rioch, Alan Curbishley and George Burley, have described the First Division as becoming ever more competitive. If that is the case this only compounds the failure of Wolves to get out of the division when the conditions were altogether more favourable.

The 'bigger clubs' are left to navel gaze, unsure as to how to come to terms with the levelling off that has become a striking feature of the First Division. They satisfy themselves with the idea that when their turn comes to climb into the Premier it will somehow be different and that their potential will see them through. It took almost five full seasons before a league fixture at Molineux drew an attendance of less than twenty thousand. Since then the 20,000 barometer has dipped below on a handful of occasions, but by and large Wolves have benefited from the massive support of a loyal following. During the 1990s season ticket sales averaged between fourteen and fifteen thousand, putting most Premier League clubs to shame. As a one-club town, Wolves manages to retain the support of most youngsters in the immediate area, which extends north to the Shropshire borders. The nearest club to the north of Wolverhampton is Stoke, some fifty miles away. However, as Charles Ross points out, 'Each year that passes without real achievement dilutes ever so slowly the hold that Wolves has. Heritage matters but heritage also depends on maintaining quality. Wolves have drunk deep from the reservoir of support that the glory days of Cullis and Wright provided; but even the deepest reservoir eventually proves harder and harder to draw upon, and now is the time to replenish a little.'

TWELVE

At Molineux, the historical sin which brought the club to its knees was one of ill-timed overambition that not even Hayward's millions have been able to rectify. Looked at from a Hawthorns' perspective, it's hard to see why Wolves fans get upset. At least there was ambition at their club, at least there was an attempt to keep pace with Liverpool, in spite of the fact that throughout the 1970s the team wasn't quite good enough. In West Bromwich, the best team in the country was assembled and then dismantled thanks to neglect, small-minded parochialism and perhaps even cowardice. For just a couple of seasons, a window of opportunity opened up. Had it been seized, Albion would now be a Premiership club, without question. Instead, the directors failed to accept the challenge, slipping back into the historical Albion mindset of making do, of taking no risks, of muddling along from day to day without ever stopping to look at the bigger picture. They never saw the Premiership coming, and when it did, it caught the club square between the eyes, mowing it down like a rabbit in the headlights. In the intervening years, Wolves have managed to maintain at least some hope of a Premiership future thanks to Hayward's millions, but for Albion, the 1990s have been a long, dark, depressing decade, while the new millennium holds out little promise of any rapid improvement.

One of Albion's greatest problems has traditionally lain in its internal workings, operating as a 'gentleman's club' in the rarefied air of the boardroom. The directors have historically held on to power with an iron grip and have rarely shown any desire to introduce new blood or new money to the club. As Bryn Jones points out, 'In a funny sort of way, because Wolves and Blues all but went to the wall, it did them good, where at the Albion, the revolution never really went to the wire and they were able to limp along without fundamental change. Outsiders came in to the other clubs, but Albion carried on with the same small-time people. Albion are the quintessential parochial club, because of the old constitution which wouldn't allow anybody to buy into the club. That still lives on, really – the rules have changed but the ethos and the values are the same.' Although a wider share issue was made – in the early 1990s, at the not inconsiderable price of £100 – that made little real difference to the amount of participation the ordinary supporter could have. The share issue was instituted because of its promise of a small fortune for team rebuilding. Without the riches offered by the Premiership at Villa Park, by Hayward at Molineux or by Sullivan and the Golds at St Andrews, stock market flotation seemed the panacea for Albion. Fans certainly looked at it in that way. Their oft-aired viewpoint, in fanzines, local radio phone-ins and the like, can be summarised as, 'When I bought my Albion shares I saw it as a way of buying into my heritage. The idea I would get some sort of return on them never entered my mind.' Such was the high cost of the shares and the limited number available, the role of these new shareholders was limited to asking a few awkward questions, which generally went unanswered, at the AGM. The club's major shareholding still rested in a few hands – chairman Tony Hale, Jersey-based millionaire Graham Waldron and the one significant outsider brought in in recent years, Paul Thompson, head of the Sanderson Computer group.

Albion had been so mismanaged for so long that by the time Hale took the chair in 1995, the club's finances were in a parlous state. The team's ability to hold on to Division One status once promotion had been achieved under Ossie Ardiles was vital to the survival of the club, particularly once some Sky money began to trickle into the First Division. Credit should be given to Hale for investing his own money, for playing his role in bringing the club's constitution into the twentieth century and for attracting

Thompson's money to the club. Hale played an important part in at least steadying the Albion ship. However, as a relatively small-time businessman, certainly when one compares him with his Midland counterparts Sir Jack Hayward, Doug Ellis and the Gold brothers, there were always going to be limits as to how far Hale could take the club. Had he stepped down in the summer of 1998 and perhaps given the reins to either Paul Thompson or perhaps someone from beyond the football club, Hale would have been seen as a successful chairman and an historically important one.

Unfortunately, for his own sake as well as that of the club, Hale continued to hold power. It became clear during the course of the 1998–99 season that the Hawthorns boardroom was dividing into two distinct camps with very different views of the club's future. In February, Paul Thompson resigned as a director. By the summer, backed by two directors, Clive Stapleton and Barry Hurst, who had resigned in Thompson's wake, Thompson had called an Extraordinary General Meeting to oust Hale as chairman. The battle was lengthy and acrimonious before Hale finally prevailed, largely on the strength of the block vote, notably that of Graham Waldron. Bryn Jones, an Albion shareholder as well as supporter – greater gluttony for punishment hath no man – was at the meeting and believes, 'Thompson won over a lot of the small individual supporters with his ideas to take the club forward, but he was kept out by the block vote. The prevailing argument was that Tony Hale is an Albion man, which he is in the sense that he's a supporter. Sadly he's an Albion man also inasmuch as he embodies the traditional make do, shuffle around, don't have fancy ideas, don't commit yourself outlook. And there's a huge culture of secrecy at the Albion, which is one of their biggest problems, because the supporters are kept in the dark and don't know what the problems are, or if there are any. In the past it was okay, but people won't accept it any more. And if you say nothing they assume it's because you've got something to hide. In the past you'd go in a pub and find Tony Brown, or your mate lived round the corner from Jeff Astle, or you'd see Cyrille in your local. Now they all live away from the club out in the suburbs, and they're even more rarefied beasts than they once were, so it's even more important that there is some channel of communication with them via the media. Clubs like Albion do have to bring in young players from lower division clubs and some of those young players do look overawed by it. I think that a lot more could be done to help them cope, be it sports psychologists or whatever, grooming them to get the best out of them. Nowadays, speaking as an industrial sociologist, businesses are run where human resource management, PR and so on are fundamental pillars of their overall strategies. Most clubs don't have this but they should, particularly because of where they want to be going. Again, that especially applies to Albion. It goes back to the Black Country base where for years you made stuff, you sold it, you had captive customers that were always there, that was it. Football – you pick a team, the punters turn up. Those days are, if not already gone, certainly going.' As Jones says, Albion is a club that has traditionally lacked vision, one which has had no pro-active role with the wider community for many, many years, certainly since the demise of the Throstle Clubs in the early 1970s.

To fulfil the clichéd prophecy, Hale won the battle at the EGM, but it was inevitable that he was going to lose the war, despite Thompson apparently turning his back on further fighting. Speaking on local radio just a few weeks before the start of the 1999–2000 season, Hale said categorically that Denis Smith would be the manager for the new term. Well before a ball was kicked in anger, Smith was out and Brian Little installed in the Albion ejector seat. Whether Smith was the man for the job is a moot point in Albion circles, but fans all respected the effort and honesty he put into the club and were universally angry at the manner of his dismissal, especially after Hale's backing of him just a few days before. And not only was Smith dismissed, it was announced as a footnote to a memo to the Stock Exchange which announced the arrival of new directors onto the board, apparent confirmation of the priorities at the club. Whatever the requirements of the Stock Exchange, such as their demand that they be informed first of major managerial upheavals, they do not stipulate the order in which items are to be set out on a press release. Where a football club is concerned, the key appointment is that of the football manager. For the fans, no other club matters have anything remotely approaching that impact. But the announcement of Smith's sacking was way down the list, almost as though the club were changing caterers.

Hale's apparent promise of £2.6 million for the manager to spend – later downgraded, as much of it was said to have been spent on a pay rise for Lee Hughes – never materialised and Little was forced to make do with the players he had. By December 1999, the club's finances were such that Albion were said to be losing £30,000 every week as gates fell, a reaction to the club's failure to invest substantially in new players. This was all the more frustrating when it had its best nucleus in years – Kevin Kilbane, Enzo Maresca, Hughes, Matt Carbon. In one astonishing week, Hale was forced to settle a libel case in favour of Paul Thompson (a case emanating from their battle prior to the EGM) and Albion's Irish international Kilbane was suddenly sold to Sunderland for £2.5 million, a sum that appeared to be a fraction of his true value. Hale tried to justify this on the grounds that Kilbane would be able to leave on a Bosman transfer 18 months down the line, but such was the backlash from supporters that Hale's position became untenable. Brian Little gave an interview to local radio which made it perfectly plain that he had been sold the Albion job under false pretences and left little doubt that he was on the verge of resigning. Before Little had time to go, Hale announced his own resignation instead.

Even this wasn't enough for a club that loves to make a drama out of a crisis. In subsequent days, several other directors left the board, most notably Jim Driscoll who had been introduced to the club in the summer by Hale. He told the local *Express and Star,* 'The events of the 24 hours leading up to me resigning left me very disillusioned. I learnt late on Monday that there had been discussions between certain plc board members which I was not consulted about. Albion are supposed to be a public limited company. Not a gentlemen's club. Don Colston got a call and he lives in Cyprus, while I only live in Stourbridge. What's the problem? Even if they had said to me, "Look Jim, you don't figure in the future plans of the club," then I'm big enough to take that. But I heard absolutely nothing despite leaving messages. In business you don't treat clients like this and I felt I had had no alternative but to resign. I can't work in that sort of environment.' Subsequently Thompson has taken the chair for an initial period of three years and will hopefully bring in the modern-day business practices that made Sanderson such a success. Initial results have been less than encouraging. Within six weeks of Thompson taking charge, Enzo Maresca was on his way to Juventus for a fee said to be around £4.3 million. In fairness to the club, this was literally a dream move for the brilliant young Italian and it would have been unfair to stand in his way. Nevertheless, it was galling to lose his quality so soon after Kilbane and, again, at a price that many saw as being on the cheap side. The local mood was hardly improved when it was revealed that Brian Little would be given just £3 million of the money for rebuilding, but at least that was an improvement on the Kilbane situation.

Somewhat incomprehensibly, a month later Little still hadn't spent any of the money. The team – shorn of its two most, maybe only, creative footballers who had not been replaced – was in a dismal run of just eight points from forty-five and had fallen into the First Division relegation zone after a comprehensive 3–0 defeat at home to Birmingham City. After the game, Little launched a blistering attack, saying that ever since he had arrived at the club he had been lied to, accusing those in the boardroom of refusing to let him manage the club as he saw fit, and of making decisions behind his back, an allegation refuted by both Thompson and John Wile. One bone of contention appeared to be a letter sent out to the clubs in the lower divisions under club secretary Dr John Evans's signature, asking if they had any promising young players they might like to sell to the Albion. Little said he had not been consulted on the matter, a statement again denied by John Wile. Two days after the Blues débâcle, Little was summoned to a board meeting and was relieved of his position, saying that whoever replaced him would receive a phone call to put him fully in the picture.

Yet again, Albion had managed to make themselves a laughing stock in the football world, with one key question left unanswered. If £3 million was available, how was it that Little hadn't spent it? With all due respect, if he thought the team he had couldn't be improved, then he deserved to lose his job. If, on the other hand, obstacles were placed before him in his search for players, he had every right to be angry.

So Little managed just seven months, a short tenure even by Hawthorns standards. Surprisingly, scores of applications were received for the vacant job, with vaguely promising names such as Colin Todd, Jan Molby and a John Trewick–Cyrille Regis pairing, the fans' preference, all mooted. Ultimately, Gary Megson was the man chosen to sup from the poisoned chalice. He deserves everyone's backing and best wishes if he's to find anything approaching success from the current situation.

In fairness to the Albion board, it is increasingly apparent that the task of finding success in the First Division is getting bigger by the day, just as the gulf between that and the Premiership is growing exponentially – it's reached a point where, in old Division terms, we have a Division One but no Division Two, so low is the quality. Having spent successive evenings in early March 2000 watching Albion play Tranmere then Forest play Norwich, of the 50 or so players on show, anyone would be hard-pressed to compile an eleven of any quality at all.

Contrary to the earlier wisdom, that task has not been eased by Albion's rush to the stock market, a move which a number of clubs have been left to rue since Tottenham Hotspur made football's first foray into the murky waters of the City in 1983. The move wasn't repeated until 1989 when they were joined by Millwall. In June 1991 the, two London clubs were joined by Manchester United. It is worth remembering that United's arrival on the stock market was an ignominious flop, bearing absolutely no resemblance to its current-day glamour rating as part of the FTSE Mid250.

Unaffected by the news coming out of Old Trafford, a clutch of clubs, including Aston Villa, Leeds United, Newcastle United and, lower down the football hierarchy, Sheffield United, Preston

North End and Birmingham City, all struck a claim in football's gold rush. The timing seemed right. After all, football was fashionable again, shedding the memories of Heysel and Hillsborough, covering itself in operatic drama, Gazza's tears and an evening with Gary Lineker. With brand loyalty support that Marks & Spencer would kill for, and becoming increasingly appreciated by those looking to make investments, the game offered exciting potential. As Sky transformed the game, that exposure would attract new and more lucrative sponsorship deals, merchandising sales and legions of converts to the impressively constructed stadiums. It was, apparently, a sure-fire recipe for success.

More importantly to clubs that had traditionally lived hand-to-mouth lives, there was a big pot of gold waiting to be had. As wage bills escalated, as stadium rebuilding programmes became essential, clubs needed the money. A few were already in a financial position to meet Stock Exchange requirements and took the plunge. Most were left to look on, curious and jealous in equal measure, asking themselves if they had missed out. They needn't have worried. The honeymoon was over almost before it began.

It was the economics of short-termism. The market could not handle the number of clubs that had become listed. It quickly realised that, with very few exceptions, most were unlikely to generate the long-term returns demanded by professional investors. The banks were not involved for philanthropic reasons; they wanted to see returns, dividends, profits, something they soon realised was not going to materialise. Football is not a profit-generating industry in the way that supermarkets can be. There's an altogether more complex relationship at work between club and supporter than between Tesco and consumer. With the short-sightedness for which it is legendary, Britain's banking system failed to notice this obvious truism and as a result is largely to blame for dispensing some dismal financial advice and the resulting difficulties that have beset many clubs. It's not a difficult equation. Supporters don't want their club to make a profit; they don't pay good money to see cash sitting in a vault. If there's excess money around, they want it spent, they want to see it out on the pitch. And if they don't and if the failure to spend leads to failure on the pitch, they'll stop coming, as will the profits. Football is not like the grocery sector. Every supermarket can, theoretically, make money, their definition of success. In football, there are only a handful of trophies up for grabs, and those trophies define success in that sector. You don't win trophies, you lose fans; you lose fans, you lose money; you lose money, you're a bad investment. It's a fact of footballing life, the number of winners is very restricted. Presumably the banks' retort is that 'responsible' banking only works when you have responsible borrowing, essentially saying, 'We offer our professional advice, but if we get it wrong, don't blame us.' Unsurprisingly, since 1997, most clubs have seen their share prices fall because of financiers' concerns.

One of the more significant recommendations by the Football Task Force is that ordinary supporters should have the opportunity to become stakeholders in their local football club. In more recent times the successful takeover of AFC Bournemouth by a group of supporters has given great encouragement to those fans whose clubs are experiencing similar difficulties. During the 1980s a few clubs, notably Manchester City, invited a supporters' representative onto the club's board. The difference between the Bournemouth and Manchester City models is that the latter was tokenist, whereas the former was about giving fans a genuine voice, and therefore influence, in the decision-making processes. The Task Force has recognised that football clubs continue to be run by directors in a way that is detached from the real concerns and interests of their fans, the more so where Stock Exchange quoted plcs are involved.

With very few exceptions club executives and directors seem to be satisfied that by giving fans the opportunity to comment upon the quality of toilets, refreshments and stewarding, they are fulfilling their duties to their customers. But, as Mick Finn, a Wolves fan, argues, 'We are not just customers. Our involvement goes deeper, much, deeper than that.' Any attempted comparison between football fans and customers of Marks & Spencer, Tesco or Sainsbury, for example, is inappropriate. Finn is very critical of the failure of *his* club to effectively engage supporters in more meaningful areas. He goes further by arguing that some of the poor decisions taken in the past could have been avoided had the club entered into a different form of dialogue with it's supporters. Finn cites the philosophy of the Brazilian company Semco, whose success is attributed for the most part to a willingness to listen to ideas of staff and customers. 'But how can we feel involved when the sum total of our involvement is to rate the quality of the Bovril and the cleanliness of the urinals? What a waste of potential. Twenty thousand people, all with ideas, all wanting to contribute, but sadly with no voice.'

Football directors often describe clubs as a 'bottomless pit' of expenditure. This description aptly summed up the predicament facing the directors of West Bromwich Albion when they took the decision to place the club on the Alternative Investment Market. AIM was the only available route for football clubs unable to show that their companies had had three or more successive years of profitable trading. Albion fans had grown heartily sick of the million-pound purchases that Wolves and Blues had been making with great regularity. They demanded that their club should stop shopping at car boot sales and instead move up to Rackhams. The directors were also mindful of the stadium's inability to maximise commercial possibilities and the continued absence of good quality training facilities, a significant factor in the club's failure to attract both senior and junior players. The strategy appeared to be simple, sound and potentially lucrative. The millions raised from the flotation would provide the manager with the funds to buy four quality players, forming the backbone of a promotion-winning team. Once promoted to the Premiership, Sky TV money and new commercial sponsorship would enable the team to be strengthened, a further share rights issue would be reinvested into the infra-structure, giving Albion a stadium and training facilities worthy of their shortly to be acquired Premier League status. If only life were that simple.

The share issue was not an overwhelming success and Albion's room for manoeuvre was affected accordingly. Manager Ray Harford broke the Albion transfer record to make Kevin Kilbane the club's first million-pound man and also brought in cult-hero goalkeeper Alan Miller from Middlesbrough, but questions have to be asked about the wisdom of buying both Mickey Evans and Graham Potter. Playing tediously defensive football, Harford's team rode it's luck and flirted with the play-off zone before, in typical Albion fashion, the uncontracted manager walked out on the club. Fans remained sceptical. Harford's replacement, Denis Smith, was given some money, buying Matt Carbon and James Quinn among others, but Albion were back to gambling on comparatively small-fee footballers once again. That's the problem with a share issue – it's a one-time deal, you don't get that money again. With the transfer kitty exhausted and little left over for ground redevelopment and training complex the club was wholly reliant on attendances. But how many people want to pay to see a poor side? The club was heading for the inevitable loss-making operation it has become as revenues failed to match the growing expenditure. Worse still, any remedial measures would be dictated by faceless investors demanding their pound of flesh, insensitive to the fans' wishes that the likes of Kilbane, Hughes and Maresca be retained. Where in the past a cosy relationship with the bank manager or the occasional interest-free cash injection by the chairman or his fellow directors would have sufficed, now institutional shareholders wanted to see the club run at a profit, cash in the coffers. Therein lies the real problem facing West Bromwich Albion plc or, for that matter, Sheffield United, Bolton Wanderers and a host of others.

Losing £30,000 a week, financial imperative now propels the club and will do so for some time to come. One feature of Thompson's arrival that initially encouraged hardcore fans is his willingness to tell supporters of the plight that is facing their club. Thompson has accepted there are no quick fixes and that West Bromwich Albion face a two-year battle simply to stabilise things and then get into a position whereby they might be able to challenge for promotion. At least there will be no more rose-tinted, 'this is the year' pronouncements from the boardroom, raising hopes that must inevitably be dashed.

This long overdue realism gives Albion genuine hope for the future, but it's also a recognition of just how the football industry has changed. The game has passed Albion by. Where in the 1980s they had sufficient money to buy footballers – generally the wrong ones at the wrong time and at the wrong price – that is no longer possible and nor, in the post-Bosman world, is it desirable. John Wile is now the club's chief executive and says, 'There are things this club can't afford to do and we have to keep that in mind or we go down the same route that we did in the early 1990s. Clubs have to be strong in negotiations, you have to have the knowledge you can walk away, accept there are some players you cannot afford. All football clubs have to recognise there is a point at which you have to draw a line. It is worrying that money that used to stay in the game is going to players and agents, it's not circulating and that's a downward spiral. Players will only stay with clubs for a long time if they are very successful, and that prevents supporters identifying with players, which is a pity. The danger for the clubs is having players who stay at the club because they're not quite good enough, so they know the next step is down, and we've had some of that here over this decade. That movement is a problem for managers trying to build a team. He gets his defence right, moves on to strengthen the midfield, but by the time he's got that right, two of his defenders have left. I think you can develop that continuity by bringing players through the ranks, because then there is an attachment to the club. And you can then increase their remuneration package in a sensible way as they improve and become more valuable to the club. Players will stay if they're successful. If the players succeed, it generates money for the club and we have to recognise that that has to be passed on to the players. You have to pay them what they're worth, but not more than that. The problem with the game in general is players think they're worth more than they actually are because of Bosman and all the TV money and so on. We as a club – and football as a game – should only pay what it can afford to pay, and only pay it to those who are worth it. We've all been guilty in the past, this club in particular, of paying over the odds to players who weren't worth it. That's not easy to change because supporters have favourites, but the manager's opinion has to be the only one that counts. If he doesn't want to pay what the player wants, we won't pay it. Players need representatives, advisors, but I think it's unfortunate that these days you can negotiate for a player without talking to him personally, that's a great shame. It does put the thought in your mind that they are only interested in the money if they don't meet the people they're going to work with. Agents should advise, particularly on investments for the future, using the money wisely. I did a deal with one player and spoke to six different people to conclude it. So if six people are taking a slice of the action, that's got to drive the costs up.' In recent years, Albion have lost players like Andy Hunt and Paul Peschisolido because they wouldn't meet their demands, and that does affect the club, taking a backward step just as they seem to be moving forwards.

It is a hugely frustrating situation for all connected with the club, but one they have to get used to, as underlined by John Trewick. 'It's very disconcerting now. I really feel it's so hard to manage, unless you're at Chelsea or Manchester United, where you can buy the best players. Nowadays people patch together a team rather than build one, because of the demands. I don't mean that disrespectfully, it's not a case of "you'll do", you select your players carefully, but if you have to do that, the teams with the most money will do the best. That makes it harder for clubs lower down, like Albion at the present, to plan and to build. When we had that successful period, it was a time when footballers were content to stay at their football club, work hard together and get a real feel for each other. That was the thing, the team spirit, we all had something to offer. The problem here is we bought too many players too often. Here we had Raven and Burgess as central defenders, then at various times we've bought Mardon, Murphy and others who really haven't improved the situation, so you might as well stick with the two you got originally and either wait until the right player becomes available or until you produce another one yourself. Until recently, we've been spending two or three hundred thousand pounds and you don't get the right one for that. If you buy, it has to be an improvement and you have to pay a million. We spent money and got no better. Recently we've had more success with players like Kilbane, Hughes, Maresca, Miller; they've improved us. But there is a temptation to buy for the sake of it, to give the supporters a new face, and that's not reason enough.'

As with Wolves, Albion's future lies in youth development. In that, the club is particularly fortunate to have the services of former midfielder Trewick who has, in tandem with his assistant Richard O'Kelly, transformed a system that had been failing miserably for a decade or more. Trewick had worked with the first team and had a brief spell as caretaker manager, but it as Youth Development Manager that he is currently making his mark. 'Getting youngsters through is a lot of hard work. You need people committed to the cause, who'll do a bit more over and above what you're supposed to do. When Alan Buckley came in as manager, I was reserve-team man, but he wanted Arthur Mann to do it. I was a bit miffed but I came into the youth side with Richard. We got together and at that time, there was nothing happening. The players in the system, all of them, weren't good enough, people weren't working hard enough to make it happen. And then you have to take time because even at Under-15 it's hard to get lads in because the good ones have gone.' It's been a long haul back after a spectacular piece of short-sighted stupidity in 1988 left Albion without its own training facility – the Spring Road ground was sold for just £298,000, condemning the club to a peripatetic lifestyle, training here, there and everywhere across the Midlands, leaving them looking little better than an amateur club. As Trewick says, 'For any club, selling its training ground is a strange decision, panic measures maybe. Birmingham had a similar situation of never owning their training ground. And that's your bedrock. We've had a long period when we didn't produce any young players at all, maybe Dave Burrows who was here at 14, I think. And when we do produce, we let them go – Ugo Ehiogu wasn't really a product of the Albion, he came here at 16, but then Villa picked him up. You've got to look after players to keep them, and that comes down to the overall philosophy of the football club. It was in place in the '60s and '70s, it reaped dividends – Tony Brown, Bobby Hope, Asa Hartford, Len Cantello, myself, Bryan Robson, Derek Statham, many more. For the cost of bringing them in as lads, peanuts in the big picture, you end up with so much. Then for years we didn't address it and we lost out.'

Gradually, Albion's youth system has grown in stature. It's a difficult path and one that will, by definition, take a long time to bear fruit. Trewick is rightly bullish about the advances made, but, as Larry Canning points out, recruitment can be difficult, and not just at The Hawthorns. 'In the postwar period, the fact that Albion, Wolves and Villa had such tradition helped them attract the kids who wanted to play football, and they had their pick of the best. Once you've got that, it snowballs, because you're a good side, you get the best youngsters, you continue to be a good side. That takes some stopping. Once you've lost it, it's even harder to start it again. While you've got poor teams, the youngsters growing up won't want to go. Anybody under the age of about twenty-five has never seen a good team at Albion, Wolves or Birmingham. So gradually you lose your tradition, and then you can't get it back. Preston had tradition, Blackpool had tradition but now it means nothing. And in another few years, the same will apply round here.' As Bryn Jones says, tradition is a double-edged word. 'Expectations are a good thing in that they demand raised standards. But they demand them immediately and so you're always liable to have short-termism and that then makes it difficult for managers to succeed. At clubs like Leicester or Wimbledon, there were no expectations, so they just got on with it and arrived at where they are now.' Even so, BBC Radio WM's Tim Beech feels that the tradition is still alive and kicking and that, on balance, it's the heartbeat of the club. 'The expectancy is a good thing, it may drive players on. Football managers bemoan the past, they say it's only today that counts. In one sense they're right, but in another they're very wrong. That tradition means these clubs are still alive – it was only tradition that meant Wolves had to stay in existence. New tradition has to be built, but you've much more chance of that if you're building on a solid past. It is futile in a way to talk about the past, but I think that supporters refusing to accept second best is a very good thing. In the last few years, it's the one thing that has sustained them. You go to supporters club meetings and if Tony Brown turns up he gets a tremendous response because they associate him with greatness. That's good. Even for younger supporters it is good to see Albion were once great and could be again.'

In building that new tradition, John Trewick can point to some success stories, such as Daniel Gabbidon, who is now making his way in the first team, and Adam Oliver, on the fringes. 'We started by looking at the Under-14s and we got Adam Oliver in. He was a ball boy here, from Menzies High School down the road. I used to see him in the tunnel. He'd first come here at 11 and then left because he said it was terrible. So I used to get him in the tunnel at half-time and have a bit of friendly banter: "come here you, when are you coming back? You'll enjoy yourself, good coaches, we'll sort you out. If you don't you won't be playing at 20." So we used to have a bit of a laugh and eventually he said, "Can I come in next week?" So I said, "No son, we've got better players now. I'm only teasing, come in, we'll have a look at you." And that was an improvement right away. Then we got the Chambers lads, which was hard work. Their dad's a lovely man, very protective, concerned, but they all came in for a chat; we set his mind at ease. Then we had Justin Richards, we got a few others and that was the year we really started.

'We got Daniel Gabbidon in from South Wales when he was 16 – he came up for a couple of days, lovely mover. He looks like a footballer, got a bit of everything – quick, stamina, two-footed, tackles, heads it, good temperament. He needs to develop the vocal side of the game and needs to impose himself, because what you've seen, he can do a lot more of. That's understandable; he lets the senior players rule him a bit, and he needs to stick his chest out and realise he's bloody good, but he's started nicely. We got a goalkeeper, Chris Adamson, from contacts I've got in the north-east, and he's been doing well. It's hard work – you have to get out there. We have steadily improved but there's a long way to go. A lot is down to finance and traditionally we haven't had the finance they've had at Wolves or Villa or Birmingham. Wolves spend £2 million a year; Forest, Leicester, Villa, Coventry all spend about £1.5 million a year. At present we cannot match that. We have improved the standards 100 per cent, but that standard may still not be good enough – for me it isn't; I want to produce more and better players. At this moment, it's impossible to do that. We have good youngsters. Now we want to get in eight-, nine- and ten-year-olds, the very best of them, and work at that age because at 14 a lot of bad habits have already been learnt. But that's a ten-year programme. We may see some fruits of that in 2008, but if the rules aren't changed, we'll have Villa and Coventry nicking them which is what happens. As far as players are concerned, it is about money – you need to have money to attract players, particularly at first-team level. But that filters down, to a lesser and lesser extent the younger the age group. When clubs are recruiting at eight, nine and ten, money doesn't come into it much, but I do think that as we go on, we're going to really have to look after our outstanding youngsters. We as a club have to give them all they need in terms of coaching, encouragement and in terms of buying them the odd pair of boots, tracksuits, bits of kit, otherwise other clubs will come in and literally pinch them.

'Gareth Barry moving from Brighton to Villa is the best-known example, but it goes on at a lot of clubs. They do look at talented players that other clubs have and take them; it's happened to us. But the powers that be don't adhere to the rules – they let clubs get away with it. We had a player, Sean Hope, signed on the only forms available for his age group, set up to come to us on a scholarship. He hadn't come through the system, I'd scouted him if you like, been to Lincoln to watch him, made lots of enquiries about him. He'd been signed at Sunderland, they released him, and we were first in, liked what we saw, had him here a week. We offered him a scholarship place, he verbally accepted it, and then signed an agreement to say he'd come down here and sign a scholarship form. He was then poached by Coventry. We've written to the FA, Premier League, Football League several months ago, and, as yet, we've got nothing back except a letter from the FA. It baffles me sometimes why the powers that be do what they do. Unfortunately, we have to get on with our jobs within the rules. There are rules to prevent it, but they don't apply them, they let people get away with it. As long as they do that, people will break the rules, they won't care who they upset, and that creates bad situations between clubs. Kids will become more mercenary because they know they can move without any problem, they're not going to be punished. We have to address that situation properly within the game, but I'm not too hopeful it will be addressed because it's the Premiership boys who benefit. The bigger the club, the more advantage they have and they do whatever they please. And that filters down. The financially poorer Premier League clubs exploit the First Division, they poach from the Second Division and so on. The rich get richer.'

That creates further problems. For the Albion, the period covered in this book started with the arrival of Johnny Giles, a great player coming to the end of his career who was willing to drop down a division. That happens less and less. As Bobby Gould says, 'The gap is huge in salaries, you don't get the likes of a Paul Ince or a Mark Hughes dropping down because they'd be taking a ten-grand-a-week pay cut to do it. Would you? And if they did, you get a divided dressing-room because there's one guy getting twice as much as everybody else.' Cyrille Regis is now a first-team coach at the Albion, having also had responsibility at reserve-team level. For him, a key obstacle to progress is the difference in pressure and expectations. 'At the Albion, you're generally not buying from Premiership clubs, you're buying potential from the lower divisions, as we did with Kevin Kilbane from Preston. And it's a step up, these lads haven't been under pressure, they haven't seen the big stage, they come from Rochdale and they don't realise the pressure of playing at The Hawthorns where the atmosphere is all about getting promotion, where the fans harp on about me and Laurie and Jeff Astle! Pressure, pressure, pressure which they've never been exposed to. That's good, it becomes the heartbeat of the club, keeps it driven. We were top six regularly not that long ago. But for the players, it takes time because they're generally young lads. If, say, Paul Ince had gone to one of the local clubs instead of Middlesbrough, he'd have strolled through it, and brought on the likes of Enzo Maresca. But that doesn't happen any more. Money has changed things. You don't see players putting in transfer requests if they're out of the side. It's less about playing now, and that's inevitable given the money. You have players who might be earning £70,000 or £80,000 a year. It depends on the person you are, but that might be all you need, you might not care about playing. The player situation has changed completely, they do have too much power now. There has been progress, but maybe it's gone too far and the clubs will eventually put a stop to it. You can't sustain these wages forever, it's not possible.'

But as wages escalate, so the club has to generate more money. As chief executive, John Wile is at the forefront of that exercise. 'Everything in football is blown out of proportion at every level, on and off the field. Every nook and cranny of the club is scrutinised. There is greater emphasis on earning money because it has become so expensive to run. Supporters don't like that much, there's a feeling that if you run it as a business, it's in conflict with the football, but in reality it is not. The only way you can now be successful on the field is to run the business well. You can have fleeting success without it, but not consistent success. We look to get progressively better each year and if you work on that basis, you will ultimately get there and the success will be sustained. But the two go hand in hand. There aren't that many areas of revenue. People through the turnstiles, money from the Football League and the TV money, then your commercial activities and merchandise. And then on a bigger scale you look at share issues, but that's not something you do very often. On the gates we don't generate enough to pay our way. Our support is very good, but it's not enough and that's probably true of most clubs, certainly in this division. It's very expensive to run a football club and the costs are continually going up, particularly on the playing side. Players' salaries don't go up by two or three per cent like they do for the rest of us, they go up dramatically. With the Bosman ruling, clubs lower down the scale will lose out on the transfer income that kept them afloat. That doesn't necessarily apply to this club, but, in the main, there will be less transfer fees in future. Part of the development has to be linked to the new stand to replace the Rainbow stand which will give us facilities we can use seven days a week. It will have a banqueting suite to hold up to 600 people, it will have other suites for conferences, exhibitions, whatever, holding up to 200. That's essential. We plan to generate income seven days a week. It's an £8 million development and the hardest thing is to make the commitment. The board has to know the money is in place before we go ahead because we don't want to impact on the team. Supporters say, "If you've got £8 million, why not spend it on the team?" The answer is the money wouldn't be forthcoming for a player, because it's basically secured against property, like a mortgage.'

As the experience at Molineux shows, it's a delicate balancing act, spending on ground development while still improving the team. As gates have fallen because of prolonged failure on the pitch, it hasn't made life any easier. That's even more the case because clubs like Albion have to invest in youth, as John Trewick makes clear. 'We're looking at land for building an academy, awaiting planning permission, and if it comes off I'll be absolutely delighted. Eight or nine grass pitches, a couple of AstroTurf pitches, indoor sports arena, accommodation for the kids, it sounds fantastic. There comes a point when you can't afford not to have that kind of set-up, because a club like this has to grow their own players because the transfer prices for good players are too high for us at the moment. We need to take the medium-term, patient route to build for the future, which requires substantial investment. It does take patience and you do have to communicate that to supporters. My philosophy is that supporters aren't daft. They watch, they listen, they talk football, they're the lifeblood of the club – without them, we haven't got a football club. You have to be honest with them. You can go along trying to kid them a bit, "we're nearly there", "if only", but I reckon it's best if you're just straight with them. "We're not good enough", the gulf is substantial between where we are and where we need to be. We're putting a five-year plan into operation, this is what we're doing over that time, we expect a year-on-year improvement and in the end we'll be like Charlton, Ipswich – solid, good, better-than-average teams who can look at promotion as a realistic target." Why not tell people that? Some say it's naïve. Why is it? Tell it as it is. People appreciate that, I think.'

What has been lost down the years, and which is only now being addressed again, is the club ethos, that there should be such a thing as an 'Albion Man'. Wolves saw the value in it when Sir Jack Hayward got involved, as John Richards points out. 'Sir Jack was very keen on that, he brought Billy Wright onto the board, he was a voice on the board for the fans, United did it with Bobby Charlton, and that's how it should be. You have to keep that link between club and supporters. With plcs getting involved, there's a danger of a distance, and if you get that, if you have supporters thinking the club only cares about money and shareholders, you start losing that bond, their love and commitment to the club. Supporters are the only people who are loyal in football. In recent years, non-football people have come in to deal with finances, and that was a worrying development for fans. From there we've had former players like myself and John Wile coming in at a senior level. I can only see that as healthy, because it's people who have an affinity with the club, they know we're 100 per cent for the club. We wouldn't make any decisions detrimental to the club. They might not agree with them all, but I hope they realise they're made with the best interests of the club at heart. We will make mistakes, but I think supporters will see they're honest mistakes.' Tim Beech agrees. 'Bringing in Wile and Richards is a good thing, because football is about emotion. You have to make rational business decisions nowadays, but there has to be an element of romance about sport. That concerns me, I think we are in danger of losing that, the glory of winning is secondary to the pursuit of money. I think that is completely wrong. There has to be the romance, there have to be figures people can identify with, and if they're good at the job, it's a dream ticket. Supporting a club is irrational – it is about passion, investing hopes and ambitions in a team that represents you, escapism. If you break that link and the fans feel ripped off by *my* club, the players don't care about *my* club. they're not representing *me*, they're representing themselves – then the passion will die. If the supporters don't feel they identify with the players any longer, you lose their loyalty. I don't think wages are the issue, I think it's more about players constantly changing clubs, contracts – that leads to cynicism and that can mean a lot of trouble. With money comes responsibility and supporters expect the players to do the right thing and that's perfectly reasonable. The introduction of figures from the glory days does help ground the club with the supporters.'

Albion have followed that plan, as Wile points out. 'It's been a deliberate policy to get former players working here. I felt there should be a natural progression, that people with something to offer shouldn't be allowed to leave. People like Cyrille, John Trewick, Bobby Hope, who works in our youth development system, they are synonymous with high standards at the club, and they know what it takes to get there. I hope that filters down to the current players, or helps in attracting players here, when they can see that if they have a good career as a player here, there is the opportunity to continue with the club if they have something to offer. High standards are what we have to be about, something we have to reintroduce to the football club. We are asking questions a bit earlier, being more ruthless. A youngster should be in the reserves at 17 or 18, pushing on the fringes of the first team at 18 or 19, and if he's not, you have to wonder if he'll be good enough. You've got to have high standards, and generally we didn't have them. This club had been in a terrible position. When Tony Hale came in as chairman, we had no money and were in a pretty parlous state. Compared with when I'd been here previously, things had dropped. A fine history isn't worth anything when you kick off on Saturday, but it does give you something to work from. The players didn't have high enough standards, the staff didn't ask enough of them. You can demand that – winning is something you can work hard at, it's a culture you need to instil. We're in the business of winning football matches. That starts at the ages of 11, 12, 13. You develop young players, their technical ability and so on, but they have to be made aware very early on that if they want a career in professional football they have to win games. We're now breeding more competitive players, winners. You think of Bryan Robson, Ally Robertson, Tony Brown, Len Cantello, they didn't want to lose. They didn't want to lose in five-a-sides in training, never mind on a Saturday. It's a culture you can get in a club and one you have to get. Maybe some players had been here too long, were too comfortable because the demands hadn't been great enough, maybe they couldn't handle the demands because we are a big club in waiting and our supporters have high expectations. That's a mental thing and it's something we've worked on. If we aspire to be a Premiership club, let's set Premiership standards. We've been fortunate that we've got a clutch of good young players coming through together and a lot of credit has to go to John Trewick and Richard O'Kelly who have done a lot of good work and demanded those higher standards. We have a few ready to make that next step: Adam Oliver, the Chambers twins, Daniel Gabbidon, Max Iezzi too, who will make a big impact at this club. If we keep them together, they'll have the bond of fighting for each other and the club. That has been the biggest single thing we've missed, that continuity and that spirit.'

As the sales of Kilbane, Maresca and Keane have made perfectly clear, it will not be easy for the Black Country rivals to find good players and then keep them. That is the biggest challenge that faces them. It may be that the imminent and inevitable arrival of 'Premiership Two' will appease supporters in the short-term. With new TV contracts to be negotiated, there's little doubt the opportunity will be taken to reduce the Premiership to 18 clubs, with an upgraded, and perhaps hermetically sealed, Division One as a sop to those clubs who will find it ever harder to make it to the top flight. It's extremely likely that Division One as it stands will become an 18- or 20-team Premiership Division Two, with minimal relegation and bolstered by the same sort of minimum stadium requirements that confront hopeful Conference sides. Attendance and financial criteria may also be added, making it impossible for smaller clubs to get their noses into the trough. The two top divisions will be marketed as 36 or 38 élite, big clubs, and the likes of Bury, Walsall and Crewe can just disappear. Quietly please. That is the next big fight on the horizon for football fans, and they need to start gearing up for it.

Even if Premiership Two arrives, after the novelty has worn off it's not going to be enough for the ambitions of Albion or Wolves supporters. There is little doubt that, if only they could get into the Premiership, both would draw excellent crowds and would be able to compete happily enough in the middle tier of the élite division. The days when they could fight for titles have gone, but they have the potential to supplant Coventry, Leicester and Wimbledon. And to talk about that as the extent of their ambitions shows just how far the mighty have fallen.

That is the crux of the matter. That, more than anything else, is the reason why Wolves and Albion still struggle. They are still trying to recover lost ground and with every passing year away from the pot of gold, they lose more ground. They were in the wrong division at the wrong time, had their slump at the worst possible moment in footballing history and got left standing on the platform, watching the Premiership gravy train recede into the distance, not waving but drowning.

BIBLIOGRAPHY

Atkinson, Ron, *Big Ron: A Different Ball Game* (Deutsch, 1999)

Bains, Jas and Sanjiev, Johal, *Corner Flags and Corner Shops: The Asian Football Experience* (Gollancz, 1998)

Bowler, Dave, *Three Lions on the Shirt: Playing for England* (Gollancz, 1999)

Denselow, Robin, *When the Music's Over: The Story of Political Pop* (Faber and Faber, 1989)

Harding, John, *For the Good of the Game* (Robson, 1991)

Hebdige, D., *Subculture: The Meaning of Style* (Methuen, 1979)

Johnston, Willie, *On the Wing* (Arthur Barker, 1983)

Ross, Charles (ed.), *We Are Wolves* (Juma, 1997)

Savage, Jon, *England's Dreaming: Sex Pistols and Punk Rock* (Faber and Faber, 1991)

Willmore, G.A., *West Bromwich Albion: The First Hundred Years* (Robert Hale, 1979)

Willmore, Glenn, *West Bromwich Albion F.C: The 25 Year Record 1972–97* (Soccer Books Ltd, 1997)